jumping the Line

A Novel

Michael G. Harpold

BOOK PUBLISHERS NETWORK

Book Publishers Network
P.O. Box 2256
Bothell • WA • 98041
Ph • 425-483-3040
www.bookpublishersnetwork.com

10 9 8 7 6 5 4 3 2 1
Printed in the United States of America

LCCN 2013950435
ISBN 978-1-940598-05-5

Editor: Julie Scandora
Cover design: Laura Zugzda
Interior design: Stephanie Martindale and Leigh Faulkner
Cover art by Ketchikan, Alaska artist David Rubin

For

Dominica, Michelle, Kathryn, Elizabeth, Sarah, and Elaine

Acknowledgements

 Writing my first novel required the help of many in this small, isolated island community in Southeast Alaska, battered by storms and deluged with over thirteen feet of rain each year. Little is accomplished here without the assistance of others. Returning from travel "outside," we walk down the C or D Concourse at Seatac airport in Seattle and instinctively search for people we know. Although we might not know each other by name, our eyes meet in mutual recognition that we are neighbors and we can depend on each other. The glance is our fist bump.

Thanks go to many neighbors in the Alaskan sense of the word. Dave Rubin, my neighbor and friend, after reading an early draft of *Jumping the Line*, designed and painted the cover. Leila Kheiry, a reporter and editor for the *Ketchikan Daily News* at the time, edited the book and came up with the title. English Professor Rod Landis at the Ketchikan Campus of the University of Alaska helped me start the transition from retired bureaucrat to fiction writer. Most helpful of all, Professor Elizabeth McKenzie at the Sitka Campus worked patiently with me through six semesters of distance-delivered writing classes and never allowed me to give up on myself. I've wanted to write this book for many reasons, and I wanted to show Liz I could do it.

Luis Orta who came to Ketchikan as a busboy and through hard work became the owner of our most popular restaurant, Oceanview Italian, helped me fill in the details of family life in rural Mexico and what it's like to come alone to *el norte* with nothing but a dream, and make good. His sister, Gabriela Horta, who before she would permit herself and her daughters, Angie and Karina, to be posed by Dave for the cover painting, insisted that *Jumping the Line* be a "good" book, that it relate the story and sacrifice of her countrymen sympathetically.

My wife, Elaine, and daughter Dominica accompanied me on long days as I revisited the San Joaquin and Imperial Valleys and the border, renewing old memories and reacquainting myself with the scenes I use in my story.

Readers Harry Martin, Lupe Hansen, Biz Robbins, Miguel Torres, Scott Bowlen, Charlotte Glover, and Dave Kiffer dutifully read my early drafts and did not dash into doorways when thereafter they spotted me on the street.

Most particularly, I thank my writing group: Biz Robbins, Sharon Nobilio, Donna Hartley, Nicole Caple, Barbara Larmon Falling, and Sharon Monrean.

Victoria Lord at the Ketchikan Area Arts and Humanities Council helped me apply for grants.

Finally, thanks to Sheryn Hara and her crew at Book Publishers Network, especially editor Julie Scandora, whose patience and skill have contributed to this book.

1

Mexicali, Baja California, México, January 1965

 Miguel Hernandez-Ochoa gazed across the wind-blown street at the border fence. Lit by a lone incandescent bulb, the barrier rose from a concrete footing and towered above a hedge of twisted brambles. It was more than twice his height. The interlinked, heavy-gauge wire formed small diamonds wide enough to admit the toe of a pointed shoe or two fingers of a desperate hand, but on top of the panels, held open in a *V* by metal brackets at the top of each post, six strands of barbed wire were stretched taut. Imagining himself at that height trying to wriggle over the sharpened barbs, Miguel's muscles tightened, and his heart pounded. Sudden dizziness made him take a half step backward. He was forced to look away.

Edging back into the shadows at the side of a building, Miguel shoved his bare hands under his armpits. The night was cold, and his thin coat had no pockets. For two days and nights, he had trundled across the deserts of northern Mexico in open freight cars. He had eaten little and was tired. Fighting despair, his thoughts shifted to his wife, Concha, who remained behind in their small adobe-and-thatch house in Zacatecas. Concha would understand his fear, he thought, but she would count on him to get across the fence. *I've got to find a way*, he told himself. *I can't let my children go hungry.*

He shuffled back onto the sidewalk, but he had no place to go in this unfamiliar city and no money to pay for even the barest lodging. Drawn by the lights, Miguel meandered along the street towards the bars and shops that stood across from the two-story port-of-entry building. At the far corner of a blue-walled cantina, he lingered in the yellow glow of a neon Corona sign and listened to the foot-stomping polka blaring from the jukebox inside. Abruptly, the music changed to a *corrido*, a familiar song about a *campesino* like him, but it made him all the more lonely.

Preoccupied by the fence, he had ignored the aromas drifting with the music through the open doorway, but the scent of *carnitas* searing on a hot grill prompted him to glance into the brightly lit room. Two men stood at the bar bantering with a waitress. From their work boots and worn jeans, they appeared to be farmworkers like him, but unlike his own battered *sombrero campesino* and thin plaid jacket, they wore tan *tejanas*, and their jackets were lined with fleece.

Despite the open door and the chilly evening air, the waitress wore a low-cut blouse. Dark curls fell on her bare shoulders. She smiled at Miguel. For an instant, he considered asking for some scraps from the kitchen, but the men appeared to be *norteños*, and Miguel did not want to beg for food in front of them. But before he could move on, clued by the girl's glance, the men turned and stared.

"*¡Mojado!*" the heavier of the two snorted before turning back to the bar. His companion laughed.

Wetback! Miguel had been called out as if he were a thief about to sneak into another man's house in the night. His muscles tensed like a coiled rattlesnake's. "*¡Cabrónes!*" he hissed, but the men pretended not to hear. The waitress smiled nervously and slipped behind the bar. Miguel lunged across the threshold.

"*¡Cabrónes! ¡Putos!* Come outside, and we'll see who's a man!" he shouted.

A large man in a white apron suddenly appeared and blocked his way, grabbing Miguel's raised arm in an iron grip. "Calm down, *señor*. You're just getting yourself in trouble," the bartender warned sharply.

"One day you will know what it's like, *pendejos!*" Miguel shouted over the bartender's burly shoulder. "Then we'll see who laughs!"

The men turned and looked coldly at Miguel. The bartender spun him around and pushed him out the door. "Go! Get out of here!"

Unable to shake the insult, Miguel seethed as he strode on along the street. The men had made fun of him as if his poverty was a betrayal of his homeland. *The* gabachos *treat me as if this is their country and I am the trespasser*, he fumed. *They are the foreigners, soft* norteamericanos. *I can outwork them any hour of the day and all day.* But the stark truth of the slur deepened his sense of alienage in this unfamiliar border town. He felt worn, dirty. His pace slackened.

Clutching the strap of his small canvas backpack, Miguel stepped back for three passersby, two men and a woman, well-dressed norteamericanos, hurrying along the sidewalk. They did not acknowledge him, and he stared at their backs while they crossed the street and disappeared around the corner of the stucco port-of-entry building. He hated their wealth, their self-assurance, and that they were headed for warm houses.

Miguel glared at the fence, hating it too, dreading it, yet knowing he had to cross it. The taunts of the norteños in the cantina, *wetback, mojado,* rang in his head. His mind flashed back to the day, intent on helping his father repair the roof of the church, he had tried to climb the spindly ladder propped against the high wall but panicked and froze. Coached by onlookers, he tried to inch his way down but loosened his grip and cascaded over the final rungs to the ground amid jeers and laughter.

Concha had been there, but she had not laughed. Shamed, he did not try to climb the ladder again, but Concha did. She had worked on top of the roof with his father doing the job that he had meant to do as he had slunk away calling the spunky girl names. He could not quit this time; he was a father, and he and Concha had children to feed.

The melancholy *corrido*, carried on the night air from the jukebox in the cantina, faded, replaced by the sharp notes of a trumpet and a baritone voice belting out a *ranchera* tune.

I've got to do it, Miguel told himself. *It might as well be now!*

Miguel strode back along the sidewalk until the fence was again in darkness. Hesitating for a moment to avoid the headlights of a passing car, he ran across the street and brushed his way through the waist-high shrubs. He jumped as high as he could and grabbed the steel chain link above his head. Breathing heavily from the adrenalin rush, he pulled himself up, but the blunt toes of his boots could get little purchase in the small, diamond-shaped openings.

He dropped back and tried again. Struggling to remain calm, he hooked his fingers through the links and tried to walk his lower body up the panel. But the flat soles of his boots could not get traction, and he was able to raise himself only a few feet above the tops of the bushes. The dead weight of his body was cantilevered out from the fence, and the wire links cut into his fingers. A passing motorist honked and jeered.

On the other side of the fence, a Jeep pulled into the near-empty parking lot and bathed Miguel in its headlights. A dark-uniformed *patrullero* stepped out. Peering into the bright lights, Miguel could see just a silhouette of the man: the outline of the official's broad-brimmed hat and the handle of a revolver jutting from his hip. He let go of the fence and dropped clumsily into the brambles.

"Go ahead, señor, climb the fence!" the patrullero taunted. "I'll be waiting. If you get stuck in the wire and I have to climb up and cut you loose, you're going to go to the *corralón.*"

Miguel scrambled to his feet and fled back across the street, narrowly avoiding being hit by a car. Once again on the sidewalk, he felt safe enough from the official, but after the patrullero departed and his heart stopped racing, fatigue and pessimism returned.

Defeated, resigned to another night in the open, Miguel walked slowly back to a small plaza next to the cantina. At the late hour, it was vacant, and he sat down on a concrete bench.

Despite his failure to scale the daunting fence, Miguel reminded himself over and over that his destination was close at hand. Tomorrow he would look for a place to cross, he thought. It was clear that, at least in the town, the fence was closely watched. He would walk to the end of it if necessary. He did not know how far that would be, but he reasoned the barrier had to end somewhere.

Miguel shifted to a bench at the rear of the plaza. Hunching into his coat, he pulled his sombrero down over his eyes and folded his arms across his chest. The multi-colored lights of the cantina cast a soft glow on the trunks of the surrounding palm trees. Staccato notes of a trumpet and the resonant strum of a guitar drifted on the cold night air. Arranging his backpack as a pillow, covering his body with a piece of cardboard he had retrieved from a trashcan, Miguel curled up on the concrete seat.

The government in los Estados Unidos says my labor is no longer welcome, Miguel ruminated as he tried to drop into slumber. He did not want to break the law, but Concha and the children, his mother and father needed to eat. Crossing the border was his only hope.

On the other side, el otro lado, *I'll find work,* he promised himself. *I'll find a farmer who needs me. How wrong can that be?*

2

Clinging to the edge of consciousness, Miguel sensed the whir and thump of rubber tires on the potholed street. He could smell the un-combusted gas and oil from worn-out engines as the cars of early-morning commuters slowed and began to queue up at the port of entry. Huddled in his thin coat on the concrete bench, he felt his shoulder and hip joints aching from the hard surface and the cold. He prayed that the sun would come soon and warm him.

Soon he heard the footfalls of pedestrians hurrying past on their way to jobs on the other side of the fence, and when his eyes reluctantly opened, he saw their dark shapes in the dim light. Trying to escape the cold and the gnawing emptiness in his belly, he fought for a few more brief moments of sleep.

Grey light filtered through the fronds of tall palm trees. Women hurried through the plaza, clutching the hands of their children: girls dressed in dark blue skirts, white blouses peering out from dark sweaters, and boys wearing blue sweaters and grey pants. The children were headed to schools on the other side of the border, their mothers to clean the houses of well-to-do people in Calexico and El Centro or to clerk in downtown stores. The women turned their heads, shushing their children past the bench where Miguel lay. Feeling out of place, he sat up and pulled his *mochila,* which he had been using as a pillow, close to his side.

At the front of the plaza, three men, hunched into denim jackets, lunch buckets in hand, waited at the curb. Miguel stood and, working the stiffness out of his legs, edged towards them.

"*¡Hola!*" he called out hopefully.

The nearest, a young man wearing a straw tejana, turned. His companions glanced over their shoulders and looked at Miguel curiously.

"Do you know where I can find work?" Miguel asked.

The trio eyed him suspiciously. "*Pues,* they're picking winter vegetables down in the valley," the man in the tejana said, gesturing toward the south.

"No, I mean on the other side, al otro lado," Miguel stammered, gesturing towards the fence, which loomed tall and strong on the opposite side of the street.

The men looked at each other and then back at Miguel. "Well, they're picking carrots up by Holtville," the spokesman replied. "But you have to have papers in order to pass through the *garita.*"

"Well, no, I don't have papers anymore," Miguel temporized.

"That's too bad."

A dark-green pickup pulled to the curb across the street. Miguel watched as the men scrambled across the traffic lanes and piled into the open bed.

"Señor," one of the men called as the pickup started to pull away. Miguel looked up just in time to catch an apple arched his way. The apple was mealy but tasted moist, and he gobbled it down.

The gesture softened the men's rebuff. Still, they had jobs, and he did not, and Miguel fought slipping back into the melancholia of the previous evening. He watched the battered pickup slip into the line of cars, inch ahead, and then disappear under the stucco canopy at the port of entry

Miguel picked up his mochila and shuffled to a drinking fountain in an obscured corner of the plaza. The worn pack was not heavy. On the night before he left their small adobe house in San Pedro Piedra Gorda, Concha had folded two clean shirts, wrapping them in white tissue paper and tying the package with a bow. He rummaged beneath it, under a clean pair of worn jeans and a single change of socks and underwear, and retrieved his toothbrush and a small, flattened tube of toothpaste that had worked their way to the bottom of the bag.

Holding the spigot open with one hand, Miguel brushed his teeth in the cold water. He splashed more water on his face and wiped his hands over his mustache and the black stubble on his chin. Miguel's eyes were bright and friendly, and he smiled easily, but his unlined face was coarse, burned from the sun and wind on the high plateau of his native Zacatecas. When he finished at the fountain, he carefully wiped around the porcelain drain with his hand.

Miguel slung his mochila over his shoulder and ambled to the front of the plaza. He stood for a moment gazing at the imposing fence. It looked less frightening in daylight, and he spotted the outline of the unmarked garita that in previous years had been reserved for the *braceros*. For an instant, he recalled the élan he and other young, healthy men headed north for farm work once felt when they trotted through it.

Behind the gate was a low corrugated metal shed. In the building, men had once stood, laughing, their belts loosened and arms held out while a worker wearing a white coat had sprayed delousing powder up their sleeves and down their pants. *Not this time,* Miguel mused. Los Estados Unidos no longer wanted the braceros. The Mexicans still needed work, but the shed now was dark and looked abandoned. The padlocked gate was just another flat grey panel in a barrier that stretched along the street as far as Miguel could see.

On the other side of the fence, directly across the street from where he stood, was a silver water tower. Miguel suffered a moment of dizziness when he looked up. Suspended beneath the curved underbelly of the tank was a green and white cabin, big enough to hold a man. Windows looked out from all sides, and in one of them was a dark-green uniformed patrullero, *la migra*. The official showed no sign that he had noticed him, but Miguel quickly looked away. He did not retreat beneath the palms but, instead, turned onto the sidewalk and headed east, walking against the flow of pedestrians headed across the border to work.

The new day offered hope, and Miguel was buoyed by the sunlight and the bustle of the morning commuters. He decided to scout out the fence; it might not be as well guarded or maintained once past the town, he reasoned. There might be a hole; perhaps it would end before he had to walk too far.

The January sun offered little warmth, and he walked facing into the wind and dirt blown up from the street. Miguel's coat and sombrero offered little protection. His walk settled into a rhythm, but the gnawing emptiness in his stomach returned. The cold made his hunger seem worse. He had a few pesos, but he put searching for food out of his mind. The money could buy him little, and he might need it later.

Miguel paused at an intersection and admired a row of neat frame houses on the other side of the fence. They were painted blue, white, and yellow and stood facing him across a paved street. Their small fenced yards were mowed, the shrubs trimmed. These were not the homes of rich people, he thought, but of workers like him.

On his side of the border, the street was rutted and dirty, the houses of adobe with dirt yards. Miguel put the difference out of mind. If life required a fence between the two parallel streets, he did not question the sense of it. Philosophy was for men with full bellies, his father taught him. It mattered only to get to the other side and earn some money to send home.

Further on, the street turned south. If he wanted a job on this side of the line, in the Mexicali Valley as the men in the plaza suggested, that was the direction he should take, he thought. If there were not too many other men already working, he might find work and eat a meal that night.

Miguel tried again to push his hunger aside. Even if he were hired, the job would pay little: two, maybe three, dollars a day. Even that was uncertain, and it would not be enough to be able to send anything back to Concha. He could earn as much as ten dollars a day in California, but either way was a gamble, he acknowledged. He looked once more down the highway, then crossed, and continued to walk east along the fence. Jumping the line offered a better chance than staying in Mexico, he concluded.

On the other side of the fence, rich, green alfalfa fields supplanted the neat rows of frame houses. The street on his side was now dirt, the neighborhood clearly poorer. Most of the houses were made of unglazed adobe bricks. In the center of each intersection, round sewer pipes topped by iron manhole covers rose from the dirt, vestiges of a paving and sewer project grandly begun but never completed. Now out of view of norteamericano shoppers and tourists, the fence was topped by loops of concertina wire.

Miguel saw a low cloud of dust puffing through the fence ahead of him. When his angle to the fence permitted him a clear view through the chain links, he was startled to see a green-and-white Jeep grinding in low gear along a dirt strip next to the fence.

The Jeep dragged a heavy metal bar trailing short lengths of chain that created a pattern of parallel ridges in the leveled dirt. The patrullero drove slowly, all the while peering out his side window at the ground. It dawned on Miguel that, even if he could get over the fence, his tracks would be discovered by la migra and he would be pursued. Clearly, climbing the fence was out of the question. On one hand, Miguel felt relieved, but he still would have to find the way around it and get past the formidable patrulleros.

With no clear plan other than to reach the end of the fence, Miguel continued to walk toward the morning sun. Near the outskirts of the barrio, he came upon a *taquería*, open on the front, cardboard and lathe walls supporting a flimsy tin roof. An old man grilled carnitas over a charcoal fire. The searing meat smelled delicious.

Welcoming the chance for warmth and someone to talk to, Miguel paused. If he continued in this direction, he might soon be in open country, and he thought he might as well use his few pesos while he could.

"*¡Hola, chaparrito!*" Peering out from the shaded interior, his face deeply lined and toothless, the old man grinned at Miguel.

"*Buenos días,*" Miguel responded formally; he was offended by the old man's reference to his short stature but said nothing. "Can you sell me some tortillas, *por favor*?" Warily, he retrieved a couple of coins from his pocket, hoping not to have to take his sole five-peso note from his wallet.

The old man grabbed two corn tortillas from a covered clay pot and rolled them into a piece of waxed paper. "*Veinte centavos,*" he said, sizing up Miguel and taking note of the small coins he was fingering.

Miguel passed the coins to the man's gnarly hand and grasped the warm tortillas.

"Going to *al otro lado, the other side*?" the old man cackled, again startling Miguel who had hoped he was not being so obvious.

"*Sí,* if it is possible," Miguel admitted. He hesitated, and then asked,. "How far does the fence go?"

"Oh, about three more *kilómetros.*" the vendor answered, gesturing towards the east. "And then the canal runs along *la frontera* for about fifteen kilómetros. But it turns north. Then you can cross through the desert, but watch out for the *coyotes*. Coyotes like *pollos,* chickens!" He cackled at his own joke.

Miguel had not known about the canal, but at least he now had an idea of how far he would have to walk. He should reach the desert in the afternoon light, he thought. The old man's warning scared him; devils, both humanlike and animal, could be found in the desert, and he feared encountering them in the dark.

Beyond the barrio, open alfalfa fields extended along both sides of the fence. He walked past a watchtower, perched on a tower of latticed steel girders. It appeared to be unoccupied, and he speculated that the patrulleros manned it after dark.

Soon, Miguel saw a high bank angling towards the border. When he reached the point where the fence was closest to it, about fifty yards away, it turned abruptly up and over the earthen bank. He climbed to the top of the levee and saw a broad, fast-moving waterway about fifty yards across. The fence continued its march out into the water; the last post was wound in concertina wire to keep anyone from swinging around it. To the east, the waterway stretched in a straight line, a continuous barrier along the border as far as Miguel could see. On top of either bank was a dirt road. Behind him, the fence blocked the trail, but his way to the east was unimpeded.

At the edge of the water, among the reeds where the current was slow, a white crane stood on one leg. The other was folded against the underside of its body, the intertarsal joint appearing like an arrow pointing north. It reminded Miguel of an iron rooster perched on top of a weathervane. It was a good omen, he thought. But the current in the middle of the canal was clearly too swift to swim.

3

 Miguel walked for about an hour along the top of the canal bank. He was approaching a group of children playing on the path when a little girl broke away from her playmates and raced to intercept him. Her feet were bare, her print dress dirty, and the blue-knit sweater she wore was torn at one shoulder.

"¡Hola! ¡Señor!" the waif called out. When she reached him, she fell in step at his side. The grime on her face was streaked with snot. She brushed back a tangled dark tress as her bright, earnest eyes pleaded up to Miguel. Pressing her hand into his, she asked, "Do you want to go to el otro lado, señor?"

"Maybe," Miguel said. He guessed her age to be no more than six or seven.

"I will take you, señor, if you give me one hundred pesos—por favor?"

Miguel laughed. "No, no, *mija*. That's impossible. I don't have a hundred pesos."

"Yes, you do, señor! Yes, you do! You're going to *el norte* to make a lot of money—become a rich man. You give me one hundred pesos, and I will show you a place to cross. La migra will never catch you. You give me money—por favor?"

The imp had spunk. Miguel was piqued by her offer, but further along the canal bank, a group of older youths watched and were starting to move in his direction. "Look, mija, I have no money. But I have a little girl like you. Her name is Lupita. What is yours?"

"Juanita," she said, her eyes turning solemn. Seeing the older kids approaching, the child hung back, tugging Miguel's hand, but the ragtag crew soon surrounded them. In good-natured banter, they also offered to take him to a crossing place and begged for money.

"Give us some money, señor," the urchins pleaded. "You're going to el norte. Get rich. Drive a big car!"

As the pack neared a *colonia* of thatch-roofed hovels, crowded against the base of the canal bank, their pleas grew more insistent. The wattle and cardboard shacks clustered around a small stream. Partially hidden by a tangle of bushes and reeds, the running water seemed to disappear beneath the canal bank. It dawned on Miguel that the bushes concealed a culvert.

"Is this the crossing place?" Miguel asked the gang. "A sewage drain under the canal?"

"You've got to give us money first, or you can't go through," a wiry boy in a dirty T-shirt and dark trousers threatened.

"I don't have any money, *hijo*," Miguel replied. "I am poor just like you, and I have a family to feed."

"It doesn't matter," a boy at the back of the throng shouted. "You've got to pay!" A chorus of jeers reinforced the demand.

Hoping to spot a parent, Miguel glanced at the silent shacks. But no faces appeared. It seemed only children lived in the hamlet, at least in daytime. "I'm sorry, hijos," he said finally and clambered down the bank. Parting a cluster of reeds, he found the concrete culvert. He was about to step down into the brown water when a clump of caliche smashed into the back of his neck, crumbling and forcing dirt inside his shirt collar.

"¡Pendejo! ¡Mojado!" the youths taunted, their thin arms whipping hard chunks of clay at him.

"Stop it, *chamacos!*" Miguel yelled angrily, raising his arms over his head. But the rain of missiles did not stop, and finally he scrambled back up to the top of the bank. Only then did the barrage slacken, but the taunts continued.

"*¡Pinche cabrón! ¡Chicano!*" the urchins called.

Perplexed, breathing heavily, Miguel turned and stalked off along the top of the canal bank.

"*¡Cincuenta pesos, hombre! ¡Veinte pesos!*" the rabble beseeched, futilely trying to extort even a few pesos for access to their zealously protected crossing.

Indignant, Miguel did not turn his head, not even to look back at Juanita, who was the last to give up following him. But the child had stirred thoughts of his own little daughter, Lupita, and he considered going back and giving her his five-peso note. *She ought at least to have sandals,* he thought. Bested by a gang of brats, he felt humiliated. *The others would simply take the money from her,* he rationalized finally and kept going.

Walking through the afternoon, from his vantage point on the top of the levee, Miguel admired the farmland to the north: straight rows of bare-branched citrus trees, broad green expanses of hay and alfalfa, and towering date palms, their fronds forming a grey-green canopy over a darkened grove. *That's where I want to be,* he thought, looking at the fields with envy. He had never cultivated fields that large, but he could. He had rented a tractor by the day to plow his field in Piedra Gorda. It couldn't be that different, he thought. And he could irrigate. He had never worked in a date grove, but he had harvested citrus and peaches when he was a bracero.

The sun had arched over him, and Miguel could see his shadow growing longer on the path. He was approaching a low concrete weir lying across the canal. When he reached it, he was not surprised to find that a padlocked chainlink gate barred him from crossing the structure. The gate was only slightly taller than he was, and Miguel considered climbing over, but he saw a Jeep approaching on the opposite canal bank, leaving a long, low tail of dust in its wake. Instinctively, he scurried down the bank, stopping when he reached a trail that appeared to mark *la frontera.* Searching for cover, he stepped behind a row of ocotillo that once had served as a fence for a now-abandoned *casita*. But the whip-like stalks of the cactus plant did not hide him.

The patrullero driving the green-and-white Jeep glanced cursorily in Miguel's direction and pulled up at the weir. Ignoring Miguel, he got out and carefully studied the dirt at the edge of the concrete deck. The official's trousers were neatly creased; a bronze badge glinted on the breast of his green-satin jacket. His fur collar was turned up against the blowing sand, and a light-colored Stetson sat squarely on his head. Miguel noted the man's tan, clean-shaven face. All the patrulleros appeared young, tall, and able, and they seemed to be everywhere.

Miguel looked around for one of the concrete obelisks that periodically marked la frontera, but he saw only clumps of creosote bush and the sandy path. Uncertain if he was indeed standing on the Mexican side, he prepared to run, but the patrullero did not seem to pay him any attention. Retrieving a wood-handled rake from the bed of his Jeep, the official let himself through the gate and, at the edge of the concrete deck, raked the dirt in a wide parallel pattern. He paused when he found the tracks Miguel had left, seeming to study them, and then briskly raked them out. Satisfied, the patrullero threw his rake into the back of his Jeep and drove off.

Miguel did not climb back up the canal bank, but stayed on the dirt trail. He had not walked far before the canal curved off to the northeast. The trail continued straight, however, passing an occasional concrete obelisk, but now there was a new feature. Immediately to the north of the markers, a strip the width of a one-lane road had been cleared through the brush. The sandy surface was dragged smooth, similar to the strip along the fence he had seen a patrullero groom that morning. Wary of leaving a track, Miguel stayed on the footpath.

Soon, the canal bank was just a low flat line fading away to the northeast, and Miguel's horizon became an endless sea of low dunes and creosote bushes. Far to the east lay a range of mountains. Brightened by the setting sun, the beige slopes blushed red. He did not think he would have to walk much farther; the old man said he would be able to turn north once the canal veered away from la frontera.

Rather than risk having his footprints discovered in daylight, Miguel decided to continue on the border trail. He feared the terrors he might encounter in the desert in the dark, but it was clear that he would not be able to evade the patrulleros, at least in daylight. If he waited until after dark, he reasoned, la migra would not be able to find his tracks until the following dawn. He hoped to be well past la frontera by then, circling back into the cultivated fields he had seen from the canal bank, where he might find a warm place to sleep and maybe something to eat. With the stars to guide him, a trek through the desert in the dark seemed not quite so hard.

His destination within reach, success seemed close at hand. The barriers, the high fence, and the canal were gone, and knowing he could step across *la línea* at any time exhilarated him. That afternoon, he had stood close to a patrullero and held his ground, as if some of the official's presence and confidence had transferred to him. Miguel did not think any more about the old man's warning.

When the sun was no longer powerful enough to make his shadow, Miguel turned and watched the lifeless yellow orb grow large and, then, like an apparition, fade from sight. Wisps of high silver clouds streaked the eggshell-blue sky. Still, he trudged towards the east through sand and scraggly clumps of creosote bushes. It was getting colder, and he tilted the brim of his hat so the blowing sand would not pepper his face. In the fading light, the far-off mountains turned chocolate.

Deciding he had come far enough, Miguel squatted on the hard caliche and swung his mochila to the ground. Retrieving the tortillas he had purchased from the old man, he picked away the cheap waxed paper. Tearing each disk in half and folding it into quarters, he savored the familiar corn flavor. He had no water, a matter he would have to address later in the night. Meager as his meal had been, Miguel regarded it as a reward, congratulating himself for having reached this point in his quest.

As if pausing to plot its course, the wind stopped. The small, thick, yellow-green leaves of the creosote bushes left a faint oily scent on the air. The desert was quiet, except for the chirping of the night birds. A pair of mourning doves startled him. Miguel jerked his head up and vainly tried to follow the zigzagging silhouettes against the darkening sky.

The evening star, Venus, was out, and Miguel admired it glowing brightly above the western horizon. Venus would guide him, he decided. He would walk north with the bright planet over his left shoulder and then turn toward it, working his way through the dunes and back into the cultivated fields. He would find work, maybe even on one of those farms. But, first, he had to get past la migra. It was lonely in the desert, but lonely for the patrullero, too. Miguel was confident they would not be able to find him in the dark. *The odds had turned in his favor.*

Miguel stood and shook the stiffness out of his legs. In the deepening grey, he surveyed the rounded crests of the low dunes and the dark creosote thickets stretching endlessly to the north. Involuntarily, he shivered. He reached inside his collar and pulled out the scapular bearing the image of the Virgen de Guadalupe that his mother had given him at his confirmation. He pressed it to his lips. Feeling very much like the poor campesino the Virgin had appeared to on a wintry night four hundred years before, Miguel beseeched her to watch over him and his family. He thought of Concha and the expected arrival of a new baby. Then he made the sign of the cross three times, kissed the sacred image, and returned it to its place against his breast.

Miguel glanced once more at Venus. Then, not bothering to hide his tracks, he took a long stride toward the north, then another, almost breaking into a run. In the ambient light of the stars, he threaded his way between dark clumps of creosote bushes. His heart raced; he was uncertain if it was from elation or fear.

He was across the line.

4

 As Border Patrol Inspector Bill Garner lurched in low gear along the uneven drag road, a spotlight mounted on the rear bumper of his Jeep lit up the ground passing directly beneath the driver's side window. Protecting his eyes and face from the sting of wind-driven sand with the brim of his Stetson, his right hand steadying the steering wheel, Garner leaned out the window and studied the groomed sand. The low angle of the beam created a distinct shadow behind every irregularity, including the three-toed footprints of peripatetic lizards and the ladder-like elongated letter *S* of a prowling sidewinder. These he ignored, but he glanced up occasionally to correct his course and be watchful of obstacles on the trail.

Tonight, Garner was working the east desert alone; during the winter months, there was not much activity. A norther had blown into the valley, and the temperature was near freezing, colder still because of the wind. Although Garner's Jeep was retrofitted with a metal cab, it had no heater. On many such quiet nights, he would meet the Yuma PI patrolling west along the Algodones Dunes, and they would get out of their Jeeps and build a greasewood fire to warm themselves. But border patrol gossip was not on his mind tonight. Instead, he thought of getting home to his warm house in Calexico and his warm bed. He hoped he would not cut any sign before his shift ended, at least not human sign, and would get off his shift at midnight.

Tonight would be a good night to cuddle up, Garner thought, and he imagined crawling naked between the warm covers and snuggling up to his wife, Margie, in her flannel nightgown. He often did not get home until two or three in the morning, but she had been a good sport about his shift work. In her slumber, she invariably rolled onto her side and gave him her back. When he was sure his fingers had warmed and would not be slapped away in protest, he would slip his hand up under the hem of her nightgown and cup her soft, full breast. As often as not, feeling his erection pressed up against her, she would awaken and make love to him.

Garner wondered about the Mexican he had seen late in the afternoon at the Alamo check. The man wore a faded, plaid jacket and a flat sombrero with a feather tassel dangling from the back rim, a sombrero campesino, Mexicans called it, a farmer hat. Men from the interior states—Jalisco, Michoacán, Zacatecas—workers who for many years had come to the United States as braceros, wore the distinctive hats with the fly-flickers. *His thin jacket won't keep him warm on a night like this*, Garner thought.

It was apparent the Mexican was seeking a place to cross, and Garner knew it was not likely he would turn back. Despite the predictability of the man's intentions, he hoped he would have second thoughts and seek out a warm place to stay in Mexicali instead. *Wets deserve to be home on a cold night like this, too,* he thought. If the man did cross, Garner hoped he would make his move early so he could catch him and deliver him to the corralón in El Centro before the end of his shift.

A shadow on the brightly lit sand outlining the distinct curve of the outer edge of the sole of a shoe caught Garner's attention. Without lifting his eyes, Garner jammed in the clutch and stomped on the brake, shoving the floor-mounted gearshift over and up until he engaged reverse. On the wind-blown surface, a faint heal mark was also visible. *The man's weight is on the balls of his feet.* Pointing north across the drag road, a second footprint appeared ahead of the first.

Garner got out of his Jeep and examined the tracks in the beam of his five-cell flashlight. The man's stride was long and deliberate. *The "fresh-start stride,"* he mentally labeled it: purposeful, vigorous, the tracks of a hungry man, desperate to cross the border. Later in the night, when the man tired or became disoriented, the footprints would tell a different story.

Though the ridges in the sand were worn by the wind, the deep serrations in the sole and heel of the man's boot left a distinct pattern of rectangles. *The Mexican's wearing tan-topped work boots, the kind braceros wore,* Garner thought. *This is the guy!*

Garner followed the tracks far enough to ascertain that the Mexican was indeed headed north. At this point, the alien still had to cross the All American Canal, which had curved away from the border but lay across his path two miles ahead.

Because of the blowing sand, it was tricky to estimate how much of a lead the alien had. Since he still was able to make out the tread, Garner calculated the tracks were about an hour old. Possibly the man already had reached the canal. The crossing at Drop #4 was lighted, a beacon in the empty desert. Once the alien reached the canal bank, seeking a place to cross, he would walk along the water's edge toward the light. With any luck, Garner thought, he could beat him to the crossing. He turned off his sign-cutting light and sped across the desert hardpan toward the drop.

Arriving at the crossing, it did not take long for Garner to find the work-boot tread in the sandy soil at the edge of the lighted concrete apron. In the stiff wind, the exposed tracks were fading rapidly. With the aid of his sign-cutting light, he found the tracks again on the north side of the drop heading onto a dirt road that led directly north to State Highway 98. The highway was less than a mile away. Garner did not bother dogging out the tracks, but hastily disengaged the four-wheel drive, shifted into third, and raced to the junction with the highway.

Garner found the tracks again at the edge of the highway. Fresher now, they led first onto the asphalt, then back to a clump of brush at the base of a mesquite tree. He got out and searched the area with his flashlight, but instead of finding the Mexican as he expected, he discovered the tracks headed back again to the highway. *He must have tried to hide from the headlights of a passing car,* Garner thought.

On the shoulder, Garner found a set of tire tracks made by the worn front and rear wheels of a vehicle that had partially pulled off the road. The boot prints, some partially covered by the tire tread, shuffled back and then disappeared. A spray of loose gravel indicated the car had spun its tires when it took off. *The guy must have seen my lights,* Garner thought.

Believing he had been only minutes behind the alien, Garner cursed his bad luck. The car had picked up the Mexican, he concluded. "El Centro, this is twenty-two fourteen," he keyed the Motorola and waited for a response as two clashes of static told him the transmission had hit the repeater tower and been forwarded to the radio room at Sector Headquarters.

"Go ahead, two-two-one-four," the night dispatcher, Gwendolyn, responded.

"I have a got-away at Highway 98, just north of Drop #4, about four miles east of the East Highline Canal. Looks like he was picked up in a vehicle."

"Ten-four, two-two-one-four."

5

As he approached the turnoff to Drop #4, Chuy Gallegos took his foot off the accelerator of his '57 Ford. He was headed home after an afternoon at a card room in Algodones, and at this time of year, he was not especially looking for pollos. Nevertheless, he had encountered wetbacks at this intersection before. If a man was hungry enough, he would jump the line, even in midwinter. He flipped his headlights off and on, a signal to any potential hitchhiker who might be hiding in the creosote thickets that dotted the side of the highway.

Chuy made a living smuggling, but his livelihood depended upon being constantly ready to grab an opportunity. One night, he had picked up a group of eight line jumpers at this corner, crowding them into his aging four-door sedan. It made no difference to Chuy whether his cargo were humans or drugs. Farmers needed workers; kids wanted drugs. The appetites of both led to big profits for him.

Chuy was pleased when his high beams caught a lone figure crouched near a small mesquite tree off to the side of the road. The man carried a small pack over the shoulder of his plaid coat and wore a white farmer hat. Chuy pulled across the empty highway and beckoned to the man who, after a moment's hesitation, approached the open car window.

"Where are you going, hombre?" Chuy asked in Spanish.

"I'm looking for work, señor," Miguel replied. He had not expected the car to stop and was prepared to run when it crossed to his side of the road and the driver rolled down the window. The man spoke to him in Spanish, but something about him, his too-familiar manner, told Miguel to be cautious.

"There's not much going on right now," Chuy temporized. He mentally ran down the list of possibilities but could think of no one needing workers. Farmers were harvesting winter vegetables, but because there was little work further north in the winter, there were plenty of workers available in the valley and green-carders from Mexicali.

Chuy was an American citizen and could cross the border at will, but he never risked the loss of his car by smuggling through the port of entry. Instead, he met intending line jumpers in the cantinas in Mexicali or San Luis Rio Colorado, drove them to a crossing point, and picked them up again on the US side of the border. Chuy delivered the workers to farmers or labor contractors who asked no questions and paid him a fee for his service. If the pollo had money, Chuy made him pay, too. It was lucrative, but seasonal.

"How about Los Angeles? I will take you to LA."

Miguel grew uneasy. "I have no money, señor."

Chuy was not surprised by the answer, but he knew the pollo would try to conceal what he had. He wanted to find out how much the man had, peaceably if he could. Even if he did not give him a ride, Chuy did not intend to drive away empty handed.

"Well, you're not going to find any work around here, hombre. I'll take you to LA for fifty dollars."

"No, señor. *Gracias,* but I don't have fifty dollars," Miguel said. The tone in the man's voice made him uneasy. In the glow of the dash lights, he was startled to see that beneath the narrow brim of the man's hat, he had only half an ear. The portion that remained was a grotesque stump.

"All right! Give me ten dollars, and I will take you to El Centro," Chuy barked. *The guy's a shithead*, he muttered under his breath, losing patience. He had not stopped just to be stiffed by a pollo. "La migra is going to catch you for sure, but I'm not going to take you any further."

"Señor, I don't have ten dollars."

"You need me, pendejo!" Chuy flashed. "Why am I bargaining with you? You don't have a chance. La migra is going to have your fuckin' ass by midnight."

Alarmed by Chuy's outburst, Miguel stepped back, but it was too late. Chuy grabbed the .45 he kept un-holstered beside him on the seat and pointed it across his chest at Miguel. "Give me your wallet!" he hissed.

Miguel froze. Reaching slowly into his hip pocket he pulled out his thin, plastic-wrapped, wallet and put it in Chuy's outstretched palm. Chuy tore away the flimsy covering and examined the contents under the dashboard lights: family pictures, a green cardboard Cartilla Militar and a five-peso note. Chuy ripped out the bill and threw the wallet in the dirt.

"¡Chinga tu pinche madre, cabrón!" Chuy yelled, disgusted with his small take. He gunned the car angrily. The wheels spit gravel as he pulled back onto the highway.

Stunned by the sudden assault, Miguel groped in the dirt for his wallet. He had been robbed, but to whom could he complain? He felt vulnerable, helpless. In Mexico, the powerful always abused the weak. One knew that and adapted to it, but he was in los Estados Unidos now, and the *bandido* acted with the same impunity as the thugs in Mexico. It was if he had crossed the border only in his imagination. Nothing really had changed.

Anxious not to be spotted by another car, Miguel hurried across the pavement and, in the dark, threaded his way among the sand dunes and creosote bushes. Fearful he would encounter another terror, his heart pounded. He prayed to the Virgencita to keep him safe from more robbers and away from the clutches of la migra.

Miguel had counted on the patrulleros not being able to track him in the dark, but alone in the desert, griped by fright, he fantasized that they might have supernatural powers. *La migra might be watching right now, hiding behind the next dune, ready to rise from the earth and grab me,* his panicky thoughts raced. A rattlesnake might strike him; they climbed into greasewood brambles and low mesquite trees. If he brushed against one and it drove its fangs into his arm or his face, it would be fatal. He might stumble into a den of *javelinas* and be torn apart by their sharp tusks.

The exhilaration he had felt when he had strode across the drag trail, across la linea, was gone. The unexpected encounter with the bandit left him somber, depressed, and fearful, but turning back was out of the question. Necessity pushed him on.

The wind had picked up. Miguel kept his head down against the blowing sand and wrapped his arms across his chest. The half-moon that had lighted his path earlier in the evening no longer seemed as bright, and Miguel stumbled frequently into low creosote brambles that slowed his progress.

From time to time, Miguel glanced up. Venus, his magical star, still hung above the western horizon. He thought about the star that had shone above Bethlehem on La Noche Buena, guiding the shepherds and the kings to the infant Jesus. He let himself believe that the Virgencita had placed the planet there to guide him, and gradually, he turned toward the west, toward the star. The steady, celestial beacon soothed him. His gait became more confident, and he stumbled less. He felt warmer and let his arms swing freely again.

Miguel's thoughts returned to finding a place to sleep and something to eat. The star gave him confidence in his reckoning. It would not be long before he was out of the desert and back into the fields and orchards he had seen in the afternoon. The men standing at the curb that morning had said they were harvesting carrots. There must be other vegetable crops as well, Miguel thought, radishes, celery, for certain, lettuce. He would be able to forage from the fields once he was out of the desert.

6

Several hours had passed since Miguel had been robbed. He had gotten past his panic and was now preoccupied picking his way between prickly clumps of greasewood. The moon had set, and the meager light of the stars provided little help; he kept his hands ready to break a fall. With the aid of Venus, maintaining his direction was easy enough, but constant sidesteps and detours slowed him. Finally, he heard the faint sound of rushing water. To his front, against the star-speckled night sky, a dark, level horizon loomed. Miguel thought it might be the top of a berm.

Miguel steadied himself with his hands as he climbed up the bank. At the top, although he could not see the water, the gurgle of the current was close. Kneeling, steadying himself against the clay bank with one hand, he eased himself down until he could dip the other in the cold stream. The fast current flowed north, and he thought this must be an offshoot of the big canal that ran along the border. Careful that he not slip into the canal, he cupped his hand and lifted the water to his desiccated mouth and throat. He dipped his hand repeatedly until his belly felt relieved.

The top of the bank was free of brush, and Miguel followed it north. He had not gone far when he arrived at a bridge that carried a road across the canal. Standing on the pavement, he could see a dome of light on the distant horizon, which he recognized as the glow of a city. Above it, beckoning, the steady blue light of Venus shone in the black sky.

The wind seemed less harsh. Gone was the dry odor of greasewood, replaced by the rich aroma of cultivated fields. Leaving the canal behind, Miguel walked west on the blacktop road, but he realized he needed to bear north, more toward Venus and the distant city lights. Abandoning the pavement, he clambered through a ditch onto the even surface of a field. Striding northwest directly toward his guiding star, his boots swished through growing alfalfa.

The familiar smell of the crop encouraged Miguel, and first his shoulders and then the rest of his muscles relaxed. He had negotiated the desert safely and arrived as planned in the cultivated fields of the Valle Imperial. He had encountered neither la migra nor wild javelinas, and he forgot about his panic. But he was cold, starting to tire, and his mind turned to finding shelter for the night, possibly something to eat.

As he hiked across the field, Miguel was engulfed in a black expanse that was the perfect inverse of the star-filled sky. He nearly stumbled when he arrived at the edge of a dirt road, and then he was crossing another field. In the distance, well below the horizon, a single pinpoint of light appeared. He did not consciously decide to go to it, but nonetheless, if only out of curiosity, he felt drawn.

When Miguel got closer, he saw that the source of the light was a seemingly unattended lantern that had been placed on the bank of a field lateral. In the circle of light, he could see long, straight furrows, like the corrugations of a washboard, extending at right angles from the lateral. In the narrow channels, shimmering black fingers of water stretched off into the black field.

Preoccupied by the light, Miguel nearly stumbled into the pickup truck parked at the edge of the field. It appeared to be unoccupied, but he skirted it carefully. The man tending the water running onto the field was around somewhere, and he did not want to be mistaken for a thief. *It's best to be cautious,* Miguel thought. *The man might be the owner of the field and object to me being on his land.* He stopped well short of the lantern.

At the far edge of the light, the irrigator appeared. He wore knee-high rubber boots and carried a shovel on his shoulder. He was dressed in a heavy canvas jacket and a hood. A red bandana protected the lower part of his face from the cold. Stepping carefully from furrow to furrow, the man occasionally stopped to remove a clod of dirt from a channel with a short jab of his spade.

The irrigator was not tall like many *gringos*, Miguel observed. He worked like a *mexicano* and on such a cold night. *Maybe he's the patron; how careful he is to make sure the water doesn't overtop the beds and flood the plants.*

Miguel was puzzled. On past trips to California, he had worked only with braceros. *Norteños don't like hard work,* he believed. *Yet this irrigator is taking as much care with his task as any man tending his own crop. Is it possible that he is able to hire me? Could it be as simple as walking up to him and offering to do the work?* Miguel crouched outside the reach of the light and watched, shivering as the cold wind blew across the wet field.

7

Satisfied that the water from the field channel was flowing uniformly through the sugar-beet beds, Ohscar Romero picked up his lantern and walked to the edge of the field. He set it down at the foot of a large cottonwood, dropped his spade, and took a seat with his back to the tree. In the stillness, compressed gas rushing through the throat of the lantern made a hollow, rasping sound and then combusted on the white-hot mantles. He took a thermos out of his lunch bucket. The hot coffee steamed in the cold air.

Ohscar was about to peel back the foil from a burrito his wife had packed for his dinner when some instinct made him look up. At the outer edge of the lantern light, a solitary figure stood gazing at him. The apparition appeared so unexpectedly that he thought at first it was a ghost. The man's arms were folded across his chest, like a corpse Ohscar once had seen laid out in a wooden coffin. His heart stopped; he grasped for the handle of his spade and pulled it close to his side.

The man wore a flat-crowned sombrero and a faded plaid coat. His skin was dark, and he had a small mustache like Ohscar's. Squinting into the bright light, he shuffled forward and crouched facing him. With a start, Ohscar realized that he had seen the man before, at the cantina La Frontera, across the border in Mexicali where he and his friend, Juan, had gone for a few beers. Juan had taunted him, but the Mexican did not appear to recognize Ohscar. *Juan should not have called the man a wetback*, Ohscar thought.

"Where are you going on a night like this, señor?" Ohscar asked in Spanish.

"Do you know where I can find work?" Miguel responded.

The man's forthrightness startled Ohscar. This close to the border, Mexicans walked through the fields in the dead of night for only one reason.

"Did you jump the line?"

"Well, I have no papers."

Juan was right. The man is indeed a wetback, Ohscar thought, and instinctively he became wary.

"There is no work around here, señor," Ohscar replied. *What if this guy asks the boss for a job? Would Mr. Pinchney give him work?* This was the first steady farm job Ohscar had had, and it had been a boon for his family. *What if this wetback says he'll work for less or that he doesn't need a house? Would Mr. Pinchney hire him and let me go? That's the way the system works.*

The Mexican stiffened. His thin jacket was no protection for the cold night, and he shivered. His eyes and face were weary. Softening, Ohscar freshened his cup with hot coffee and held it out to the stranger. The man grasped the steaming cup in his bare hands, savored the warmth for an instant, and raised it to his lips. Undoubtedly, he was hungry, Ohscar realized, but he stopped at passing the Mexican his second burrito that lay in the bottom of his lunchbox.

"Gracias," Miguel said. When he finished, he handed the cup back and, as if searching for a reason to remain in Ohscar's presence, swiveled on his heels and looked out at the neat rows of sugar beets.

"That's a big field," Miguel observed. "Much bigger than I have in Mexico. I grow corn and some vegetables."

"Sí," Ohscar replied, his unease returning. "If you want to find work, you need to go further north . . . and west, past El Centro. They're cutting lettuce up there."

Miguel looked blankly at Ohscar, sensing his impatience. He rose stiffly. "Pues, gracias, señor, I'm going now." Hunched into his turned-up collar, he turned and trudged north into the black night.

Ohscar noticed the feather tassel dangling from the rear of the man's sombrero and his worn work boots. *He's come a long way,* Ohscar thought. *But he knows what he's about; he's been here before—probably he was a bracero.* Ohscar waited until the Mexican disappeared before unwrapping his second burrito.

Ohscar's lantern, which before the intrusion had provided a warm, comforting light, no longer seemed as cheery, and he began to worry about his family. The Romeros's kitchen was a happy place in the evenings. After finishing the dishes, Javier, Rita, and Mirabele worked on their homework at the kitchen table while listening to the Beatles and Elvis on KICO from El Centro. But the lights would be turned off in the kitchen by now, and Carolina and the children would be in bed.

The older children slept in the living room, and the youngest shared the single bedroom with their parents. Ohscar worried about the heater, a natural-gas panel set into a wall in the kitchen. During cold snaps such as tonight, people died from carbon monoxide emitted from unvented heaters. Before he left that afternoon, he warned Carolina to leave a window partially open. There were so many cracks around the cheaply constructed window casements and worn-out doors that opening a window seemed superfluous. Still, Ohscar worried.

The small, white, clapboard house had sat vacant and decaying on a far corner of the Pinchney Ranch until Mr. Pinchney allowed the Romero family to move in. The cistern had been removed for other uses on the ranch, and Ohscar had to carry water in milk cans from the pump-house at the ranch headquarters. Yet, Ohscar and Carolina felt lucky to have the place. As migrant workers following the crops up and down the state, the family rarely had been able to stay more than a month or two in one place.

Mr. Pinchney paid Ohscar a dollar an hour, but deducted fifty dollars from his monthly earnings for the house. Since the work was steady, Ohscar and Carolina felt it was a fair exchange. Mr. Pinchney grew sugar beets, and during the long growing season, the plants required water every ten days. The Pinchney Ranch had enough fields that Ohscar was kept busy almost every night. Because several of the fields were at a distance, Ohscar was permitted to gas up his old Ford pickup from the tank the grower kept for the tractors.

Ohscar was a hard worker, impressing Mr. Pinchney with his willingness to put in long hours. He could also drive a tractor, cultivate, and help prepare the fields for fall planting. Mr. Pinchney had talked of keeping him on for that purpose after the harvest.

The Mexican's appearance on the very farm where only months before, in a stroke of good fortune, Ohscar himself had found work unnerved him. His cousin had held the job previously but, at his wife's urging, had left for Los Angeles to find a factory job. Before leaving, he had arranged for Ohscar, who was picking citrus near Yuma, to meet Mr. Pinchney.

Ohscar finished his second burrito, folded the foil wrapping, and put it back into his lunch bucket. A raw wind blew across the wet field, and he pulled his red bandana back over the lower half of his face. He tried to shake off the memory of the Mexican's visit by getting immediately back to work.

Ohscar jabbed his spade into the side of the field channel, deftly removing three shovels full of reddish-tan clay. The freed water spilled through the breach and into a new furrow. He stepped carefully to avoid crumbling the bank and repeated the process until water flowed into a half-dozen furrows, enough to ensure a rapid flow to the far side of the field yet not deplete the supply in the field channel too quickly. To provide nourishment to thirsty roots, the water had to rise to a depth of six to eight inches, high enough to infiltrate the steep walls of the furrows and soak into the soil under the beds.

Making crops grow was in Ohscar's nature, and he liked the work. His parents had been tenant farmers and fled north across the border to escape the violence of the Mexican Revolution. They came to California, yearning to own a small farm. But they never were able to accumulate money beyond that needed to feed and house their family. Mexican, migrant, they were unable to get credit. They worked in the fields through the boom years of the twenties and then the bitter depression years of the thirties, years when there were too few jobs, setting race against race and worker against worker.

Ohscar was born in Sunset Camp, a migrant camp run by the city of Arvin. An Anglo public health nurse visited his mother shortly after she delivered. His father wanted his son to have an American name, Oscar, after a farmer for whom he once worked. Following what she understood to be best practice, the nurse carefully spelled out the name on the birth registration form exactly as she heard it, "Ohscar." A local Catholic priest who visited the camp on Sunday to celebrate mass for the migrant families baptized the baby.

Ohscar grew up speaking Spanish at home, but his father wanted him to learn English and did his best to see that the boy attended school. At the outbreak of World War II, fearing conscription of their sons, many immigrant families returned to Mexico, but the Romero family remained. Farmworkers were needed to produce food for a nation at war, and Señor Romero was proud to play a part.

When Ohscar was nineteen, he married sixteen-year old Carolina, herself the daughter of a migrant family. Soon after, war broke out in Korea, and the United States, once more, needed men. Ohscar was drafted into the Marine Corps. His father encouraged him, and Ohscar, looking for a way out of life as a farmworker, was eager for the adventure. Their first child, Javier, was born shortly after Ohscar left.

Home from Korea two years later, Ohscar enrolled in adult education classes in Delano under the GI Bill. He planned to complete his high school diploma and go on to a trade school. Carolina was very supportive, but a second child was on the way. It became apparent that Ohscar's parents' small frame house would not be large enough to house two families.

Ohscar's GI education benefits did not pay all the bills. He and his father got plenty of work picking grapes that fall, but by late October, the harvest was over. Pruning lasted a few more weeks. Ohscar searched for winter work close to home, but Filipino crews picked the asparagus crop, and whites picked potatoes and onions. Picking end-rows of cotton after the machine harvest on big farms on the west side of the valley was a black job. Ohscar had to leave Delano to pick lettuce at the southern end of the valley, near Mettler, and then went down to Yuma to pick melons. He had to abandon his adult education classes.

After the birth of the new baby, a daughter they named Mirabelle, Carolina and the children joined Ohscar. With his discharge money, he had bought a used pickup that he equipped with a camper back. The family moved up the coast to Santa Maria for strawberries in the spring, south to Riverside and Oxnard for oranges and lemons, to Salinas and Watsonville in the north for lettuce and artichokes, back to the San Joaquin Valley, Arvin and Delano, for grapes in the fall, and then down to the Imperial Valley for winter vegetables. They searched for temporary housing in towns near where they found work, sleeping in the truck when they had to.

At the height of each season, harvest work paid well. Often an older woman, either in the camp or in the shade of the row of farmworkers' cars and trucks parked at the side of the field, took care of the picker's babies, and Carolina and Ohscar could make as much as two hundred dollars a week on piece rate. But over the course of a year, only seven or eight such weeks were possible. Often, after driving hundreds of miles, they would arrive to find that the jobs were already taken or that the grower had decided to use Mexican braceros that year. Sometimes, due to low market prices, the grower paid so little they barely covered their costs for gas and food.

Harvesting meant lugging heavy totes. Weeding and thinning required working along a long row, bent over in the hot sun wielding a short-handled hoe called *el cortito*. The work was always hard. For many, the tasks were crippling.

Despite the hardships, Ohscar's family grew. By the time Javier was ready to start school, he had three sisters and a little brother. California law required children to be enrolled in school by age seven, and that year, Carolina successively enrolled Javier in schools in Delano, Yuma, Arvin, Salinas, Santa Maria, and Oxnard.

Knowing that education was the only way their children could break free of the cycle of work and poverty that ensnared them, Ohscar and Carolina tried to piece jobs together that would allow them to remain in one place during the school year. But farmers did not plant crops so that their workers' kids could stay in school; they planted according to growing season and market demand.

By the time Javier was fifteen, he was two years behind in school. Perceiving no other future, he wanted only to get out in the field and work with his father, but his parents and the State of California would not allow it. Until Ohscar began working for Mr. Pinchney, the boy had been growing increasingly rebellious. But Ohscar's steady job on the Pinchney Ranch changed the family's prospects and, much to Carolina and Ohscar's relief, Javier's perception of his own future. It looked as if the family would be able to spend the entire school year in one place and maybe the next year, too.

Javier was enrolled in the seventh grade at Holtville Junior High School, The younger children attended the Verde School, near the Pinchney ranch. It appeared that, for the first time in their lives, they all would be able to complete the school year at the same school they started in the fall. A future for his children seemed possible. *If only I can hold onto this job,* Ohscar thought.

Ohscar worked hard to make sure Mr. Pinchney would want to keep him. Mr. Pinchney had been happy to pick up an experienced hand so easily, but Ohscar knew the grower could hire someone else just as quickly, *even a wetback.*

Picking up his lantern, Ohscar walked along a dry furrow to the far side of the field. He had to be constantly wary lest the water overtop the beds. Immersion could rot the leafy tops of the young sugar beets.

8

 Miguel sensed he was close to the edge of a ravine. The dirt road he was following had played out into a fallow field, and once across it, he could make out a dark horizon of small trees and brush. He stumbled in a fissure and fell forward, breaking his fall with his outstretched hands. Regaining his footing, he backtracked until he encountered a field road running north. Before long, the dirt road intersected a blacktop road. He turned west again, toward Venus. Feeling the hard surface under his feet, he sensed that it would take him safely across the ravine.

Having trudged through the day and a good part of the evening, Miguel was tired; his steps were short and uncertain. The bright star in the west was fading in a gathering haze. He tucked his hands back under his armpits for warmth, and without the balance of his arms, he swayed from side to side with each step.

Crossing the border, even being robbed, was a distant memory. He thought of Concha and vowed not to let her down, but his dreams of tomorrow were supplanted by a pressing need to find shelter, a barn or a shed, where he could slumber for a while and then sort things out. Miguel dozed as he stumbled on, grasping at an illusion of warmth.

His mind flickered in and out of consciousness. He considered simply lying down in a ditch.

Far down the road, a single pinpoint of light appeared, suspended in the blackness like a low-hanging star. Miguel played with it, squinting until it turned into an elongated prism. As he drew closer, he realized the light was mounted on a pole in the center of a cluster of farm buildings. Next to them, set back from the road, was a broad, single-story house. There were no lights on in the house, but a lone bulb illuminated the empty carport.

A dog barked a low, paced warning. A second dog joined in, and the barks grew vigorous, competitive. Although Miguel did not think he had anything to fear if he stayed on the road—the dogs were confined behind a chainlink fence—he considered making a detour. But he was drawn to the tractor shed and the barn under a broad, pitched roof. He continued forward cautiously, coming abreast of the fence.

No one from the darkened house came to check on the barking dogs, and Miguel began to feel he was on the verge of good fortune. He was so weary he could barely keep his feet under him. Perhaps he could find an unlocked door to the barn, he thought. Surely, there would be straw inside, an old blanket, somewhere he could sleep. Tentatively, muttering soothing words to the dogs, he turned up the driveway.

☀ ☀ ☀

Cold air streaming through gaps in the retrofit cab of his Jeep drove Garner to scrunch into his fur collar. After losing the tracks at the highway, he had driven to a high point on the East Mesa to eat the supper of chicken and noodles that Margie had packed for him in a wide-mouth thermos. From that vantage point, he could see for a dozen miles or more and easily spot the headlights of a car if it were prowling the desert trails near the border. The warm meal and hot coffee raised his spirits, and he decided to drive back to the drag road and cut for sign from east to west. He would be close to Calexico by the time his shift ended.

Garner briefly considered stopping and removing the round metal plate on the floorboard that accessed the brake fluid refill cap but decided to wait until he reached the drag road. The warm air streaming off the hot exhaust manifold and up through the opening as his Jeep chugged along in low gear would at least warm his feet and ankles.

Garner rued losing the alien at the highway. It was a loss of face for him, but it was possible the Mexican would be caught later at the traffic checkpoint north of Westmorland. At that point, all the roads on the west side of the valley narrowed into a single highway passing along the west edge of the Salton Sea. Or, if the alien stayed in the valley and found work, there was a good chance he would be caught by one of the border-patrol farm-and-ranch check crews.

Garner believed a passing local had picked up the Mexican in a chance encounter on the highway. Lone line jumpers did not often make arrangements with smugglers; the coyotes cost too much money, and the alien would not have been poking around the gate at the Alamo Check if he had. Probably, he was wrapped up in a warm blanket somewhere, Garner thought in a passing moment of envy. He slowed and prepared to shift gears as he neared the highway.

"Twenty-two fourteen." Garner's radio crackled to life and he recognized the voice of his supervisor, Senior Patrol Inspector Zeno Smith. The transmission was not followed by a burst of static, which meant that the senior had used the local channel and was nearby.

"Two-two-one-four," Garner responded.

"Meet me at the location you called in that got-away," Zeno said cryptically.

"Ten-four," Garner replied and hung up the mic. With a sinking feeling, he turned onto the highway. His senior was the best tracker in the station, often able to pick up a trail when less-experienced PIs had given up. In less than five minutes, he pulled up behind the supervisor's Jeep and cut his lights. The older man was waiting beside the road, and as Garner joined him, he illuminated the now very faint boot and tire tracks with his five-cell light.

"Is this what you saw?" Zeno asked.

"Yeah. It's a work boot. It looked to me like he was picked up by the vehicle making those tracks there." Garner had been in the patrol just over a year. Even though he now was off probation and more confident of his relationship with the supervisor, Zeno was still the teacher, and Garner was anxious to establish that he had mastered his lessons. "The boot print and the tire track were made about the same time, although the tire tracks cover one of the boot prints. The driver could have been waiting for him."

"I doubt it," Zeno replied. "Why don't you go across the road and take a look."

Spirits sagging, Garner obediently crossed the asphalt and cast his light on the soft shoulder of the highway. Directly in front of him, too faded by the wind and blowing sand to make out the tread, a sequence of oval indentations led off across the desert floor and disappeared between the clumps of creosote bushes. Sheepishly, Garner rejoined his supervisor.

"He's got two choices," Zeno said. "He can thrash around in the brush and eventually hit Highway 80—probably about dawn. Or he can work his way west and try to get back into the valley. Which do you think he'll try?"

"Well, he was wearing boots, not street shoes. I'm pretty sure he's the guy I saw on the south side while I was raking out Alamo check. He was clearly from the interior, flat sombrero, *trique* bag. Like you always say, they follow the lights. I figure he'll follow Venus up there." Garner gestured toward the western sky. "I'll run up and check the Verde Road crossing."

"Good! Looks as if he has a couple of hours on you, maybe an hour and a half."

"I don't think I was far behind him."

"You probably weren't, then." Zeno headed for his Jeep.

An offshoot of the All American Canal, the East Highline Canal flowed north, and once past Highway 98, there was no way to cross it until the Verde School Road bridge. Garner calculated that by following Venus, the alien would come upon the canal at a point south of the bridge before he reached the road.

When he arrived at the bridge, Garner checked the dirt shoulder of the approach with his sign-cut light and was not surprised to find the work-boot tread, the same pattern of small rectangles he had seen earlier in the evening. The tracks were fresh, less than a half-hour old, and angled up to the roadway from the canal bank.

Garner crossed the bridge on foot and searched the road shoulder with his flashlight until he found a set of tracks angling off toward the northwest into an alfalfa field. He cursorily swung the beam across the field but did not spot a human figure. He snapped off his light and returned to his Jeep.

The tracks confirmed that the alien was guiding on Venus, and his course from now on was easily predictable. When other PIs were available, Garner could radio for a fellow officer to lie in wait ahead of the alien while he dogged out the tracks. Working alone, Garner had fewer options and needed to plan carefully, or the chase would go on until after dawn. He knew Zeno was giving him a chance to redeem himself and would cover the line for him while he pursued the alien.

Wary of damaging the farmer's crop, Garner did not attempt to follow the alien across the open field in his Jeep. Nor did he attempt to follow on foot; the alien would see his light and could flee faster than Garner could follow his tracks. If he cut for sign on the edge of the field, the alien would turn in circles, and the chase would become a cat-and-mouse game until after dawn.

Garner knew that if the alien continued northwest, as he had so far, he would encounter the chasm of the Alamo River. The stream drained irrigation water, polluted with agricultural chemicals and salt from the cultivated fields of the Mexicali and Imperial Valleys, north into the Salton Sea. The banks were unstable caliche, overgrown with a tangled jungle of mesquite and brush and often crumbled. Garner had seen rattlesnakes slithering along the low branches of mesquite trees. If the alien panicked and fled into the river bottom, Garner would have to follow him, and he did not want to go in there, especially in the dark.

When the alien arrived at the edge of the ravine, if he did not think he was being pursued, Garner figured he would likely backtrack to a road and follow it north and west until he found the Hunt Road bridge. He decided to head there and lay in.

As he sped toward the crossing, Garner spotted a night irrigator's lantern far across a field. Possibly the alien was headed towards it if he was not there already. The irrigator was most likely a local and would probably tell him if he had seen the illegal alien. But once the alien spotted Garner's Jeep, he would be off in a different direction, ruining any chance for an apprehension.

Garner wondered whether the irrigator would himself one day be replaced by an illegal alien. The US Border Patrol had been able to keep them out during the years of the Bracero Program, mainly because farmers knew they would lose their braceros if they also hired an illegal alien. Now with the braceros gone, there was no law preventing a farmer from hiring a line jumper. No one in the patrol thought the hundreds of thousands of former braceros would stay home in Mexico, unemployed, for very long. They would become the first of a new wave of illegal aliens jumping the line to take American jobs. The alien he was tracking tonight was probably an ex-bracero, and there were not enough PIs to stop them.

Once across the Hunt Road bridge, Garner continued for a few hundred yards and then cut his lights and made a sharp *U*-turn. As quietly as he could, he nursed his Jeep back toward the bridge, stopping a few yards short of the low-railed structure. Allowing his eyes to adjust to the dark, with the aid of his binoculars and the ambient light of the star-filled sky, he could see enough of the bridge surface to detect the moving figure of a man if he crossed. At that moment, he would get out and crouch in wait just short of the railing.

Taking off his glove and absorbing the warmth of the cup in his hand, Garner poured the last of the coffee from his thermos. He thought about the Mexican working his way toward him, hoping for the man's sake, and his, that he would not wander into the river bottom. The alien had been smart so far, but now Garner was ahead of him, and he was confident the chase soon would end.

9

When John Pinchney saw the border patrol Jeep parked on the shoulder of Hunt Road, just short of the Alamo River bridge, he dimmed the lights of his Lincoln Continental. *He must be watching for a Mexican,* the grower thought. *It's a cold night for that!* But when Pinchney crested the far bank of the Alamo River ravine and the familiar yard light next to his barn came into view, his curiosity about the drama being played out at the bridge quickly faded. The green-and-white Jeeps were ubiquitous in the valley, the officers doing an essential job protecting the border, and unless one ventured onto his land, Pinchney was little concerned. The light, however, he considered a beacon in a dark sea, guiding him home after a meeting that had gone too late.

A pair of round, red reflectors marked his driveway, and Pinchney slowed to make the turn. His headlights swept the low chainlink fence and decorative shrubs at the edge of the drive, briefly illuminating the wide, single-story house set back from the road. As the heavy car straightened onto the gravel drive, Pinchney noted that there were no lights on in the house and Laura's Chrysler was not in the carport. She was at a meeting that night, too, he remembered.

Further down the drive, Pinchney saw their two black Labradors, Pell and Mell, restrained by the fence, barking agitatedly. He braked to an abrupt halt and flicked on his high beams. Off to the left side of the driveway, a brown-skinned man wearing a white, flat-crowned sombrero stood motionless. Hunched into his plaid coat, his hands thrust up under his armpits, he looked away from the bright lights.

Pinchney felt a twinge of fear shoot along his nerves and down his spine. He leaned across the wide bench seat, opened the glove box, and took out his .45 caliber Colt Python. He laid the heavy revolver across his lap, his finger on the trigger, and inched the car forward until he was directly abreast of the man. He lowered the car's electric window.

"What are you doing on my property?" Pinchney demanded.

Alarmed at the sight of the grower's gun, Miguel thrust his hands out as if to protect himself and stepped backward, "¡No inglés!" he pleaded. "¡No inglés!"

Pinchney contemplated the shivering figure. There was little reason for a local to be out on a night like this. The flat crown of the man's hat and the small, feathered tassel dangling from the back edge of the brim reminded him of the Mexican braceros who used to work for him, men from Jalisco or Zacatecas. He decided that the man meant no harm. *You're a long way from home,* Pinchney mused silently, *and cold. I'll bet you're hungry too.*

Remembering the border patrol Jeep at the bridge, for a moment Pinchney considered putting the Mexican in his car and driving him back there. *There's probably a connection,* he thought. *On a night like this, turning him in would be a mercy. They'll put him up and then send him home.* But as he looked at the Mexican's dirty garb, he hesitated at putting him in the car. *Hell, he's just looking for work,* Pinchney rationalized. *It'd be a shame to turn him in.*

Pinchney slipped the gun into the pocket of his sheepskin jacket and motioned for the man to step back from the car. Stepping out, he grasped the brim of his silver belly Stetson by the front and the rear and squared it firmly on his graying head. He towered over the shivering man in the plaid coat. John Pinchney had broad, muscular shoulders and the confident stride of a man who at midlife had found business and social success.

"¡Vengarse!" he said to the Mexican, and motioned for him to follow.

Stepping inside the door of the barn, Pinchney threw a switch, and a line of shaded light bulbs dimly lit the unpainted interior of the building. Motioning again, he led the Mexican past a row of stalls and opened the door of the tack room at the far end of the building. Long unused, the room contained a single metal cot. Grabbing a thin mattress, its cover stained and yellow with age, the grower flopped it onto the frame. Motioning to the Mexican to stay put, Pinchney went to the house and returned in a few minutes with some old blankets and a frayed comforter. "Here," he said, flopping his load onto the cot.

Pinchney surveyed the room. The man would be all right here, he thought, a little cold, but certainly warmer than he would be out in the night. There was one thing more to do. He returned to the house and came back with a stack of sliced bologna and the remains of an opened loaf of bread.

"Gracias, señor," the man mumbled, forcing a nervous grin and raising his hand as if to salute. "Gracias."

Satisfied with what he had done, Pinchney returned to the house and, in the light from the hallway, fixed himself a Scotch and water at the wet bar in his den. He sank into his leather couch and found a music station on the radio. Easy-listening music, the station called it. Laura teasingly called it supermarket music, but it served his mood. He did not know what he would do with the Mexican shivering himself to sleep in the tack room, but he was sure he had done the right thing. *We'll see what he looks like in the morning.*

Strange, that the man should show up tonight, Pinchney thought. The speaker at that evening's Farm Bureau meeting, an agricultural economist from the University of California at Davis, warned that now that the Bracero Program was over labor was going to be scarce. If growers wanted Mexican field hands, they were going to have to use a new program called "H-2." First, they were going to have to prove there were not enough domestic laborers present to harvest their crop. If their application was approved, they were going to have to pay the Mexican workers $1.40 an hour. The last point brought hoots of disbelief from the audience.

"The average wage increase in the Imperial Valley would be thirty cents an hour," the economist continued after he regained his audience. "A wage increase of 27 percent. Growers are going to have to either find a new source of labor to get in their crops or mechanize."

The economist discussed a range of options, including building housing for migrant domestic farm laborers and their families and planting crops that would come in during the off season so that local farmworkers would have enough work in a vicinity to support themselves year-round. He cited the proliferation of new almond orchards in central and northern California as an example. Almonds ripened in late January and February, a slack time for other crops. Workers who had finished pruning grape vines and fruit trees in the early winter would be available to harvest the almonds before the summer citrus and grape cycle started again.

Pinchney needed large crews for thinning and weeding his sugar-beet fields in the spring, and those crews had always before been braceros. When the green, leafy tops of the beets began to emerge from the soil, they appeared as a thick stand of several seedlings, and they had to be thinned down to a single plant. That required stoop labor—men using a short-handled hoe—a job most local workers avoided if they could. When Pinchney asked about that, the economist warned that if farmers wanted to attract enough local workers to do the job, they were going to have to start using long-handled hoes. *That could mean a lot of damage to the plants*, Pinchney thought. He would allow it if he had to, but only as a last resort.

One of Pinchney's neighbors, old August Luttig, had gotten ponderously to his feet. "Vat if vee jest go back to hiring vetbacks?" he asked in his thickly accented voice. The question had been in the back of everybody's mind, and the farmers in the room laughed that it had taken Augie, one of the early pioneers and an immigrant himself, finally to ask it.

The speaker shifted nervously behind the podium before answering the question. It was not the direction he had wanted to take his audience. "Nothing," the economist admitted. "There's no law that says you can't hire an illegal alien."

For now, Pinchney had Ohscar Romero to irrigate his sugar-beet fields and drive the tractor. Like most of the growers, he did not trust locals, but Ohscar had been reliable and was all he needed until thinning started.

He was not the only grower in the Imperial Valley who was going to need farm laborers. Together, the farmers would meet the challenge if they had to, just as an earlier generation had brought water to the valley by working together, forming the early irrigation districts, and diverting water from the Colorado River. In mere decades, they had transformed waterless desert into one of the most productive agricultural districts in the nation. It was simply a matter of sizing up the challenge. No one knew yet how many former braceros would come back illegally, or if the US Border Patrol would be able to stop them, but somehow valley farmers would find labor.

Pinchney punched the select button on the veneer console of the radio, and the dial shifted to KGO, a clear-channel station broadcasting from San Francisco. He liked to listen to Ira Blue, who hosted a new type of radio show that encouraged listeners to call in and talk on the air. He caught the tail end of a rant against criminalizing LSD. *The guy must be a beatnik*, Pinchney thought. A new caller wanted to talk about Ayn Rand's book, *Atlas Shrugged*.

"What if farmers stopped innovating?" the caller posited. "What if they left every decision to government bureaucrats? We wouldn't be able to feed ourselves after the first harvest season. The only thing that keeps this country ahead is the profit motive, every man looking out for himself. That's America."

Pinchney smiled and crunched an ice cube. The caller sounded like a farmer, like himself, or at least believed like one. There was too little appreciation of the role of innovation in bringing wealth and plenty to this country, he thought. He had not read the book, but Laura had and urged him to read it also.

The hallway door opened and closed. "Hel-lo," Laura called. Her greeting was followed by the tap of high-heeled shoes on the tiled hallway to the kitchen and the rustle and thump of groceries being unbagged and stacked in the cupboard and refrigerator. The domestic noises amplified Pinchney's feeling of satisfaction, and presently, Laura joined him on the couch.

"How was your meeting?" Laura asked.

"Interesting," Pinchney replied. "We had an economist from Davis talking about farm labor and what to do now that the braceros are gone. How was yours?"

"Joan Dixon wants us endorse Ronald Reagan for governor even before the primary," Laura answered. "Did the guy from Davis have any practical answers?"

"Yeh," Pinchney said, grinning. "He said go out and hire a wetback, and so I did." Laura sat up and turned toward him. "You're kidding," she said, slapping him playfully on the shoulder.

"'Fraid not," Pinchney answered. "I just bedded him down out in the tack room."

Laura leaned back on the couch, allowing her head to rest against her husband's outstretched arm. She realized he was no longer joking.

"He was standing in the driveway when I got home," Pinchney continued. "Cold as a plucked chicken in a meat market. I got him some old blankets from the spare room and something to eat."

"How do you know he won't kill us?" Laura asked, semiseriously. The thought of a strange man intruding on their property in the dark disturbed her.

"This guy is straight off the hacienda," Pinchney reassured her. "He even has one of those fly-flickers dangling from the back of his hat like the braceros wore. I'll check him out in the morning and send him on his way."

"That's good," Laura murmured snuggling into her husband's shoulder.

But Pinchney was already thinking about taking the Mexican on as a second hired hand.

10

Unable to sit longer in the cold, Garner got out of the unheated Jeep and walked down to the bridge over the Alamo River. He hoped moving around would warm him or, at least, break the tedium. He had waited for over an hour for the alien to appear, but the only traffic had been a white Lincoln, a local grower headed to his place down the road and, a little later, a Chrysler. Garner thought the woman behind the wheel of the Chrysler might have been the grower's wife. He paid them little mind. White people who could drive fancy cars did not pick up Mexican hitchhikers in the middle of the night.

The adrenalin Garner felt in his veins earlier had faded, and he was ready to call it quits. At midnight, he listened to the chatter on the radio as a new shift came on. Garner knew his senior would not quit for the night if a chase was still going on, and he could not either. Just as well, he thought. He still burned with embarrassment at so easily being thrown off the alien's tracks and was reluctant to return to the station just yet.

Turning to go back to his Jeep, Garner was startled to see his supervisor's Jeep, its headlights off, ease silently to a stop behind his. Zeno got out, and the two men stood in the chill night air for a moment without speaking.

Zeno Smith was sixty, old even for a senior patrol inspector. He was erect and did not carry a paunch. He rarely joined the younger PIs at the Border Café for coffee at the beginning or end of a shift, and he and his wife never attended a border patrol party. But he knew the mettle of each of his officers, observing them, working with them on chases, or helping them follow difficult sign. He did not tolerate one of his PIs quitting before the alien was found. SPI Smith made it his responsibility to teach young officers, whether they served in his unit or not, the sign-cutting skills and desert lore they needed for the job and for their own safety. Even so, Garner found him easy to talk to on long desert nights. Despite feeling sheepish, he was glad to see Zeno now.

Striking a match, cupping his hands around the flame to shield it from the wind, Zeno lit a cigarette. The flicker illuminated the underside of the brim of his Stetson and highlighted the older man's craggy, wind-worn face. Wedging the glowing cigarette between his index and second finger, he leaned back against the hood of Garner's Jeep. The heel of his hand rested on the butt of his revolver, which rode high on his hip in a quick-draw holster. The smell of burning tobacco lay faintly on the air, mingling with the dank smell of the river bottom. Garner took it as a sign that the senior felt a further stakeout at the bridge was futile.

"It's a cold night to be a wet," Garner volunteered.

"Yeah," Zeno answered. "They get cold too. By now he may be holed up in some farmer's outbuilding."

Struggling for conversation, Garner said, "Margie put together a box of old clothes the other afternoon, and I dropped them off to those kids that play on the canal bank by Alamitos. Shoes, sweaters, and stuff our girls have grown out of, but I didn't have nearly enough for them all."

"A lot of the guys drop their kids' hand-me-downs off there, and at some of the other colonias too." Zeno said. "Sometimes the women get into it and organize stuff. But there's nothing you can do to change the way those kids live."

"So, what do we do?" Garner challenged. "As Christians, I mean."

"The first thing you've got to remember is that you're just one man. You're no more than one of those little stars up there," the older man said, lifting the brim of his hat towards the lighted sky. "One star doesn't light up all that heaven."

Garner felt relieved to have shared the incident, relieved to find that he was not the only PI who delivered clothing to families on the other side of the line and that his gesture seemed to meet the senior's approval. At times, he found it difficult to tell how his peers felt about their job. Subject to dismissal without cause during their first year and a long way from home, trainees were careful about discussing their feelings with older officers. Some affected a macho, hardline attitude toward illegal Mexicans that Garner suspected was mostly show. One of his fellow trainees had quit saying he no longer wanted to be one of America's hangmen. Garner's probationary year was behind him now, and he felt secure enough with the senior to pursue the conversation.

"You know, one afternoon out by Midway Wells, I apprehended a wet from Michoacan. He was no older than me and said he had two young daughters. I couldn't help wonder why that wasn't me. And how I would feel if it was."

Zeno took a long drag on his cigarette. "I've never met a man who stayed in this outfit who hasn't asked himself the same questions," the old man remarked, his voice even, serious. "No one can answer that. No one can answer any of those questions for you. In the meantime, we have a law that tells us what we have to do with the people we apprehend and how we have to do it.

"Those stars up there don't have a choice about what they do, but we do," the senior continued. "We get to decide whether or not we want the job. That's a decision that all of us have had to make, sometimes more than once. Most of the men decide it's their duty. They can do it as well and with as much compassion as the next guy and go on with their lives. But that's up to you."

The two men gazed at a heaven so laden with stars it was difficult to imagine it could hold any more. *He's right,* Garner thought. *I have a choice to be part of a system that in this imperfect world down here is doing the best it can because all of us in it are doing the best we can.*

"Let's go in," Zeno said, snubbing his cigarette on the heel of his boot and flicking the butt into the night. "There's no sense in you hangin' around here any longer. If that Mexican hasn't showed up by now, he's holed up somewhere, maybe down in that river bottom, and you ain't gonna find him tonight."

11

When John Pinchney took his seat at the breakfast table, he noticed immediately that his juice glass sat empty. During their long marriage, thirty-three years, John and Laura had each come to rely on the predictability of the other. Laura timed their breakfast of waffles and sausages to John's expected arrival in the kitchen. A tall water glass filled with fresh orange juice always sat at the top of John's plate.

John liked his habits, and Laura adhered to them mostly because it was a way to remind her husband that she loved him. But Laura also had learned that stepping out of habit, like failing to pour his orange juice, was a convenient way to signal that she had something on her mind.

"John," she asked a moment after taking her seat, before he could ask about the missing orange juice, "what are you going to do about that Mexican in the tack room?"

John buttered his perfectly browned waffle and smothered it with maple syrup. "If he's still out there, I might see what kind of work I can get out of him."

"But you've already got Oscar." Laura refused to pronounce the hired hand's name as Ohscar, believing the name had been given to him as a cruel joke.

"Yeh, I know, but you never know how long these locals are going to work out."

"Oscar's done fine so far, hasn't he?"

"Yes, but locals always want more pay or want off because someone in their family is sick or something like that. You could depend on braceros. They worked hard, and if something went wrong with one of them—if he was sick or something—you just had to take him back to the camp and get another. I guess what I'm saying is we just don't know where we're going from here without the braceros, and I want a little insurance, another hand to fall back on if we lose Ohscar."

It made sense, Laura thought, but not entirely. There really was not enough work this time of year for two hired hands. Oscar had proved himself reliable and deserved some loyalty in return. They had taken at least some responsibility for him and his family by renting them the old Nakamura house. The whole idea of giving them a place to live was to encourage Oscar to stay, she recalled her husband saying. Still, she had seen workers come and go, and although John had always been restless about his hired help, it generally did not pay to question her husband's judgment on such matters.

For all her life, Laura had listened to her father, and now her husband, complain about hired hands. The locals were not all bad, she knew, but having a willing worker available when help was needed was important, particularly at planting and harvest. In recent years, the border patrol had finally gotten rid of the wetbacks, the illegal Mexicans the farmers once depended on. And, after a Mexican had crossed the border and murdered a woman in Calexico, the city had built a border fence, walling itself off from the filth, crime, and poverty of Mexicali and impeding the flow of illegal workers who once had simply walked across the border through the neighborhoods of the small town.

The braceros seemed to have been a good thing, she thought, although a lot of Democrats thought it was unfair that locals had to compete with foreign workers. The braceros provided farmers, like her husband, with the reliable help they needed. They had been treated well, fed and housed in clean camps, and paid a wage that was pretty good when compared to what they could make in their home country. The farmers had found they could rely on the braceros and the green-carders, the legal Mexicans who lived in Mexicali and commuted every day.

Laura did not want to see the wetbacks return, and her husband's sheltering a Mexican, who from every appearance was here illegally, seemed to be a step in that direction. But John needed reliable help, and she could not deny his reasoning. She dropped the subject.

They finished the meal and talked about what they had to do that day. Laura had a garden club meeting at noon, and John had some business in town to attend to. Before she cleared away the breakfast dishes, she wrapped the remaining waffles in foil and handed the package and a small decanter of syrup to John.

"You have someone to feed, you know," she said.

"Yeh, sure," John said. "I was going to do that."

When he stepped out the door into the crisp, morning sunlight, Pinchney was startled to see the Mexican swinging a weed cutter at the tall weeds that had grown up around the foundation of the barn. He walked over, but the man appeared not to notice him.

"Here, *muchacho!*" Pinchney called to the man, holding out the foil-covered waffles and a thermos of coffee. The Mexican looked up when he heard Pinchney's voice and then took three extra swings with the weed cutter before dropping it.

"Gracias," he said, accepting the food.

That afternoon, Ohscar drove into the driveway to see whether Mr. Pinchney had any instructions before he set out to irrigate the south field that night. He was incredulous to see the Mexican with the flat hat and plaid jacket, the same man who had approached him in the field the previous night, step out from the barn.

"*Hola, señor,*" the Mexican said, warily.

Too stunned to speak, Ohscar simply nodded and walked around the pickup to the side door of the house. Mr. Pinchney came out just as he arrived.

"Ohscar, I figured you could use a little help, at least until harvest time," the grower said. "This is Meegwell. I want you to take him with you tonight and show him the ropes."

Ohscar was taken aback but tried not to show any displeasure. With the beets growing in the ground, he had to irrigate each field every ten days, and there were several fields. The schedule meant he had little time off, but the long hours also meant extra money that the family needed.

"Sure, boss," he stammered. "I can do that. Whatever you say. Anything else, Mr. Pinchney?"

"The soil in the south field is pretty coarse, and I'm a little concerned that it's not getting a good-enough soak. Let the advance get at least 80 percent across the field before you cut off the water. It's a new field, and I don't mind a little extra tail water there. And you might help Meegwell find some gear. I think there's an extra pair of rubber boots in the shed."

After Ohscar retrieved the boots, the two hired hands climbed into the cab of Ohscar's pickup and started on the short drive to the field. Neither spoke, but Ohscar's mind was racing. He had thought he had this job sewed up, that he alone would be plowing and irrigating the Pinchney Farm fields—until this wetback appeared. Now it looked as if he had to share the work.

It was no secret that farmers in the valley preferred Mexicans. Ohscar wanted to feel that Mr. Pinchney valued his work and would be loyal to him, but on another level, he realized that he would not have the job if Mr. Pinchney had been able to hire a Mexican in the first place, a bracero or otherwise. He had gotten decent wages from the grower and a place to live, but would his job last? If his future depended on the border patrol keeping the wetbacks out, it had not happened. The man riding beside him, the worker who this night he was going to have to show how to do his job was an illegal. Mr. Pinchney had hired him on the spot—simply because he was a Mexican.

"What is *el patrón's* name?" Miguel broke the silence.

"Pinchney."

"Pinch-the-nee?"

"Yeh, Pinch-knee. You know. Like this," Ohscar said, grasping his knee with his right hand, lifting his foot momentarily off the accelerator. "Pinch-knee!"

"Oh, Pinch-the-knee!"

Ohscar caught himself laughing, but stopped quickly. Miguel sensed an opening.

"Are you from here?"

"I was born here," Ohscar said with a bite in his voice.

Miguel lapsed again into silence.

Ohscar pulled up alongside the field. Miguel hopped out, quickly grabbing the two shovels and the lantern from the back. Ohscar stood for a moment, looking at Miguel across the bed of the truck. Then he reached back in the cab, retrieved his lunch bucket, and walked deliberately to a spot along the edge of the field some distance away. Miguel followed.

"Have you ever done this before?" Ohscar asked.

"Only on my *ranchito* in Piedra Gorda. Never in a field this big," Miguel answered.

Ohscar grunted and grabbed one of the spades. "You just sit right here and watch."

The Mexican looked surprised but remained standing as Ohscar walked the length of the dry bed of the field channel clearing debris and repairing the walls of the ditch that would carry the water down the long side of the field. The channel ran perpendicular to the long furrows that separated the rows of sugar beets. The leaves of the plants already had broken the surface, forming two long dotted lines of green on the top of each mound.

By the time Ohscar finished, the sun was about to drop over the horizon. He cast a self-satisfied look back at Miguel, sitting on the ground beside the truck, his spade useless at his side. Ohscar walked the length of the cleared channel to the head gate, arriving just as the ditch rider from the Imperial Irrigation District showed up to unlock the gate and release water into the field channel.

"Got a helper tonight, I see," the ditch rider said cheerily.

"Not much of one."

"Well, maybe he'll keep that spot warm for you. If you can get him to share."

"That's the problem," Ohscar grumbled. "Wetbacks don't share."

12

 The late February afternoon was warm but breezy. In another few weeks, the wind would stop abruptly, and overnight temperatures in the valley would shoot up thirty degrees. But today, the dogwoods were in bloom, and the azaleas and the lavender bushes gave off the pleasant aroma that signaled spring in a region where year-round sunshine offered few clues to the changes of seasons.

Javier Romero strolled past the broad, single-story house, roofed with sun-darkened cedar-shakes. It was one the largest in Holtville. Built on a man-made mound, it was the only house in the town where the foundation was not a simple concrete slab resting directly on the layer of silt that gave the town an aspect of unsparing flatness.

Javier was reluctant to turn up the walkway to the door, telling himself he was just curious if the address he found in the Holtville telephone book was correct and this was Janice's house. At the end of the block, he turned, trying not to look out of place, and retraced his steps. Satisfied by the name on the mailbox that the house indeed belonged to the McDonald family, he wondered whether Janice might actually be at home. On his third pass, he wondered, if he walked up and rang the doorbell and she was at home, would she come to the door.

Javier paused at the street corner. He dreaded walking down the street again, almost hoping the voices in his head would convince him that the pretty Anglo girl who lived in the house would not want to talk to a Mexican-American boy, the son of a farmworker. After all, Mr. McDonald was a wealthy farmer. Javier wished the voices would persuade him, finally, that he was making a fool of himself and he should just go home. He questioned if he really had the courage to turn up the walk to the house and ring the doorbell.

But overpowered by the yearning he felt in his heart to see the beautiful girl with soft, clean-smelling hair he had met at the Holtville Junior High geography bee and had not been able to get out of his mind since, the voices in Javier's head grew silent.

This time, Javier turned up the flagstone walkway, strode purposefully up the slight rise between the rows of manicured shrubs, mounted the low step to the tiled entryway, paced three steps to the dark, hewn-oak door, fitted with wrought-iron, and pushed the doorbell.

At age fifteen, Javier was tall and slender with fine features and intense black eyes, his skin, dark in contrast with his white, short-sleeved shirt, which he buttoned at the collar. His mother had given him the shirt at Christmas. He felt himself sweating, although the afternoon was not that warm, and shook his arms in an attempt to calm his nerves. He wiped the tops of his shoes on the back of his pant legs.

Javier's long-planned day had started early. When his father, Ohscar, arrived home after a long night irrigating one of the Pinchney Farm's sugar-beet fields and sat at the kitchen table eating his breakfast, Javier had not asked him for a ride into town. Instead, he slipped out the door without mentioning what he planned to do that day.

Since his father had found steady work, Javier had been allowed to keep some of the money he earned picking carrots on weekends and over Christmas vacation, and he felt the blush of newfound independence. With a five-dollar bill in the pocket of his freshly ironed khaki trousers, he set out on foot for Holtville five miles away. After walking for a half-hour in the bright morning sunlight, he managed to catch a ride.

Javier stopped first at the barbershop. Until that day, his mother cut his hair with her sewing scissors; there never had been money for professional haircuts. Lately, he had put off his mother's offers to trim it, preferring to let his hair grow longer, greasing it heavily with Brylcreem and combing it with a broad-toothed comb into a duck tail. Elvis wore it that way, and he had seen the style on older boys at Holtville High, not only Latinos but also Anglos, boys who were smart, from wealthy families, and popular with the girls. He was hoping to impress a girl who, at the moment, loomed much more important to him than mere school buddies, and he believed that nothing but a professional haircut would do.

At the second ring, an older Anglo woman abruptly opened the door, startling Javier. Looking as if she had just come from the hairdresser's, her dark hair piled on top of her head in a beehive, every strand perfectly in place. The lady peered at him sharply, saying nothing. Javier presumed she was Janice's mother.

"I'm Javier Romero, ma'am. I go to Holtville Junior High. Is Janice home?" he managed.

"Oh, I'm sorry. She's not," the woman said. "She's out with her friends this afternoon."

"I'm here, Mother. It's all right." Janice's voice came from behind.

Mrs. McDonald feigned surprise. "Oh, I thought you had gone out. Why, I thought you were with Jody. I had no idea you were in your room."

Janice stepped from behind her mother. In the instant her blue eyes met Javier's, her face brightened, and she smiled.

"It's all right, Mother," she repeated.

"Well, don't forget you have plans for this afternoon."

"I really don't, Mother."

"I don't want to interrupt your plans," Javier stammered. "I can come back some other time."

"No, it's really okay," Janice stepped out into the entryway and closed the door behind her.

Janice wore her light brown hair in a bob, held in place by a white hair band. She was almost as tall as Javier. Her fair skin was smooth and free of blemishes, and her broad smile revealed even white teeth. She wore a red-checked blouse, tucked in at her trim waist, and a pair of white tailored shorts, the light fabric setting off her perfectly tanned legs.

"Let's sit here." She sat down on the tiled front edge of the entryway and cradled her arms around her knees. "I hate being inside on a day like this."

Javier's mind floated. He suddenly felt clumsy. When he managed to sit down on the step with his legs stretched out in front of him, he became self-conscious of his shoes. Although he had carefully shined them the evening before, they were boxy and worn. He tried sitting cross-legged but felt even more awkward. Finally, he opted to bring his feet under his body and clasp his arms around his knees as Janice had

"I thought you did a great job at the geography bee," Janice said. "Congratulations. I never would have known where Tonga was. I would have said Africa."

"Just lucky, I guess. You did a great job, too. First place for the eighth-graders.

"Well, I had a lot of chances to study, and Mr. Hixson is such a great teacher."

"Yeah, he is." Before his father got the steady job on the Pinchney ranch that promised to allow the family to stay in one place during the school year, Javier rarely had the chance to get acquainted with a teacher. But this year, he had connected with Mr. Hixson. The young teacher seemed to spot something in the boy and took an interest in him.

Mr. Hixson's encouragement was the spark Javier needed, and he seized on it, suddenly finding an interest in school. When it became apparent to him that he might complete a full year at Holtville Junior High, Javier's self-confidence grew. His peers accepted him as a local, and friendships became possible. Teachers regarded him in a different light too, and, when Javier took a particular interest in geography, Mr. Hixson encouraged him, entering him in the school geography bee.

Javier won the seventh-grade bee, which made him eligible for the All Valley Geography Bee.

On the day of the event, Mr. Hixson had driven Javier and Janice to the competition in El Centro. Javier felt a tingle when Mr. Hixson introduced Janice and she smiled. He briefly touched her hand when she extended it. Then she popped into the front seat of Mr. Hixson's car, and shifted toward the middle, making room for him. Excited by her unexpected touch, but unsure of himself, Javier instead climbed into the back. But during the drive, she hardly talked to him, turning only when it was polite to acknowledge his presence. Javier ached for something to say, something clever that would make her notice him. He leaned forward on his seat, his back held so straight that by the time they arrived his muscles were sore.

In the days after the geography bee, Javier could not get Janice out of his mind. He lay awake in bed at night concocting impossibly dramatic scenarios in which he became her hero.

Now he could not believe his good fortune to be sitting beside her in the warm sunshine on the front step of her house.

"Mr. Hixson gave me his atlas," Javier said. "The one he used in college. That helped me a lot."

"That is so like him. He is really nice. I'm going to miss him next year."

"Are you going to go to Holtville High or El Centro?"

"Daddy would never let me go to El Centro, but I'm hoping he will let me have a car when I'm sixteen, and then I might bring the subject up."

"Do you know my name?" Javier suddenly blurted.

"Javier. Of course I know your name." She laughed.

"Good, I was afraid you might have forgotten it." He grinned in embarrassment.

"Don't be silly. I know you. You're a good student, and this is your first year in school in Holtville."

"It wouldn't be my first year if my parents didn't move so much. I'm fifteen; I really belong in high school."

"I thought maybe you were a little older. You can't help it if your parents move a lot."

"My dad has a steady job now. He works for Mr. Pinchney. In other years, we'd be in Watsonville about now."

"It must have been tough, moving like that."

"It was. It was hard to have friends. But now I can make friends without worrying about having to move on."

"It has been nice for me, living here all of my life and having friends. But someday, I want to move on, move out of the valley. I want to travel. I want to be a teacher like Mr. Hixson."

"Yeah, I'd like to do something like that, too. My parents have never done anything but farm work. Most of the guys I know just want to get out of school and work in the fields, too, but I don't want to do that. I want to go to some of the places I've seen in Mr. Hixson's atlas: Rio de Janeiro, Egypt, Paris. I'd like to go to Paris and see France. I've read *The Three Musketeers* by Alexandre Dumas. There's a lot of history there."

They talked while the shadow of the house, cast by the warm afternoon sun, moved unnoticed across the lawn and into the street. When Mrs. McDonald opened the door and reminded Janice that it was dinnertime, Javier stood.

"You know … the Tea Dance is coming up?" he stammered. Through the afternoon, he had struggled with the next step. He wanted to see more of Janice but had formulated no practical idea of how, or even whether, it was possible. Javier realized he had just seconds to make his case.

Before he met Janice, he would not have thought of attending the Tea Dance. He had no money, no good clothes, and he was not Anglo. But now it loomed hugely important. She had consented to sitting and talking with him on the front step of her house, but would she want to be seen with him at the school dance? He feared that he was placing Janice in an awkward position, afraid that by asking he would force her to say no. Summoning all his courage, Javier had decided that if disappointment were to come, it would not be because he did not ask.

"Yes?" Janice smiled.

"Well … I wondered if it would be all right … I mean, would you dance with me … if I asked?"

"Of course. I'd like to very much."

Javier was euphoric. Not once during the long walk home did he bother to stick out his thumb in the hope of catching a ride. When he was not forced onto the shoulder by passing cars, he crooked his left arm as if it were encircling Janice's trim waist and, holding his right hand in the air, shuffled forward on the pavement and then to the side, as if they were embracing the girl of his dreams in a waltz or a sensuous rumba. Then, mimicking Elvis, he would spread his feet and gyrate his hips. Swaying his arms, he crooned, "Put your sweet arms around me and love me tonight."

13

"Negroes don't need to be marching in the streets. Martin Luther King can send them here," the florid-faced speaker, the president of the California Farm Bureau Federation, thundered. "We won't discriminate against them. We'll give them a good, honest American job producing good, quality American food to put on the tables of our good American families. No one has to go hungry or go without a job in America. We'll employ the hungry, the jobless. California farms will take them. The government doesn't need to put people on welfare."

The early February weather was pleasant, but little air stirred under the broad awning sheltering the picnickers at the annual Holtville Carrot Festival. The speaker paused to wipe away the perspiration from his face with a white handkerchief. The audience of growers and families, all Farm Bureau members, glanced up from plates loaded with barbecued chicken, potato salad, and baked beans. John and Laura Pinchney put down their forks, hoping others would do the same and signal the speaker they were paying attention.

"We've fought the good fight," the speaker continued. "We've spent years and thousands of Farm Bureau dollars trying to show the American people what California agriculture produces for them: quality food at a low cost. We've had the Mexicans and, before them, the Filipinos,

Punjabis, and Japanese to harvest our crops. But now the people and Congress have spoken, and they say we're going to have to find Americans to do the job.

"Americans? By God, we want the country to know that California farmers are Americans! Good, loyal, God-fearing Americans!" The speaker pounded his fist on the podium each time he spoke the word. "And we'll abide by the law. We'll do what the people want. We'll hire every American who comes to us for a job. We invite President Johnson to send us all those people who want equality, who want dignity, freedom from hunger, and who want jobs!"

"Whew!" Laura said as she and John walked to their car in a dusty field roped off for festival parking. "Does he really expect LBJ to send people on welfare out here to work in California fields?"

"Naw," John replied. "Everyone knows that won't happen. He was talking for the benefit of those press guys up front. I recognized the one from the *LA Times*, and I heard one of the others is from New York. He's just trying to make the point that Americans won't do this work. Nobody is gonna show up, and the politicians know better than to say that they should. Laying down a challenge like that is just a way of making the press, the politicians, and maybe some people think. Nobody will show up."

The interior of the Lincoln was hot, and John lowered the windows as soon as he started the engine. He preferred fresh air to the air-conditioning for the short drive home. The speech was very much on his mind.

"We didn't create the way life is. It's just the way it is," John continued. "Crops grow in the ground under the hot sun, and they come in when nature tells 'em to. Someone's got to till the soil, chop the weeds, and bend over to pull carrots out of the dirt. If Americans won't do it, then we've got to have people who will.

"These people crying for civil rights, for welfare, for free medicine. Whatever. They're not going to come here and work. It's going to be tough on us, tough on all farmers without the Mexicans. Americans are going to have to learn that food doesn't just somehow pop out of the ground and land on their table."

"What about us?" Laura asked. "Are we going to be able to get our sugar beets out of the field this year?"

"I don't think we're going to have a problem." John answered. "At least for this year. I was talking to Joe Rodriguez the other day. So far, he's been filling his thinning crew with green-carders from Mexicali. Even Ohscar had a couple of his kids out there working with a hoe last weekend. Joe says there'll be trouble when the green-carders discover they can make more money picking oranges or strawberries up the coast or in the San Joaquin. He says, for now, the people he's got like being able to go home at night to their families in Mexicali, and that will keep 'em here at least through the beet harvest."

"I can relate to that," Laura said. "But won't the growers up north build housing for the families?"

"Some already have. But the unions and the do-gooders are saying that the growers are building housing just so they can hold another stick over the heads of their workers. It looks like the legislature is going to step in and set standards for farmworker housing."

"Is that going to affect us, too? That old house that Ohscar's in is in pretty poor shape. I see him coming over with a couple of milk cans and getting water out of our cistern."

"Yeh, the place needs its own cistern. I should have torn down that old shack years ago. Seemed like a good idea to put him in it at the time, but it's not really fit for a family, and we're going to hear about it from someone sooner or later."

"Well, it's important to him to have a place for his family, just like the green-carders. Being an American, he shouldn't have to raise his family across the border in Mexicali. But I don't want to see things go back to the way they were in the past with the wetbacks and the Okies. You didn't grow up in the valley, but I did. You wouldn't believe how those people had to live. Sometimes you couldn't get enough money out of a crop to pay them, and the poor people didn't have any place to go. I don't want us to be bringing people in here again who won't have a place to stay when there's no work."

"For Christ sake, Laura. Farmers shouldn't be responsible for providing things like family housing. One of the things that made the braceros so good was that they were all single men. Their families stayed back home in Mexico. No one had to worry about whether their kids were getting educated or their family had a roof over their head or a baby was being born."

"Yes, but don't you think we're going to have to worry about those things now if we're going to have workers?" Laura replied, hoping to steer her husband into the innovative line of thought she knew he was capable of and that had made him a successful farmer.

"Well, we'll see," John said. "We'll just have to see. I know we've got to worry about it to some extent because we let Ohscar keep his family on the property. But we've also got this Mexican fellow, Meegwell. We don't have to worry about whether his wife is sick and he has to take care of her or whether his house has water or whether his kids got to have shoes. And it looks like there are going to be a lot more Meegwells around soon enough. Maybe that's going to be the solution."

"What about the US Border Patrol?"

"I was talking to this new guy, Vic Veysey, who's running for Congress, at the dinner the other night." John replied. "The first thing I asked him to do if he gets elected is to get the patrol the hell out of our fields. They got no right to come on our land in the first place, and if we've got a fella like Meegwell working and minding his own business, why, that's our business, not the government's."

"Yes, but I don't want to see the wetbacks come back," Laura said, repeating herself. She was disappointed the conversation had come to this. "I don't want to see Oscar and his family hurt."

"That's all well and good, Laura. Both those guys are good workers. Both Meegwell and Ohscar. But don't forget that we've got a crop to get in. We've got a farm to run. We'll all be hurting if we can't get our fields irrigated or our crop in."

14

Shouldering his spade, Ohscar gazed at the rows of sugar beets that stretched the width of the field. In the fresh, early morning light, the sun's rays sparkled on the dew-covered leaves, making them appear soft and lush, like green velvet. He had labored through the night, filling the slender earthen channels with black water that cut evenly across the field like ruled lines on a page. The roots nested in twin rows between the lines. In another month, swollen by nutrients absorbed from the fertilized soil, they would be pulled from the ground, the leafy tops lopped off by the hooked blade of the harvester's knife.

Ohscar liked making things grow and had once dreamed of farming a small piece of land of his own. But it was no longer possible to homestead in the Imperial Valley, and available land was far too expensive for a farmworker like him to be able to get a start.

The Imperial Valley had once been the floor of an inland sea, and only a generation or two earlier, homesteaders and immigrants settled it. The pioneers built canals and brought water to the arid desert floor, turning it into one of the richest agricultural valleys in California.

Corporations gradually forced small landowners to sell their farms, turning the descendants of many of the original homesteaders into men who worked for wages, often on land their families formerly owned. A man with no capital stood little chance of farming his own land anymore. Still, Ohscar liked growing a crop, even if it meant working for another man.

After a last admiring glance at the perfect geometry of green rows and dark earthen furrows he had helped create, he was ready for the short drive home and a well-deserved sleep. He turned to retrieve his lantern and lunch bucket and saw a green-and-white border patrol Jeep speeding toward him on the field road. He paused apprehensively.

"Buenas dias, señor," the young, pleasant-faced officer said when the Jeep came to a stop. "Can I see your papers, please?"

Ohscar was not surprised to be asked for papers. Everyone in the valley, including white people who worked in the fields or in the packing sheds, carried their birth certificates. Most often, the US Border Patrol officers were businesslike and, like this one, tried to make it easy. Still, Ohscar felt a twinge of chagrin.

"I was born here," Ohscar said, reaching into his hip pocket for his wallet. He carefully removed the wrap that protected his papers from moisture and extracted a folded copy of his California birth certificate.

"Can I see your driver's license?" the officer asked.

Ohscar reached again into his wallet. "Sure. Here it is."

The officer scrutinized the two documents and returned them. "I'll bet you're ready to go home and hit the sack," the officer said, gazing out over the freshly irrigated field. The water in some of the channels was already starting to recede, leaving darkened soil between the beds of green.

"Yeah, it's been a long night." Ohscar did not resent the officer; it was a job that had to be done. Growers often preferred to hire Mexicans, legal or otherwise, and locals understood it was the border patrol who was trying to protect them. The only way to know who was legal was to check birth certificates and green cards.

"Well, have a good one," the officer said, putting the Jeep in gear.

"Wait!" The impulse came so suddenly that the words were out of Ohscar's mouth before he could think. "Do you want to know where there's a wetback?"

"Sure," the officer said, pushing the gearshift back into neutral.

In the weeks since Mr. Pinchney had hired Miguel, Ohscar had thought many times about notifying the border patrol. Now that he had his chance, he grew cautious.

"My boss won't find out that I told you, will he?"

"No, we never reveal the name of anyone who gives us information. Your boss will have no way of finding out."

"Well, he stays in the barn at the Pinchney ranch, in the tack room. His name is Miguel."

"Okay, we'll take care of it. Thanks." The officer touched the brim of his Stetson in a salute and drove off.

Ohscar felt a sense of relief. His hours had decreased while Mr. Pinchney accommodated the new man, and he feared that when work got slow, after the beets were harvested, he would be the one let go, not the Mexican. Mr. Pinchney no longer discussed with him the work that would need to be done between the harvest and the next planting, and he made Ohscar show the Mexican how to drive the tractor. Ohscar hoped the officer would follow through on his tip, arrest Miguel quickly, and send him back to Mexico.

Ohscar had not been able to share his dark fears about their future with Carolina. Things had been going too well; the children were all in school, the family had enough money for food and clothing, and everyone was healthy. Javier had been a worry, but now that Ohscar and Carolina had not had to move on for work, the boy was a success in school and was making friends. None of them, not the children, and particularly not Ohscar and Carolina, wanted to move on.

Ohscar decided he did not mind showing his ID if it meant that he would have a job. And sometimes you had to go further, he told himself, and tell the border patrol where the farmers hid their illegals. Ohscar did not fault the Mexican a livelihood. Every man needed work, particularly a man with a family. But he was born in the United States, and his children were born here. Work should go to US citizens first and then others, only if needed, he thought.

As he threw his gear into the back of his truck and opened the door to the cab, he whistled a happy tune, a song from Mexico, a birthday song, even though it was not his birthday.

"John, there's a border patrol Jeep in the driveway," Laura said, interrupting their breakfast routine.

Pinchney turned from his plate of waffles and sausage and peered over his shoulder out the kitchen window. Spotting the green-and-white Jeep, he dropped his fork, shoved his chair back, and rushed out the door. Stepping gingerly on the gravel in his stocking feet, he arrived at the side of the border patrol Jeep just as the officer set his handbrake. Leaving the motor idling in neutral, the officer got out.

"Looking for something?" Pinchney challenged.

"Good morning, Mr. Pinchney. I'm looking for a Mexican named Miguel," the young officer said flatly, watching the rancher for a reaction.

"Well, there's no one here by that name," Pinchney lied, trying to keep his voice even.

"Mind if I check your outbuildings?" the officer asked, starting for the barn.

"There's no need to look. I said he's not here."

"Yes, you did, but then you might not know if a trespasser spent the night in your barn."

Pinchney recognized that the border patrolman was giving him an out, but he dared not give him permission to search.

"I'm telling ya that there's no need to search my buildings. I had a fella here by that name, but he's gone. Left last week."

"What day did he leave?"

"Friday." Pinchney felt the muscles in his face tighten and the large vein in his neck throb. Fearful of offering a sign that might indicate he was not telling the truth, he stared at the border patrolman without blinking. The officer looked at him for what Pinchney thought was a long time.

"Very well, have it your way, Mr. Pinchney, but I'd better not find him on your property."

"Well, it'd be no problem for me if you did, would it?"

"You're right, Mr. Pinchney, but I'd really hate it if I found out you were lying to me."

Ashen faced by the encounter, John Pinchney returned to the kitchen.

"You didn't lie, did you John?" Laura asked anxiously.

"They got no right to search our property," Pinchney replied. "They can't prosecute me for hiring a wetback. They got no right even to ask if we got one. They ought to mind their own business."

"What if they catch him?"

"Then I guess they'll haul him off and deport him. Can't stop that, but they shouldn't come here snoopin' around. Wanted to search the barn. I told him, hell no. The border patrol got no business bothering us. They can't do anything to us if they do catch him."

"John, you shouldn't have lied."

"What was I going to do? I couldn't let them take him."

"You shouldn't have hired that Mexican in the first place, particularly since you've got Oscar. I've never liked him sleeping out there in the tack room."

"Laura, who do you think is going to get our crop in this year, Ohscar and a bunch of locals? You can't depend on the locals. I'm going to hire whoever I can get, whether they he's legal or not. I got beets to get out of the ground and up to Spreckels. That's how we earn a living. And speaking of Ohscar, I'm not going to have anyone around here who's gonna' rat me out. That border patrol officer knew Meegwell's name. How do you suppose he knew that?"

"John, you don't know that Oscar turned him in. Be careful whom you accuse. He might not have done it. Oscar has been a good worker for us, and he has a family."

"Who else would have known that we had a guy without papers named Meegwell livin' in the barn? That officer asked for him by name. It's none of Ohscar's business who we hire. I pay him a fair wage, and we give him that house. If he don't appreciate it, he can move on. But I'm not going to have a snitch living on my property. For all we know, we might have to hire a hundred wetbacks here this summer to get in our crop. That is none of Ohscar's business. In fact, it's better for him if we do hire wetbacks. We can't pay him if we can't get the beets to market. But, he doesn't seem to appreciate that."

"John, what are you going to do?" Laura asked, alarmed at the turn of the conversation.

"I'm going to get him out of that house for one thing. I ought to fire him, but I'm at least going to get him out of that house. It's only a matter of time, the way things are going, before the state makes us fix it up anyway, and I don't want to do that. Might as well get him out of there now. It's better to have sugar beets growing on that land than to have a snitch livin' there."

"John, you're just going to hurt his family kicking them out of the house. Can't you just give him a warning?"

John Pinchney pulled on his boots, grabbed his Stetson, and strode out the door for the Romero house. Laura was right, in part, he thought. He didn't want to look like a fool just punishing the man's family. Might be better just to get rid of him. There were plenty more Meegwells around these days, if it came to that. And the locals were becoming more reasonable.

15

 Grey clouds shrouded the dawn, making it difficult at a distance to make out the colors of the vehicle that had just turned onto the field road and was coming toward him, raising a cloud of dust. It was not Mr. Pinchney, Miguel decided, or an Imperial Irrigation District ditch rider; they drove white pickups. Anxious that it might be la migra, he paused, balancing a spade full of dirt in midair, and watched the vehicle approach. Too late, the light-green-and-white colors of a border patrol Jeep became apparent.

Miguel dropped his spade and bolted into the freshly irrigated field. The saturated clay pulled at his high-topped rubber boots. He was able to take only a few strides before they stuck fast. Unable to stem his momentum, he stumbled forward, stepping out of his boots to avoid falling full-face into the flooded field. The cold mud sucked at his socks forcing him to reach down and grab at them before they, too, were lost in the muck.

Realizing the futility of flight—even if he could run, the officer would simply drive around to the other side of the field and wait for him—Miguel faced the patrullero and shrugged. Grinning, the young officer got out of his Jeep and waited as Miguel pulled his empty boots out of the muck and slogged barefoot back to the edge of the field.

"¿*En d*ónde *nacio, señor?*" the patrullero asked, still grinning, knowing the obvious answer.

"*México.*"

"¿*Tiene usted papeles?*"

"*No, señor,*" Miguel answered with a shrug. "No, I don't have any papers." As Miguel held his arms out from his sides, the patrullero quickly searched him, taking his wallet and his penknife and tossing them in the front seat of the Jeep.

Miguel tried to catch his breath. His heart was pounding. He tried not to be afraid. La migra were not brutal, he reminded himself. But he was in a country not his own and in violation of the law. He had worked on the Pinchney ranch for seven months but had never been at ease with his illegal status.

After a patrullero had asked for him by name at the ranch house one morning, both he and Mr. Pinchney had been extra wary. The rancher even moved him into the old house vacated by the norteño, Ohscar, and his family, but that had blown over. La migra never returned as he had expected they would, and he moved back to the tack room in the Pinchney barn.

Still, Miguel kept a constant watch. If he spotted the green-and-white Jeep soon enough, he hid, lying down in a ditch if he was working in one of Mr. Pinchney's fields. If he could not find a ready hiding place, he affected an air of nonchalance, hoping the patrullero would think he was a local. Each near encounter left him short of breath, his heart pounding.

Once, when he went with Mr. Pinchney to the Lechuga Store to buy groceries, a patrullero came in and bought a cold soda. The officer looked at him with a penetrating gaze, forcing Miguel to quickly look away. It was not the same as the day he stood his ground within yards of a patrullero on the south side of the All American Canal. In the confines of the small grocery store, he felt trapped.

The chance encounter fueled Miguel's paranoia. The next time his boss asked if he wanted to ride along to the store, he made up an excuse. Thereafter, Mr. Pinchney picked up the milk, eggs, tortillas, and meat for the simple meals Miguel prepared on the small hot plate Mrs. Pinchney had provided.

"Okay, señor, your boss is going to be plenty mad if you don't shut off the water," the patrullero admonished. Miguel did not bother to pull on his muddy socks and boots, but walked barefoot to the head gate. After he ratcheted down the gate and returned to the Jeep, the patrullero handcuffed him, supporting him by his elbows as he clambered into the short open bed behind the metal cab. The officer tossed the muddy boots and socks in beside him.

At the Pinchney house, the officer roused the rancher from sleep. "I've got a fella that works for you, Mr. Pinchney, and you need to pay him off."

Clad in a silk bathrobe over his pajamas, Pinchney stared at the officer in disbelief. He stumbled out onto the driveway and peered at Miguel who squatted in the rear of the Jeep.

"I didn't know he was illegal—he looked all right to me," Pinchney stammered. "He said he had papers. He gave me a Social Security number."

"Be that as it may, Mr. Pinchney, you need to pay him."

"Yeah, sure, I'll pay him. But, he'll have to take a check. What about my field? Did he leave the water running?"

"No, he shut it off, and your gear is out there where he was working. While you make out that check, I'll take him to get his stuff."

"Yeh, well, he can show you where he stays ... Now, this doesn't have nothing to do with me, does it? I mean, I'm not in any trouble for hiring him, am I?"

"No, it's not against the law for you to hire him," the officer responded. "It's just against the law for him to be here."

"Well, he doesn't have much. Those rubber boots there belong to the ranch."

The officer followed Miguel into the barn and, in the dimly lit tack room, removed the cuffs long enough for Miguel to cram his belongings, including a new pair of jeans, into his mochila. He put on a fresh pair of socks and the new pair of work-boots he had purchased with one of his first paychecks. Opening the Igloo cooler where he kept perishables, he broke his remaining three eggs into a tall glass of milk and downed the concoction in quick gulps.

When they went back to the Jeep, Mr. Pinchney, dressed this time, reappeared in the driveway. The rancher gave Miguel his check and stuck out his hand. "You've been a good worker, Meegwell. You come back when you get papers."

Miguel studied the freshly prepared check, nodded, then creased it and put it into his shirt pocket.

At the border patrol coralón in El Centro, a chainlink fence, topped with rolled concertina wire, surrounded the compound. But to Miguel's surprise, the painted concrete-block barracks were air-conditioned. The food was much better than the fare he had prepared for himself in Mr. Pinchney's barn, and the bunks were clean and orderly.

On Sunday afternoon, a priest from a local church, Padre Jaime, said Mass and then heard confessions. He said he was from Irelandia, and Miguel was surprised he spoke such excellent Spanish. The young, red-haired padre spent the remainder of the afternoon playing soccer with the detainees on a soccer field in the back of the compound.

Miguel learned that he would be detained for two weeks while his fingerprints were checked in Washington, DC. One of his fellow detainees, a man from Jalisco, told him he had been foolish to tell la migra his true name.

"Certainly you didn't admit that you were from Zacatecas?" his new companion urged. "Unless you tell them you're from Mexicali, they will put you on an airplane and fly you to Leon, Guanajuato. You'll have another long journey to get back to la frontera."

But Miguel had not had a choice. The patrullero had found the *mica*, issued to him when he was a bracero, and his *Cartilla Militar* that showed he resided in San Pedro Piedra Gorda, Zacatecas. When the report came back showing he had no previous arrests, he, along with forty other detainees, all from Jalisco, Guanajuato, Michoacan, or Zacatecas, were taken in a green bus to the airport and put aboard a four-engine airplane. The pilots and guards wore the dark-green uniforms of la migra.

Miguel had never flown before, and as the airliner droned at a low altitude over the Gran Desierto of Sonora, he stayed glued to the window, staring out over the endless miles of yellow-grey sand, speckled with olive-green clumps of desert foliage. In the afternoon, the aircraft increased altitude and flew above the Sierra Madre. Anxious to see Concha and his children, particularly the new baby, Maria Guadalupe, he was happy he was going home. San Pedro Piedra Gorda was only six hours by bus from Leon.

When they landed at Leon, the Mexican *Aduana* would demand *mordida*, and Miguel wondered how big a bite it was going to be. He had been able to cash Mr. Pinchney's check in the coralón—a bank in Mexico would have insisted on holding it for up to two weeks or demanded a steep fee—but carrying cash could be a problem too. He was thankful he had been faithful about sending *giros* to Concha each payday.

All in all, his time in el norte had been profitable, and Miguel was satisfied with that. True, his hours had come at the expense of a norteamericano, a man who like himself had a family, but that was not his business. The boss could hire whom he wanted, and if Mr. Pinchney felt he was working harder than the norteño, then it was only fair that he get the job. That was *la vida*.

It did not hurt that la migra was sending him home for free. Miguel understood it was a gesture meant to encourage him to stay in Mexico. Had he simply been put through the gate to Mexicali, he would have jumped the line again the next night or the night after. What man would ride the train fifteen hundred miles back to Zacatecas?

Miguel figured he would not stay home long. There would be no more work for him in Piedra Gorda this summer than there had been when he had left in January. There never was enough work in Zacatecas. That is why so many men had gone to work in el norte as braceros. Nothing had changed in Mexico, except his countrymen jumped the line now as *ilegales*.

Miguel had earned enough money to support his family through the winter in Piedra Gorda, and he would enjoy the time with Concha, the new baby, and the rest of his children. He would not need work again until spring, he thought. Then he would return to el norte.

16

 The knob rattled in the cheap wooden door but would not turn. Javier stepped back and stared in disbelief. In the dim light of the sleeping migrant camp, the door's peeling paint faded to a dull grey. He despised the cramped cabin that was now his family's home, but he could not conceive that he was intentionally locked out. As he reached for the knob again, his hand quivered.

"Mama!" he called in a low voice, hoping not to awaken his brothers and sisters or alert other people sleeping in the closely spaced cabins.

"Mama!" he called again, knocking. "It's Javier."

The door cracked open, and his mother's face appeared. Wearing a nightgown and slippers, she pulled her worn terry-cloth robe around her slender body, catching her single braid under her collar. Barring Javier from entering the darkened room, she stepped out onto the bare concrete doorstep. Javier heard the latch click behind her.

"Javier," she said, "we must talk." He followed as his mother led the way to the cinderblock building in the center of the former tourist court that housed the bathrooms and showers, the only building showing a light.

Javier shifted awkwardly; his face hardened. He had delayed coming home until he was sure his father was asleep and then had loitered longer, not wanting to face his mother's questions either. He had spent the day at the game arcade, lingering even after school was out and it was time for him to go home. Finally, when the arcade had closed, with nowhere else to go, he had walked home. He had hoped to slip quietly into the room while his siblings and parents slept. His space on the two pushed-together beds probably would be taken, he knew, but he was prepared to sleep on the floor.

Life in the rundown camp confirmed his family's misfortune. He hated the name of the place, Camp Tia Juana, and the caricature of the fat, Mexican woman outlined in neon above the name on the faded green-and-red neon sign that no longer lit up. The red-tile roofed, faux-adobe cabins once housed tourists passing through El Centro on Highway 80. But now the sign mocked the plight of the migrant worker and welfare families who paid by the week to live in one of the shabby cabins or repurposed trailer homes.

"Where have you been?"

"I was at the Jalisco Arcade."

"I looked for you there at ten o'clock. You weren't there."

"I ran an errand for Mr. Camacho," Javier lied. Warned of her approach, he had hidden in the men's room.

"Why weren't you in school today?"

Javier did not answer. He hated Woodrow Wilson Junior High and resented the forced transfer. When he arrived in March, relationships in his class had been long established, the students ready for the end of the year, graduation, moving on. He made no friends. No one was interested in the new student, least of all his teachers who viewed him as just another of the migrant kids who came for a while, occupied a desk, and then left. Feeling betrayed by his family's return to migrantcy, Javier had become sullen and alone.

"That's what this is about, isn't it? You didn't go to school today and were ashamed to come home," his mother said.

Javier looked down, prodding a plucky clump of weeds with his toe. His mother was right, of course. They had had this discussion before, long discussions about trying, regardless, about keeping his eye on a goal, finishing seventh grade and hoping next year would be better.

About how resenting school was useless and only made success more difficult to achieve.

Javier wished he could talk to Mr. Hixson again. If only Mr. Hixson could tell him these things, he could believe. He had done well at Holtville Junior High, had actually believed he might have a future other than farm labor. But his father, who was supposed to protect him, had let him down, let the family down. He could not understand why and could not forgive him.

Javier cringed at the still-vivid memory of his father standing in front of the house, hatless, in the presence of the tall rancher wearing an expensive Stetson. He and his mother watched anxiously from the window, sensing something important was being discussed, some dire news being delivered. The two men did not shake hands when they parted. His defeated father walked back in the house and told the family that they would have to move, that he had been fired.

"Javier," his mother said, "I know what you're thinking, that your father let you down. You blame him for having to change schools and live in this place."

"The way we live is stupid!" Javier flashed. "Why do we have to move all the time? Every time something good happens, like living in Holtville, something ruins it."

"*Mijo,* I don't have the answer to that. Only God knows. But you must not blame your father. Your father is a good man. He works, and he brings home money and food to us—every day. That is a strong man. He doesn't run away from life, and you mustn't either."

"I'm going to get away from here. I'm going to get a good job. I'm not going to pull carrots for a living, and if I ever face a boss like Pinchney, I'm going to stand up to him. I'm going to tell him off, knock his damn hat off, and stomp on it."

"Javier, I hope you do get away from here. I hope you never have to raise a family in conditions like we've had to raise you. But you just remember, your father had to do the only work he could do in order to raise you. That's being a man, and don't you ever accuse him of being weak. I hope you do get a job someday, not in the fields. A steady job, so that you can stay in one place and raise a family. That's why you should stay in school and get an education. That's the smart thing to do."

"Mama … I can't. I can't go back to Wilson. I want to go back to Holtville."

"Javier, we've been through this. You can't. You've got to stand up and be like your father. Endure until the time comes you can get your diploma. Then your life will be yours, and you can get a good job somewhere."

"Mama, I can't. I'm not going to."

"Don't tell me that, Javier. You were gone all day. I worried about you. I worry about you every night. But I'll worry more if you do nothing to improve yourself. Javier, you came home tonight. Finally. And I'll let you in. But this is the last time. If you do not go to school tomorrow, I'll not let you back in. That'll be it. You'll be on your own, and you can find your own place to sleep and pay for your own food."

Javier watched the back of his mother's colorless robe as she turned and walked back to the darkened cabin. She paused at the door, not turning, then entered, and closed it behind her. Stunned, Javier stood in the warm night air, pondering, uncertain about what to do, not knowing what he wanted.

17

Javier's red bandana and the green-and-gray plaid shirt that he kept buttoned at the neck and wrists were streaked with sweat and white salt residue. Attempting to power the overloaded truck up the rocky trail, he tromped on the clutch and grappled for a lower gear, but he succeeded only in producing a grinding metallic clash. Motor racing, the drab, war-surplus ambulance, its red-and-white insignia crudely blotted out with green paint, lurched to a stop. Beside him on the bench seat, Chuy Gallegos cursed and grabbed the gearshift from Javier's hand.

"Why did I have to bring a fucking kid?" Chuy yelled above the roar of the engine. Four hundred kilos of marijuana stashed in burlap bags filled the box-like rear compartment of the vehicle. The pungent smell, mixed with the dust and the heat, fueled his ill temper.

Since turning off the paved highway west of Mexicali, they had made slow progress toward the US border, and now it was early evening. Clumps of creosote bush, its small, oily leaves clinging to scraggly gray branches, dotted the desert hardpan. The trail followed a dry wash leading to a saddle between the lonesome peak of Mount Signal, still bathed in sharp sunlight, and the Jacumba Mountains to the west. The gigantic piles of dry rocks, one to two thousand feet high, had been formed during the Pliocene era by granite boulders, cobbles, and gravel coursing down prehistoric streambeds from the tall escarpment of the Laguna Range behind them. The shadows and haze of late afternoon colored the steep slopes in obscured hues of deep purples and browns.

When they could, they stayed on the hard desert caliche, but frequently the way was blocked by crevasses, and they were forced down into the sandy bed of the wash. Despite the military vehicle's four-wheel drive and heavy-ribbed tires, the top-heavy truck bogged down often. In the 120-degree heat of the cloudless August afternoon, Chuy and Javier were forced to dig loose sand away from the wheels and stuff clumps of brush under the tires. Chuy's soft hands were soon raw.

Unable to find the right gear himself, Chuy angrily slammed the shift against Javier's thigh releasing it back to him. Finally engaging first gear, the youth let out the clutch, and the heavily laden truck lurched ahead once more.

Chuy stood to get twenty thousand dollars, big money, for delivering the drugs on the US side of the border. It was the largest smuggling job he ever had undertaken. If successful, there would be more trips. Those crazy kids in San Francisco wanted a lot of pot, and only the border patrol seemed to be trying very hard to stop them from getting it. But now that the braceros were gone, la migra was busy trying to round up all the wetbacks, and Chuy felt that the odds had turned in his favor. His business was getting people what they wanted, and his qualifications included eagerness to do it, even if it broke the law.

Chuy had gotten away with smuggling small quantities of easily concealed heroin through the port-of-entry in his nondescript Ford. Lately, taking advantage of the growing numbers of former braceros, pollos, looking for a way to cross the border to find work, he recruited small groups to mule backpacks of marijuana through the desert. Once they were across the line, he picked up the Mexicans and drove them to Los Angeles where he sold the pot to pushers.

The old smugglers' trail Chuy and Javier followed crossed the border into Davies Valley to the west of Mount Signal. He had used it sometimes for his human marijuana caravans. Always looking for bigger profits, it occurred to him a truck might navigate the trail, and he made a deal for the four-wheel drive ambulance. But he had needed help, someone to help dig the heavy vehicle out of the sand if it bogged down and drive if possible.

Until now, Chuy had operated alone; an extra hand in the drug business incurred risk. A partner might try to move in on his deal, turn him in to la migra, or hijack the load, leaving him to face angry suppliers who would force him to make good on their lost drugs. Not having to settle up with anybody after the payoff had proven to be the best policy.

Big for his age, Javier was lean and muscular. Just a boy, he would be easy to deal with after the trip was over, Chuy thought. The kid did not have much experience driving, but on a desert trail, he would be good enough. The desert was the place for kids to learn.

Fearing a rival might attempt to hijack his load, Chuy carried a .45 and rode shotgun. It was not just that he wanted to be ready if he needed to use his gun; also, when they crossed the border, they ran the risk of an encounter with the border patrol. Riding in the passenger seat, he had a better chance of making a quick escape. He might have to roll out of the moving vehicle.

Chuy had sensed something about Javier, a burning resentment of his parents, probably, barely concealed just beneath his skin. The boy was a loner, and that was good. He had seen him hanging around the Jalisco Arcade, loitering in the shadows under the stucco overhang that protected pedestrians from the harsh desert sun. The boy occasionally played foosball, pool, or pinball in the arcade with other loungers.

A sweaty local with a large mustache and his dark-haired wife operated the arcade and the businesses on each side, a grocery and a cantina. Chuy casually asked the proprietor about the boy and learned that he lived in Camp Tia Juana. The next time he saw Javier at the arcade, Chuy offered him a game of pool.

Sullen at first, uncommunicative, Javier perked up when Chuy asked if he would like to earn two hundred dollars. He was not surprised when the boy accepted. Now that the truck was moving again, Chuy tried to start up a conversation.

"You ever smoke any of that shit?" Chuy asked, jerking his thumb over his shoulder at the pungent burlap bags in the rear.

"Yeah," Javier said, trying to avoid the conversation by keeping his eyes focused intently on the rough trail.

"You ever fucked a girl, kid? Betcha never fucked a girl, have you?"

Javier tightened his grip on the wheel. He did not like the runty little man with the crumpled ear on the seat beside him. His breath was foul, and his teeth stained, and now the taunting. He regretted getting into this. Chuy had not explained exactly what he wanted Javier to do until he picked him up in Mexicali that morning. At first, Javier had been excited, although he suspected he was about to be involved in smuggling. He never had done anything illegal before, but the chance to earn two hundred dollars overcame his qualms. But as the trying day wore on, Javier grew less and less confident that Chuy knew what he was doing. As they neared the border, his fears grew.

"Aw, a handsome guy like you, I bet you've fucked plenty of 'em, maybe thirty or forty, maybe even the whole school! Have you done that, kid? Fucked any girls?"

"No!" Javier said through clenched teeth. He wanted to bail out, leave Chuy, and walk back to town, but Chuy kept his .45 at hand on the seat, and with his growing unease, Javier began to believe it was meant as a warning to him.

"Shit. I can't believe that. Never been fucked! I tell you what. When we get done with this, I'm gonna take you to a whorehouse I know in Mexicali. Get you fucked. I'm gonna introduce you to Blanca. She'll fuck your balls off."

Trapped, Javier tried to concentrate on the two hundred dollars he would get when the load was delivered. Soon this day would end, he told himself, and he would have more money than he had ever had in his life, more money than his father often made in a month. He wanted to buy a gun with the money and thought about how the situation would change if he had one now. He would not be putting up with Chuy, for sure. After they delivered the load, he would force Chuy out of the truck and drive alone back to town.

Javier believed having a gun would change his life. It would give him power, importance. Dropping out of school would not matter. He had hung around the window of the gun store on Main Street, sometimes going there in the evening after closing time to gaze through the steel grating. The row of rifles and shotguns chained to a rack behind the counter awed him, but it was the revolvers and automatics displayed in the glass-topped counter that he wanted to see.

One afternoon, hands buried in his pockets, Javier had edged into the store. But the owner, wearing a white T-shirt, his trousers held up over his huge belly by a pair of rainbow-striped suspenders, looked up from showing a customer a revolver and froze Javier with an iron stare.

"I don't sell guns to Meskins, boy," he said in a hard voice. "Now, git outa here."

Seething, Javier left the store, more determined than ever to get his hands on a gun. Having a gun, he thought, would give him the authority of the man in the store. He could stand up to a John Pinchney, and he would not have to put up with scum like Chuy.

Javier was hungry, but he was not going to admit it to the sweating runt of a man beside him. Chuy had brought along a large thermos of water, but no food. It had been a tough day, hard work driving this awkward vehicle, harder still repeatedly digging out of the soft sand.

Close enough to the entrance to Davies Valley to be in the shadow of the rock-pile mountain to the west, Javier and Chuy worked their way through a wash. The top of Mount Signal was still in sunlight, but dusk covered the slopes below. The air was hot, but the approaching darkness promised relief.

Ahead, the trail led to a short, steep grade covered with loose shale. Chuy was quiet, studying the slope. Javier sensed the crest was close to the border. With a chill, he wondered whether the border patrol was lying in wait at the top.

18

Border Patrol Inspector Bill Garner slowed as he pulled within sight of the Coyote Wells gas station. In the summer, the patrol removed the doors from the retrofitted metal cabs of the Jeeps, and the dry desert air swirling around him sucked the moisture out of his skin leaving white salt stains in the folds of his long-sleeve, green uniform shirt. He toyed with the thought of stopping and buying a Coke at the red machine standing against the front wall of the decaying white-clapboard building.

Fronting on Highway 80 in the midst of a sparse collection of wooden shacks and mesquite trees, the station and a tilted steel water tank, perched on top of a rickety timber frame, were Coyote Wells's only landmarks. A lone gas pump, the brand logo defaced with red paint, dispensed an undisclosed grade of gas at twice the price of gas stations in El Centro or Calexico forty miles to the east.

The proprietor, a grizzled desert-rat the border patrol suspected of being a lookout for smugglers, stood in the doorway watching. Garner ignored him and pulled off on the dirt side street. Reversing direction, he coasted to a stop facing the highway. He retrieved the gallon-thermos of ice water he carried in the foot well in front of the passenger seat.

Ignoring the advice of a local physician posted on the bulletin board at headquarters, Garner took a long, satisfying swig.

In the hot months, Garner endured chronic lower back pain the officers called "Jeep back." The memo warned that water held by the kidneys was the source of the discomfort. Ice water encouraged the men to drink more than they needed, the doctor reasoned, and bouncing over rough desert trails caused the loaded kidneys to tear at their supporting ligaments. He recommended they drink unchilled water instead, but few of the PIs heeded his advice.

A black sign with white, hand-painted lettering propped against the wall of the station said there was a museum inside. For an admission price of one dollar, the sign said, visitors could see a mummy. Feeling that human remains deserved the dignity of a burial, Garner never went in. PIs who had seen the leathered corpse speculated that it was a Mexican who had perished in the surrounding desert.

The Yuha Desert harbored many legends, and the mummy could have been an actor in any of them. Leading parties of colonists to San Francisco, Juan Bautista de Anza twice passed along the route, making camp on each occasion in Yuha Wash. The Old Butterfield Trail passed through Coyote Wells, carrying wagons and stagecoaches via the southern route to fledgling California towns. In life, the mummy could have been a dreamer, a sojourner, his journey to a better life interrupted by death in this meager oasis, or a passenger on a stagecoach, slain by an Indian arrow.

Or, the mummy could have been a Spanish sailor on the treasure galleon Hernando Cortez lost in a storm while exploring the Gulf of California. At the time of the conquistadors, the Imperial and Mexicali Valleys were submerged under the waters of the gulf. An earthquake in the eighteenth century lifted the land, trapping the northern waters of the gulf and forming the Salton Sea. The original shoreline was still visible among the dunes at the eastern edge of the Yuha Desert. Dreaming of discovering treasure, border patrol pilots on their way to and from the border from the airfield in El Centro flew along the shale and gravel strip, hoping that one day the shifting sands would reveal the rotting timbers of the lost galleon.

To the south of Coyote Wells, just across the border, the conical peak of Mount Signal was still bathed in sharp sunlight. To the west, the terrain rose through a series of low peaks, known as the Jacumbas, to the four-thousand-foot-high façade of the Laguna Range. The second lowest of the steps that worked their way up the escarpment, a north-south plateau between Mount Signal and the Jacumbas, was known as Davies Valley. Though it was a difficult trek, smugglers crossing the border from the south could pick up the Jeep trail that ran through the valley and follow it down out of the mountains to the highway at Coyote Wells.

The sun already had dropped behind the Lagunas, but Garner thought there was enough daylight to run down through Davies Valley to the border for a quick look. A short distance from the highway, Garner passed through a patch of crucifixion thorn cactus, named for the long, sharp needles protruding from the crooked arms of the plant. From here, the trail climbed gently, almost imperceptibly, to about five hundred feet above the desert floor and then stretched for a mile in a straight line, gradually climbing between two rock-strewn ridges to the mouth of a canyon. Garner stopped at a point where he still could look back and see the late afternoon haze over the cultivated fields surrounding El Centro and keyed his mic.

"Gwendolyn, this is unit twenty-two ten. I will be out of radio contact in Davies Valley for about an hour." Three bursts of static followed the transmission as the FM waves hit the repeater towers that relayed the message to the border patrol dispatcher at her desk forty-five miles distant.

"Ten-four, unit two-two-one-oh," Gwendolyn's voice came back, again accompanied by three static bursts.

The border patrol had adopted FM radios because they were suited to the broad, open spaces of the Southwest. But the low-powered FM waves traveled in straight lines and could not bend into canyons or curve over the top of a mountain. The radios were useless to officers working in mountainous terrain. Headquarters had not found a ready solution to the problem but believed the often-inadequate radios were the outfit's best effort.

With the end of the Bracero Program this year and the increase in illegal crossings along the border, a new threat emerged—drug smuggling. As yet, the smugglers were amateurish, tenderfoots, no match for seasoned border patrol inspectors. It had been years since an officer had been killed on the line, and complacency had set in. Elan among the PIs was high. Garner, like his fellow PIs, believed his radio was a tool, but not an essential one.

It was Gwendolyn's job to record the checks as PIs called them in, noting the time and location. A trim, middle-aged lady who wore flower-print dresses and high-heel shoes, Gwendolyn had been the evening shift radio operator at sector headquarters in El Centro since before anyone at the station could remember. She sat erect, like a school marm, at the dispatcher's desk just outside the door of the chief's office. She discouraged idle conversation. She liked to be called by her full first name and addressed as "ma'am," and every officer complied.

Gwendolyn knew every officer's habits, his idiosyncrasies, and every one of his tricks. She knew which PIs were in the habit of dropping into the Mount Signal Café for an unauthorized meal break. A PI who had gotten on her bad side could count on having his unit number called just as he was climbing onto a stool at the lunch counter. New officers quickly learned that Gwendolyn had a sense of her own importance, and it was said that she had the goods on so many of the bosses that none of them ever crossed her.

The trail grew steeper, so Garner put in the clutch and engaged the front transfer case, putting the Jeep into four-wheel drive. The four-cylinder engine roared as he lurched up the rocky trail through the canyon. At the top, the trail made a broad swing to the left into the long, narrow Davies Valley. Skirting boulders, clumps of ocotillo, and greasewood bushes, it wound along the valley floor to the border five miles to the south.

About halfway along the trail, a few rotting timbers marked the shaft of the Slim Pickens Mine. Little trace of the abandoned shaft was left, the wry name clueing the cause of its demise. Off-roaders occasionally visited the site, but with its remote and isolated location so close to the border, only the very bold camped overnight.

At the south end of the valley, the trail seemed to end abruptly at a precipice, and Garner stopped and killed his engine. In the deafening quiet of the still, desert evening, he admired the broad panorama opened before him. Far to the south, Garner could see the highway that ran from Tijuana to Mexicali, Mexico Route #2. At its western end, the single straight line split, and the lanes disappeared into separate canyons of the Rumarosa Range.

Zeno had brought him to this place on his first day back from the Border Patrol Academy, and they had sat in their Jeep enjoying the view and eating their lunches. When they had finished, Zeno had put the Jeep in gear and started forward. Believing they were going over a cliff, Garner had panicked and rolled out, landing on the ground in a lump.

It was not a cliff; it was a shale-covered slope dropping away at a steep-enough angle to not be seen from the top. Sheepishly, Garner had dusted himself off while Zeno, laughing, had turned and driven the Jeep back up the grade.

Smiling at the memory, Garner reached into his canvas trique bag and retrieved the insulated plastic sandwich pouch. Margie had packed a pot-roast sandwich, he noted with satisfaction. Next, he pulled out a cylindrical packet loosely wrapped in wax paper held in place by a thin green ribbon. He grinned. The package contained three cookies, carefully chosen and wrapped at the kitchen counter by his small daughters, Lisa and Mary Ann.

As Garner finished his meal, night birds appeared, their chirps barely audible against the overpowering stillness of the desert evening. He watched a kangaroo rat scurry from its burrow at the base of a clump of ocotillo, bound on some important errand. He wondered whether it calculated the risk from the red-tailed hawk circling high above. Or did it think it was already dark enough to be safe? Wondrous, he thought, how the desert slept during the day and came alive at night.

Mesmerized, Garner did not notice at first a barely distinct dust plume rising just above the olive-green-dotted terrain to his southeast.

19

The beige slopes of Mount Signal lay in shadows. As if resting, the air was quiet. It would soon be called upon to help dissipate the heat accumulated by the barren terrain through a long day under an unrelenting sun.

Planning to head back to Coyote Wells and begin a cut that would take him past the old Customs corrals towards Calexico, Garner started his engine. He gazed out over the still panorama one more time. Spotting a puff of dust rising to his left front, he quickly shut off the motor. He would have dismissed the plume as an incipient dust devil, except there was no breeze.

Garner reached for his binoculars. Preceding the plume, an olive-drab truck worked its way toward him through the scraggly vegetation. The boxy vehicle was still about a mile away, he estimated, and making slow progress. Off-roaders seldom approached the border from the Mexican side. It was not a camper, he decided; there were no windows or vents on the sides of the box.

Although it was uncommon to spot a smuggler in daylight, it made sense for them to try to get as close to the line as they could while they still had light. In the desert at night, headlights could be seen a long way. This guy was bold, trying to reach Davies Valley before dark, Garner thought.

Garner did not believe he had been seen and backed his Jeep a few feet away from the edge of the shale-covered slope. He got out and climbed on top of a boulder beside the trail, lying flat while he monitored the progress of the vehicle with his binoculars. It was clear that the truck was making its way to the embankment below him, although Garner thought the heavy vehicle, even with four-wheel drive, would have a difficult time making it up the slope. It was probably carrying marijuana, he speculated, and it would have to be unloaded in order to get the truck up the grade.

Garner weighed the possibilities. He was working the west desert alone. There were plenty of Calexico PIs working the line between the East Highline Canal and the Westside Main—illegal crossings across the fence and along the All American Canal had been heavy lately—but one of them would be dispatched to help him only if he were in trouble. His senior, Zeno Smith, could back him up, but Garner had not heard him go ten-eight before he had gone out of radio contact in Davies Valley. Zeno usually did his paperwork first, coming out on the line when it got dark.

Garner knew he should go back and call for backup, but the mouth of the canyon was five miles away. In the meantime, darkness would set in, and even if Zeno arrived in time, they might have to confront two or three armed men in a moving truck on the narrow Davies Valley trail. If he backed off and followed them, the truck would get down out of the valley and onto the highway. Stopping it then would require help from other officers and possibly the California Highway Patrol. That seemed like a lot of effort for an arrest he felt he should be able to accomplish alone. It was common for a lone PI to take a group of a dozen or more unarmed, illegal Mexicans into custody.

If he surprised the smugglers when the clumsy vehicle stalled on the grade, Garner thought he would have the initiative. Close to the border, when confronted, smugglers abandoned their load and ran back into Mexico rather than risk capture. That would be the worst that would happen here, Garner thought. If he acted quickly enough, he could grab at least one of the smugglers and be left with the truckload of marijuana.

He would have a good prosecution case to present to the US attorneys in San Diego.

The truck was close enough now that he could hear it grinding in low gear and make out two occupants in the front seat, but daylight was fading. It would be deep twilight by the time the truck reached his position. Garner hopped down from his vantage point and checked his Jeep, moving it further back along the trail so that it was partially screened by creosote bushes. Returning to the edge of the embankment, he checked the progress of the truck and cast around for a place to hide.

Garner was confident now that the straining vehicle would not make it up the slope and speculated that when the vehicle stalled, the passenger would get out first. He was the one more likely to be armed, Garner thought. He would disarm him and then go after the driver if he had not already fled on foot. Garner crouched behind a creosote bush to the left of the trail, where he still could see down the slope.

The truck paused briefly at the bottom of the grade. Despite the crude paint job, Garner could make out the outline of a red cross in a white circle on the side of the World War II relic. A hatless, runty-looking man stepped out onto the passenger-side running board and peered up the embankment.

The gears clashed noisily as the driver let out the clutch, and the truck lurched at the slope. It traveled little more than its length before the front wheels, and then the rear, buried themselves in the loose shale and gravel. The truck stalled, coming to rest at a steep upward angle just a few feet below Garner's position.

Cursing, the runt jumped from the running board but lost his footing on the loose shale and slipped to the bottom of the grade. Garner, gun drawn, rushed down the embankment and, before the man could get to his feet, jerked him upward by his shirt collar.

"!Alce las manos!" Garner demanded.

The smuggler hurriedly complied. Holstering his gun, Garner moved behind him and snapped a cuff on the man's raised wrist, then brought the man's arms down behind his back, and cuffed the other. The smuggler did not struggle.

His heart pounding with adrenalin, Garner quickly frisked his captive. He looked up momentarily as he caught sight of the second smuggler, a youth wearing a red bandana, sprint wildly down the embankment and disappear into the creosote bushes.

"What are you carrying in the truck, *drogas?*" Garner demanded, knowing full well the answer. Sullen faced, the smuggler did not answer.

Garner stepped to the back doors of the truck and yanked on the door handles. He jumped back as the doors swung outward, and from the tilted compartment, a dozen pungent-smelling burlap backs spilled out at his feet. Garner looked at his prisoner and smiled. "Drogas!" he repeated.

"*¿En donde nacio?*" Garner began the well-drilled immigration questions, hoping to nail answers before the man had a chance to concoct evasions.

"*México,*" the man answered.

"*¿Cómo se llama?*"

"*Juan González.*"

Garner shook his head. Juan Gonzalez was the border equivalent of John Smith. The man carried no ID, just a few bills stuffed in his pocket. Smart drug smugglers, even those born in the United States, concealed their identities and claimed to be from Mexico, hoping to get little or no prison time and a quick boot back across the border to freedom.

The truck sat only a few yards into the United States, but with a prisoner in hand, Garner would have to leave it. It would take a tow truck to winch it up the slope, a task that would probably have to wait until daylight. Garner hated to leave such a large trophy behind knowing that, as soon as he left, the smuggler who fled, and possibly other accomplices, could return and move the load back into Mexico. To make sure that he had some evidence against the smuggler he held in custody, Garner picked up one of the marijuana-filled bags before pushing at his prisoner to start him up the embankment.

Full twilight had fallen. Taking care not to slip on the shale, keeping his eyes on the dim outline of the handcuffed man struggling up the embankment directly in front of him, Garner did not see the two men standing at the top of the slope. The prisoner spotted them first, stopping in his tracks, and then scrambled up the remaining few feet.

"Put your hands in the air, border cop!"

Garner straightened, his eyes searching the gloom for the disembodied voice, finally making out the outlines of the men standing above him. Directly in front of his eyes, he saw the short, round barrel of a gun.

"Don't be dumb, border cop, or you'll be dead!" the voice demanded.

Incredulous, Garner slowly raised his hands over his head. The second man scrambled down to his side, grabbed his .357 out of its holster, and pushed him to the top of the slope. The gunman wore a bandana sweatband over his long hair and a leather vest. Garner recognized the squat, square shape of an Uzi pointing at his chest. The man who had taken his revolver wore a denim jacket with the sleeves cut off.

"Get me out of these, guys! Get these fucking cuffs off me," Garner's prisoner bleated.

"I don't know why, asshole," the gunman replied. "You got us into shit!"

"I didn't know. How could I know? It was that fuckin' kid … I couldn't go any faster. You guys knew the chances."

The denim-jacket man searched Garner's pockets, finding his handcuff key. "We gotta use these for the border cop," he said to Garner's former captive, releasing him. "Otherwise, you'd be going over a cliff in 'em."

"Guys, look," the freed man pleaded, "I couldn't know. It was dumb fucking luck. I'll help you guys. I'll help you get this stuff outa here. We're in this together."

Denim-jacket moved behind Garner. "Don't do anything dumb, cop," he said to the back of his head, "and you might live to see your kids." Expertly bringing the officer's hands down one by one, he handcuffed them behind Garner's back and walked him past two heavy motorcycles to his Jeep. He ordered Garner to squat down against the Jeep's front bumper. Removing the steel cuff from one of his wrists, he guided Garner's free arm behind the channel-iron bumper, and recuffed the PI's hands behind his back.

Garner's head throbbed. His heart pounded. He was too stunned to think. *Why didn't I draw and fire?* he recriminated. But the gunman had the drop on him, and instinctive self-preservation had prevented him from acting. Now he had no way of knowing what to expect. Even though his captor had held out the hope of sparing his life, Garner imagined the worst. He felt shamed, inadequate, violated, as if he had been sodomized. Becoming a prisoner of a criminal was something the patrol had never trained him for, a fate he had never contemplated.

Verging panic, Garner thought about his family—Margie, his two little blond-headed girls, Lisa and Mary Ann, at play on the swing set he had installed in their backyard. *I could be dead*, he thought in a daze. He was thankful he was not. But he realized the ordeal was not over, and he still could die.

He wondered whether he was locked in a nightmare and began a desperate search for some tangible thread that would lead him out of his dream back to consciousness. But he could not seem to wake up. That was his .357 in the smuggler's waistband; he had felt its cold, smooth steel brush the back of his hand as he had been cuffed. *It's not a dream! What will they do to me? Are they going to kill me? I have to escape! How?*

What would his fellow officers think when they found out he had let a couple of thugs get the drop on him? What would Zeno think? The chief? He should have gone back to the mouth of the canyon and radioed in, he remonstrated.

The iron bumper dug into his armpit, and Garner eased himself to a sitting position. *How do I get out of this?* He had heard of animals chewing off a paw to free themselves from a trap. He would do that if he had to. Was there some way to get his arm past the frame of the Jeep and slip off the end of the bumper? *How is the bumper attached?* It was bolted to the frame, he was sure. Overloaded with fear, his mind raced back to the night he and Joe Arnold were busting tumbleweed and bent in the bumper of Joe's Jeep when he ran into a clump that turned out to be wrapped around a concrete-filled pipe. They had worked frantically to straighten it out. *Yes, I'm certain. It's bolted, not welded!*

Garner struggled to his knees, bending forward, painfully adjusting his position until he could feel the hexangular outlines of the bolts that held the bumper. *If I can get the bumper off, I'll be free.* He could hide in the rocks; they would never find him in the dark. By then, he would be missed, and Zeno would be hunting for him.

Garner's mind raced. *Gwendolyn will notice I haven't called in. I told her I'd be out here for an hour. How long has it been? That was well before dark; it must be over an hour. I'm sure. She's probably been calling my unit number already. She's sharp. How many times will she call before Zeno notices I'm not responding? Not many. Zeno will be on his way soon. Maybe he's on his way already. God, hurry. How much time do I have?*

Garner could not turn the bolt. His fingers could not tighten enough on the angled steel edges. He tried another. The pads of his fingers were numb, but he kept trying. He could not tell if he had cut them or whether the flesh had opened to the bone. *Jesus help me. Mary, mother of God, help me. Don't let me die here.* He switched his body around; straining to bend forward enough to get his fingers on the head of a bolt on the other side of the frame. But the bolt would not budge either.

Defeated, Garner succumbed to panic and sobbed. *They're too tight! Too tight! Chew off your hand, the only way! The only way! Jesus! Jesus!* But his hands were behind him. He tried to saw his wrist against the steel edge of the bumper, biting his lip to keep from crying out with pain. Mercifully exhausted, he slumped, held up by the bumper. He was trapped, and there was no way out. *I can't do it! I can't do it! No way! Margie! Margie! Jesus! God!*

Lighting their way with flashlights, Garner's captors had scrambled to the rear of the truck and unloaded the burlap bags, pitching and passing the bundles to the top of the embankment. When they finished, they packed brush and rocks under the wheels. Rocking the clumsy vehicle, shoving, cursing, engine roaring, they wrestled it to the top of the embankment, and it finally rolled free on the trail.

The headlights of the former ambulance lit up the hatless border patrol officer kneeling on the ground tethered to the front bumper of his Jeep. Denim-jacket walked toward him, drawing the officer's .357 from his waistband. Garner looked up. Staring into the headlights, he could see only the man's silhouette and the outline of the heavy gun clasped in the smuggler's right hand. The silhouette stopped, legs spread apart. The gun disappeared in front of the black mass of the man's torso.

Every muscle in Garner's body froze, his mind seized. He did not hear the lead bullet crash through his skull and into his brain.

20

 Alone in the darkness, Javier tried to take stock, but panic prevented him from thinking rationally. He had fled headlong through the brush, stumbling and falling repeatedly into thorny creosote bushes. Looking back at the dark outline of the mountains, he discovered he had not actually gone far. He decided to hide until he recovered his breath and his senses. He did not see any lights, and it did not appear he was being followed, at least not yet.

Javier thought maybe he could sneak past the border patrol officer and walk home on the American side of the border. When the headlights of the truck unexpectedly came on, like the flame of a candle in the black night, his instincts took over, and he cautiously started back. As he drew closer, Javier could see men pitching burlap bags of marijuana up the slope. They were not wearing green uniforms, but jeans. One wore a cut-off denim jacket. At the crest, two motorcycles were illuminated in the truck's headlights. One of the men scrambling up and down the slope was Chuy; he did not appear to be a prisoner.

Puzzled, Javier hid in the brush while the men stuffed branches under the wheels of the unloaded truck. Finally, after much shoving and cursing, the truck's motor roaring, they wrestled and rocked the clumsy vehicle to the top of the grade. There, the men reloaded the drugs.

Still perplexed, fearful of being left alone in the darkness but afraid to reveal himself, Javier scrambled up the grade and crouched just behind the truck. He arrived just in time to witness the officer's execution. Horrified, fearing that the killers would now search for him, he turned and fled down the slope toward the distant lights of Mexicali.

In the moonless night, he crashed repeatedly into greasewood brambles, finally slowing his pace to a walk. As he gradually regained his senses and began to understand his predicament, he formulated a loose plan. He would hang out in Mexicali for a while. He would have to live by his wits. After time passed, he would slip back into the United States and lose himself in the barrios of Los Angeles. He could get a job in a factory and build a new life.

Javier thought of Janice and was swept by sadness. If there had ever been a chance for him, a normal life in a home with a wife and children, it was gone forever. Damning himself, he cursed his stupidity.

At dawn, Javier walked into a barrio on the outskirts of Mexicali. Smoke rose from early-morning cooking fires. Dogs barked. Early risers stepping out of crumbling adobes and cardboard shacks to visit the *excusado* eyed him suspiciously. Javier's shirt and khaki trousers were torn by countless blind encounters with the scraggly branches of creosote bushes, his arms and face streaked with welts.

He had meant to stay on the back streets, but the curious stares of the residents of these neighborhoods drove him to better-traveled thoroughfares. On a busy street, a lone pedestrian was not unusual, he reasoned, but he still felt the stares of the people he passed. Javier bought some *huevos* folded into a flour tortilla from a street vender. Standing on a corner, he ate ravenously, washing the meal down with a small carton of milk.

Uncertain where to go, Javier feared the inspectors at the port of entry might be watching for him, and he wound up in the broad river bottom that bisected the city. At its center, a small stream flowed north, passing under the chainlink border fence a few hundred yards from where he stood. Wanting to clean up, he made his way down to the bank, but the smell was so foul, and he could see raw sewage in the dark brown water, so he quickly turned away. Returning to the edge of the gully, he sat down on an outcropping of caliche facing the morning sun and pondered what to do next. A row of adobe houses stood at his back.

"¡Hola, muchacho!"

Javier turned to see a middle-aged man wearing striped dress pants and a blue satin shirt standing a few feet behind him.

"A beautiful morning, isn't it?" the man said.

Javier did not respond, but the man approached and squatted at his side.

"Such a beautiful morning for a handsome young man to be sitting in such a place so alone."

Surprised, Javier's instincts demanded caution, but the man sounded sincere and sympathetic. Flattered, Javier's guard dropped.

"Sí, I'm a little tired," he responded.

"And a little *triste* too!" the man replied quickly. "Did your girlfriend let you down?"

"No ... no," Javier replied. "I don't have a girlfriend."

"Well a man needs companionship, even if he doesn't have a girlfriend."

Javier had not noticed the man edge closer, and now he put his arm around Javier's shoulder. Javier stiffened, but the man's clasp tightened.

"I bet a young man like you has a good, stiff cock."

Javier tried to get to his feet, but the man slipped his arms down over Javier's shoulders, pinning his arms tightly to his sides. Javier struggled violently, rocking side to side as the man mouthed filth into his ear. Only after crashing his head repeatedly into the man's face was Javier able to break his iron grip. Regaining his feet, Javier sprinted down a street past the houses.

Javier spent the rest of the day aimlessly wandering the streets of Mexicali. He walked to the rail yard and back and lingered around the white stucco government buildings. He watched schoolchildren on a playground: the boys dressed neatly in blue trousers and white shirts, the girls in blue jumpers. He avoided going to the cantinas and shops near the port of entry; he thought it would be an obvious place to search if somebody were looking for him.

As darkness fell, Javier gravitated to the downtown and found a concrete bench in a small plaza across from the busy border port. The evening air was pleasant, and he wondered whether the border patrol was searching for him on the other side. They must have found the officer's body by now, he thought.

After a day of aimless wandering, Javier had been unable to formulate a plan for the night. Despite the Spanish he learned at home from his grandparents, Mexico was alien to him. He did not know how to survive or whom to turn to for help. He had only a few dollars in his pocket and no place to stay. The memory of the queer was fresh, and he feared being beaten if he returned to the river bottom.

Worse, Javier could not shake the image of the slain border patrolman; his mind seemed shackled to the horrible event. He wondered if the memory would fade if he returned home to his family. His father was away, but Javier began to believe he might feel better, less frightened, if he were just around him. If he could get across the border, he might find his father and join him picking grapes.

Surrendering to impulse, Javier strode to a fountain in the corner of the plaza, washed his face and arms in the cold water and, throwing away his sweat-stained bandana, slicked back his hair. With the illogic of a first-time criminal, Javier had brought his California learner's permit when he had crossed the border with Chuy to Mexicali, and he retrieved it from his wallet.

Hoping that no one yet knew his name or that he was connected to the officer's slaying, Javier walked across the street to the port of entry.

21

The grape harvest had moved north, and Ohscar took the bus from Arvin to Delano. It was past suppertime when he arrived at the cluster of cinderblock buildings nestled in the middle of the Sinkevich vineyards. After checking Ohscar's work referral letter, a corpulent Anglo security guard let him through a recently erected gate. He dropped his gear on a metal cot in the first of the two bunkhouses.

Ohscar was worried about his son, and he immediately looked around for a telephone to call Carolina. In his call the night before, she had told him Javier had not come home, and she was worried about him. The boy had started hanging out with youths neither Ohscar nor Carolina liked. Still, he most always showed up after a night away, and they decided he should not make the three-hundred-mile trip back to El Centro until something definite was learned about the boy.

Ohscar walked in the gathering dusk to the mess hall. Pulling open the screen door, he stepped into the brightly lit dining room. Two large window fans noisily sucked the heated air from the single-story building. Painted wooden benches were stacked upside down on the tables. A fat Mexican-American woman, her gray-streaked hair pulled into a bun, worked at a mark on the floor with short, scruffy strokes of her mop.

A steam table separated the dining area from the kitchen. Over the roar of the fans, a small radio positioned on a shelf high on the wall played a ranchera tune. The melancholy song sounded as if it were coming from a station far away, and Ohscar wondered whether it was one of the Mexicali stations he and his family listened to at home in El Centro. A grey-headed Filipino wearing a white T-shirt and apron worked at the sink.

"Where is the telephone?" Ohscar called across the room to the man.

The Filipino dumped the rinse water out of the large aluminum pot he was washing and placed it upside down on a rack. Wiping his hands on his apron, he approached the counter.

"We don't have a telephone anymore. The boss tore it out."

Ohscar looked puzzled.

"Mr. Sinkevich, he don't want anyone talking to the men about the strike. He don't let anyone in or out of the camp and took away all the telephones so no one can organize any troubles here."

Ohscar had known that the Filipinos at the Sinkevich camp were on strike. It was at least part of the reason he had been able to get the job, but he had not anticipated being unable to use a phone.

"Well," Ohscar responded, "it looks like everybody left anyway."

"Yeah, the boys they want thirty cent an hour more and twenty-five cent a box. Just like they gonna pay the foreign workers. Mr. Sinkevich, he say, no! And when the boys say they goin' on strike, he come in here, right in this mess hall, and tell everybody to get out! They fired!" The cook shooed with his hands as if he were driving the men out the door himself.

"He didn't even let them finish supper. He even kick out the old buffalo. They work for Mr. Sinkevich thirty, maybe forty years, from before the war. When they get too old to work, he let them stay. But no more. They gone!" Dramatically, the old man chopped the tabletop with the edge of his hand. "Mr. Sinkevich say, if the Filipinos strike against him, he no longer going to take care of them. That simple."

"How about you?" Ohscar asked. "The boss didn't make you go too?"

"No, I don't pick grapes. I'm not on strike. I just cook, and my woman and me, we take care of the camp." He gestured towards the heavy-set woman who had moved to the sink and was rinsing out her mop.

"You want something to eat?" the woman asked, having followed the conversation enough to sense a break. "Cup of coffee? I can fix you something. This is not a bad place, but you come at a sad time. Mr. Sinkevich is a good man. He's taken care of the old men and us for a long time. But the younger men, they want more pay."

"Yeah, Mr. Sinkevich give us a place when we couldn't get a house nowhere because, back then, a Filipino can't marry a Mexican in California," the old man continued. "We get married in Nevada. He tell me, 'Frank, you're a good man. You're not trying to cause nobody trouble. You and your wife come and take care of my camp.' And we did. That's why we stay. He is loyal to us, and we're not asking him for no big wages."

"Are the Mexican-Americans on strike yet?" Ohscar asked.

"Not here. Not yet. We heard they had a big meeting Sunday, and everybody wanted it. But we haven't seen any pickets yet," the woman replied.

Ohscar accepted the coffee and some heated-up chicken adobo. While he ate, he admired the chrome counters and kitchen equipment. The Filipino camps, including the Sinkevich camp, were provided by the growers and were clean and modern. The workers were mostly older men who did not have families. The braceros had not had their families with them either and also lived in camps provided by the growers. Domestic farmworker families like Ohscar's were forced to stay in roach-infested hovels rented from local landlords who gouged transient workers at harvest time.

The Filipinos had worked in California fields since way before the war and suffered as much as any other group of farmworkers from the unbridled economic power the growers held over them. Ohscar sympathized, but he also believed in some ways Filipinos were given advantages the Mexican-Americans did not get. Growers first sought Filipinos for such well-paying jobs as cutting asparagus and field-packing table grapes, often excluding Mexican-Americans who could do the work just as well. The growers in the Coachella Valley had settled with the

Filipinos for $1.25 an hour, while they continued to pay the Mexican-Americans only $1.10 an hour.

Ohscar did not feel he was being malicious or motivated by envy in taking the job at the Sinkevich Vineyards. He simply needed work, and taking a Filipino job seemed an acceptable choice. And, after all, they looked out for themselves, he rationalized. As long as growers continued to treat the two groups separately, he could not see how honoring a Filipino strike could help him.

The next morning after breakfast, Ohscar started work with the largely Mexican-American crew. Squinting in the bright morning sunlight, he examined a bunch of purple grapes he had just cut from under a leafy vine. He clipped away several spoiled grapes and those that had not fully developed, shaping the clump into a cone before placing it in a flat box.

The work was slow. The vines should have been lifted on top of the trellis before the harvest began, he noted, and the bunches should have already been pointed before the harvest began. The tasks had not been accomplished because of the strike, and Ohscar was frustrated by the extra work. He had expected to be paid fifteen cents a box, earning eighty or possibly ninety dollars for the week, normal wages for a Filipino in the harvest. To his surprise, he learned the crew was being paid by the hour.

But Ohscar could think of little besides his missing son. It had been too late the night before to walk into Delano to find a phone, and wondering whether the guard would have let him go, he had not tried. Javier had been angry and resentful since the move from the house on the Pinchney ranch and had finished the school year at Wilson Junior High only because Carolina demanded it.

Ohscar had been unable to talk to Javier. The boy was old enough to come along with him for the grape harvest, and the extra income would have helped the family, but when Ohscar left for Coachella in early July, Javier refused to go. As the grapes ripened, Ohscar moved north with the harvest, sending money home and keeping in touch with the family by telephone.

As if worry for his son were not enough, a band of strikers arrived and lined the road adjoining the vineyard. Waving signs, beating on pans, they clamored for the pickers to leave the vineyard and join them.

Ohscar spotted several Filipino men among the picketers—short, slender, serious-faced men, wearing narrow-brim hats, silently holding professionally printed signs that identified them as members of the AFL-CIO. He realized with a start that the Mexican-American woman leading the strikers was Mrs. Palacios, a friend of his mother's during his childhood in Delano. Standing in front of the raucous strikers, the aging woman, her puffy brown face framed by dark curls spilling from beneath a straw bonnet, screamed into her bullhorn.

"Okay, muchachos!" she yelled. "I called you boys! You want to be men? You want to show your *cajónes?*" At that, the short woman in too-tight pants and a flowered shirt that pulled tight over her bulging hips and buttocks grabbed her crotch.

"I want men! Real men, who have the balls to tell Son-uv-a-bitch that you deserve $1.40 an hour, just like they're gonna pay the foreign workers!"

Ohscar cringed, hoping that Mrs. Palacios had not recognized him. She passed the bullhorn to a young blond girl wearing a pale yellow dress standing in the bed of an old pickup truck. The girl looked like a college student, and Ohscar wondered if she had ever in her life picked a grape.

"*¡Huelga!* ¡Sálganse! Leave the vineyard, fellow workers! Don't scab for Sinkevich!" With her free hand, the girl gestured earnestly to the workers who did their best to keep themselves mostly out of sight amidst the leafy trellises. "The National Farm Workers Association and the United Farm Workers Organizing Committee are on strike against Sinkevich. Support your brothers and sisters against the exploitive growers!" she pleaded.

The strike had followed the harvest north as the grapes ripened. The braceros were gone, but the government was holding out the possibility of letting growers import more foreign workers if they paid them $1.40 an hour. The growers felt that was an impossible wage. Although they had to turn to domestic workers to harvest their crops, farmers were taking a tough line against any wage increases.

Those who worked in the fields prayed the grape strike would succeed, that the growers would be forced to pay a decent wage to American farmworkers. The Filipinos already had been offered an additional fifteen cents an hour, and the Mexican-Americans deserved as much, Ohscar believed.

The picketers waved flags, red with a black thunderbird emblazoned in the middle, but Ohscar had yet to see any Mexican-American men he could believe were actual farmworkers on the picket line. None of the two-dozen men working with him in the vineyard left to join the pickets.

Several of the picketers were Anglo and, like the young blond girl, appeared to be college students. He told himself it was going to take more than Mrs. Palacios, who was a busybody even when his mother knew her, to convince him that Mexican-Americans really were on strike. It never would succeed unless the Mexican-Americans left the vineyard and joined the Filipinos. Although it appeared inevitable he would, at some point, be forced to join the strike, he hoped it would not happen today, not just yet. He had to work and send money home.

Hoping to distance himself from the picket line, Ohscar worked a little faster, thankful that the vines and the rough leaves partially hid him while he groped for the ripened fruit. He was relieved that the foreman had moved the scale and the flatbed truck used to collect the loaded totes to a field road in the middle of the vineyard, making it unnecessary to go near the picketers who lined the edge of the field. So far, he had picked and packed fewer than a dozen boxes and was starting to feel glad he was being paid by the hour and not piece rate.

A Catholic priest in shirtsleeves, wearing a Roman collar, took the bullhorn and read from a book. "When a strike breaker comes down the street, men turn their backs, and angels weep in heaven, and the devil shuts the gates of hell to keep him out!" the priest thundered. "No man has a right to be a strikebreaker so long as there is a pool of water deep enough to drown his body in or a rope long enough to hang his carcass with!"

Ohscar struggled. He needed to make as much as he could in the three months of the grape harvest. In a few months, there would be work close to home harvesting winter vegetables in the Imperial Valley, but his family needed to eat in the meantime, and they needed to find something better than the cabin in Camp Tia Juana that Javier hated so much. Ohscar and Carolina did not want their younger children to experience the trauma Javier was going through with another move. It was crucial to keep them in their schools for the full year. They were determined not to move from El Centro. Ohscar alone would follow the harvests, they decided.

His heart aching, Ohscar hoped Javier was simply spending the night with a friend. He vowed to find a way out of the camp that evening and call home, hoping Carolina would report that the boy had returned. But he feared something worse. Javier had refused to work when school was out, even when offered jobs by the same crew bosses who employed his father. Javier refused to talk about it, but Ohscar prayed that, before it was too late for the boy, he would.

At the end of the day of packing grapes under the wrathful eyes of the pickets, Ohscar and the rest of the crew ate pozole prepared by the Filipino cook and served by his fat wife. After the meal was over, Ohscar slipped through the heavily leafed vineyards, avoiding the camp security guards, and made his way to the asphalt highway. He was anxious for news about Javier, whatever it would be, and planned to walk the five miles into Delano to call Carolina.

22

Far to the west, heavy grey clouds rested on the low mountains of the Coastal Range, but overhead, the powder-blue sky was streaked with ordered rows of cirrocumulus clouds, colored pink by the fading rays of the sun. After the closeness of the vineyard, the early evening air felt pleasant. The workers confined in the camp were clearly under siege, and once he reached the open highway, freed from the ire of the strikers and the paranoia of Mr. Sinkevich and his foremen, Ohscar felt free.

Sensing a car approaching behind him, Ohscar stepped off the pavement and onto the gravel shoulder. A black Volkswagen beetle chugged to a stop beside him. As the engine rattled in a fast idle, a round-faced man pushed open the passenger side door. "Are you going to town?" he shouted over the noisy engine.

"Yes!"

"Hop in!"

Ohscar had never been in one of the little cars before, and he marveled at the sensation of riding so low to the roadway. His benefactor wore a light-colored, short-sleeved shirt and chinos. The man's fleshy brown face was friendly; his brown eyes appeared sad, yet had an earnest, persuasive quality. "Where are you working?" the driver asked.

Ohscar hesitated. He could not deny that he was working, but he did not want to admit that he was working in a struck vineyard to the stranger. He wondered whether the question was more than casual. The driver did not appear to be coming from working in the fields, at least not today.

"Sinkevich. I just started this morning."

There was a slight pause before the driver answered. "Sinkevich is one of the growers we are striking."

Ohscar was startled and became defensive.

"Oh. Are you with the union?"

"Yes, the National Farm Workers Association. Have you heard about us?"

"A little. I don't know much about unions," Ohscar replied. He had witnessed strikes before but never belonged to a union and was dubious about their success. True, workers often got more pay after a strike, but the unions never were able to get a lasting contract, and the gains always seemed to fade away before the next harvest.

"We just started our strike last Sunday."

"I thought it was just Filipinos that were striking around here. That's why I came to Delano."

"Well, we support them. In fact, our two unions are joining together with our demands, and the Filipinos are supporting us, too."

Ohscar shifted uneasily in the low seat. Remembering the harsh words thrown at him by the picketers, even by the priest, he wondered if he was being set up for some sort of reprisal. The driver did not look threatening, but you never could tell. Maybe he was driving him some place where others would beat him.

"I wouldn't be working, but I have to," he pleaded. "I have a family to support. I thought it was just Filipinos who were striking."

"We understand that people have to work and support their families. We are all farmworkers and have families too. If you can't join us, we just ask that you leave the vineyards we are striking and find work elsewhere. They're picking plums up by Porterville. You can support us by leaving the camp and signing a card saying that you are honoring the strike."

"Well, I'll think about that. Maybe I can do that. But tonight I have to call my wife. We are having some problems with our boy, and I may have to go home anyway."

"That's too bad. How old is he?"

"He's fifteen and won't go to school."

"Boys are difficult to talk to at that age, but it's important he stay in school." They rode in silence for a while, the driver acknowledging honks and waves from the occupants of a passing car.

"Our strike is a nonviolent strike," the driver continued, seeming to have sensed Ohscar's fear. "We do not want to make ourselves the issue. We want our cause—organizing farmworkers—to be what people are talking about. Our goal is to sign contracts with all the growers in the valley, all the way from Arvin to Stockton."

"But what if the growers just hire wetbacks?"

"They have done that in the past, and I am sure they will try to do it again. But we are working very closely with the border patrol. They have just opened an office in Bakersfield and have four officers. They have been up here already. We have met with them, and I have assigned a vice president whose responsibility is to collect information about the illegal aliens and report it to the border patrol immediately."

"That's good," Ohscar replied, glad the conversation had turned from his strike-breaking. "I lost my job to a wetback a couple months ago." Ohscar proceeded to tell the driver, who was a patient listener, his experience on the Pinchney ranch that forced him and his family back onto the migrant labor circuit.

"You see, there wasn't much you could do by yourself," the driver said when Ohscar had finished. "That's why we are organizing—the Mexican-Americans and the Filipinos. We want a better life for farmworkers, for your son to graduate from school."

The little black car passed small highway businesses on the outskirts of Delano and then row after row of identical small houses. "Where can I let you off?" the driver asked.

"I need to find a telephone," Ohscar replied. "I have to call home."

"There is a telephone here at the People's Market," the driver said. The car pulled off the highway onto a gravel parking lot and chattered to a stop in front of a broad, single-story building housing a mercantile and a cantina. Farmworkers and families bustled in and out; the atmosphere seemed festive.

"¡Hola! César!" a grinning young woman balancing a bag of groceries on her hip called out. "¡Viva la huelga!"

23

Carolina clutched Javier's arm as they turned up the walkway to the rectory, and in a few short steps, the family stood in front of the heavy wooden door. Ohscar had returned to El Centro less than an hour before and stood a little apart, fidgeting and grim. Feigning indifference, Javier nevertheless was anxious.

A tall, red-haired priest answered their ring. Father James Fogarty, SJ, greeted Carolina warmly and shook Ohscar's hand.

"Come in," the young priest said, holding the door as Javier, already taller than both his parents, crowded closely after his parents. Electric candles in thick glass and wrought-iron fixtures illuminated the foyer. "I haven't seen you in a while, Javier. I've wanted to."

"Well, uh, I didn't …" Javier's reply was indiscernible, even to himself. He had avoided the priest, avoided attending Mass, despite his mother's pressing. At Easter, when Carolina had shepherded the rest of the family to Our Lady of Guadalupe Church, he had pretended to be sick.

"I know, son. There's been a lot going on in your life, hasn't there?" the priest said, leading the way into his study. Rustic dark-wood beams lent intimacy to the sparsely furnished room. A large portrait of Jesus in the Garden of Gethsemane hung on a wall in an ornate frame. Lit by a flickering votive candle, a statue of Our Lady of Guadalupe, her palms opened to the troubled family, stood in a niche set into the thick exterior wall.

Father Fogarty directed Carolina and Ohscar to a leather couch and Javier to an armchair. He brought a straight-backed chair from beside his desk and positioned himself beside Javier, facing the anxious parents.

"Father Jaime, bless us," Carolina began. "We asked to see you because Javier is in big trouble. He was there when the border patrol officer was killed. Javier didn't kill him, but he was there."

"Oh, my!" the young priest exclaimed. His face turned serious.

Javier flushed and sat forward in his chair, anxious for his chance to explain. He was relieved that his nightmare was finally out, hopeful that someone—Father Jaime, God, even—could help ease the crushing burden he had shared only with his mother.

Fearful that he might be overheard if they talked outside by the restrooms, yet wanting to keep the details from the ears of his sleeping siblings, Javier had poured out the details in a hushed voice in the smothering closeness of the decaying former tourist cabin. For a night and a day, they had waited for Ohscar to call, anxiously listening for the ring of the single pay phone in the center of the court, and then waited another day for him to travel home by bus. While they waited, hiding the terrible events from Javier's younger siblings who knew only that something was terribly wrong, his mother had insisted he remain in the small kitchen unit, curtains drawn.

Each morning, Carolina walked up the street to La Tienda Mexicana and picked up copies of the *Imperial Valley Press* and the Mexicali paper, *El Diario*. Back in their cabin, she and Javier anxiously examined the long articles about the manhunt for the officer's killers. The Federal Bureau of Investigation was assisting the border patrol, and the Imperial County Sheriff's Department was involved, they learned. Fearful of the day that the truth would be found, as she knew it must, Carolina found little relief that there was no mention yet of her son.

Carolina had been unable to read an article about the officer's young widow and two orphaned daughters; it was too terrible for her to think about. She knew in her heart that reparations would have to be made and likely would include the imprisonment of her son. She tried to convince herself that since he fled before the actual murder and was only fifteen, he would not face worse. But what if the killers claimed that it was Javier who had killed the officer?

Through two long nights, Carolina lay awake, gripped by terror, as her thoughts involuntarily probed the possibility of a death sentence for Javier. She beseeched Mary, the mother of Jesus, to help Javier, to help her in this moment of trial, to bring Ohscar quickly home. Exhausted, she lapsed into despair, sobbing into her pillow. She would get up and, stepping over the bodies of the slumbering children, sit in the dark at the kitchen table. There she would start to pray again.

During the day while they waited for Ohscar, Javier lounged on the sagging double bed. Damp, fetid air, drawn over rotting fiber pads kept moist by a constant dribble of water and forced through a vent directly above him, cooled the room. The rumble of the ancient machine and the squeak of dry bearings provided a backdrop to long periods of silence and sporadic moments of conversation between mother and son. Short questions were followed by short answers, recriminations. Unable to relax, Javier shuffled through a stack of worn comic books, occasionally picking one to read before quickly discarding it.

Javier relived every second of that horrible night, hoping with each review to recall some detail, some fact he had overlooked in a previous running that would absolve him or allow him to believe the murder had not really occurred. Day and night, he dozed fitfully, praying that he was only caught in a dream that would go away if he could just wake up, that he would awaken in sunshine, fresh air, his memory cleansed of the gruesome execution. Instead, he awoke to the awful reality, confirmed by the daily newspaper and radio accounts, that he was at least a witness, if not an accomplice, to the murder of a border patrol officer.

The fact that he had escaped, that he was still free, provided Javier little relief. The events were too vividly fixed in his mind: the border patrolman kneeling on the ground in front of his Jeep, illuminated in the headlights of the boxy truck he had driven almost to the very spot; the bareheaded officer, captive, looking up into the barrel of the revolver in the hand of the smuggler; the officer's head jerking hideously backward; the sickening crack of the gun; the body crumpling to the ground; the shackled hands held grotesquely aloft by the bumper of the Jeep.

Javier knew his life had changed forever, that his dreams of rising out of the grinding life of field labor endured by his parents were over, smashed irreversibly by his stupid decision to participate in the ill-fated drug-smuggling venture. He desperately wished he could relive the chain of events that had led him to accompany Chuy.

What would Janice think when she found out? Javier could not bear the thought. He continued to think of her, even though he had not contacted her since leaving Holtville Junior High. Burning with shame, he had managed only to mumble that he would be leaving school that day; his family had to move on, just like the migrants they really were, he thought bitterly.

Janice had urged him to call or write. He tried to call her once, even going to the phone booth, ready to deposit a quarter and a nickel in the box at the operator's request. But as he stood there, staring through the cracked glass at the shabbiness of the place, the depressing life in the crowded cabin caught up to him, and his resolve slipped away. He could never let Janice know, never let her picture him living with his family packed into a shabby room in a squalid migrant camp. He hung up the receiver before he completed dialing.

Javier tried to put thoughts about Janice out of his mind, but he could not. He was in love with the girl. She was at the center of his dream of an education, a life of stability, achievement, and respect. The dream was his map out of a life of drudgery and defeat; Janice was to be his guide. That was all over for him, he thought bitterly; now he faced a lifetime in jail.

Javier dreaded Janice learning of his pathetic part in a stupid drug-smuggling attempt and the murder of an officer, and with it, she would learn the truth of his existence. She would see him as merely the son of a migrant laborer, destined to lead a marginal life of itinerant fieldwork, the crimes indicative of his family's economic status—poor Mexican. Even if he did see her again, how could he convince her it was all a mistake, that he never wanted to smuggle drugs or be part of a murder?

Javier looked up from his hands to the painting on the wall of Father Jaime's office, the anguished Jesus, the Son of God, beseeching his Father on the eve of his final ordeal. When he was small, Javier had lain awake at night, terrified by the image of Jesus dying on the cross, and fled to his mother's bed in tears. Now he identified with the distraught Jesus, and a boyhood question returned. *Why hadn't Jesus simply fled? Why hadn't he hid on that night?*

I can still run. Why haven't I? Javier puzzled. *What brought me here? What invisible force is keeping me in this room?* Gazing from the picture of Jesus to his anguished parents and Father Jaime, Javier understood why. *My parents would be here anguishing even if I weren't. Jesus couldn't run. His fate was real, too. Jesus had no power over the events overtaking him, and neither do I. I can't change the facts, even if I run away.*

"Carolina, Ohscar, perhaps it would be best if I talked to Javier alone," Father Jaime said. "Would that be all right, Javier? When we're alone, I can hear your confession if you wish. Asking God for forgiveness will help you sort things through in your mind and give you peace. He will forgive you, and we'll be able to talk about reconciliation with Him. Then we'll invite your parents back in, and we can talk about reconciling with them and the other things we have to do."

Javier nodded. Ohscar and Carolina rose to leave the room. Javier felt his burden ease as Father Jaime took over.

24

"That Mexican boy who is involved in the shooting of the border patrolman, isn't he the one who came to the door last February, the one you sat out on the front steps with?" Mrs. MacDonald's voice was controlled, solicitous, the words carefully chosen.

The tuna noodle casserole seemed to blend into the whiteness of Janice's plate, and she picked at a slice of avocado with the tine of her fork. She had heard the news of Javier's arrest at school. Although she often thought of him, it was the first she had heard of Javier since he had suddenly left Holtville Junior High early in the spring, mumbling only a few confused words of goodbye. She knew her mother would ask at the dinner table, but she was at a loss to respond. Without looking up, she sensed her father's sunburnt face turned to her, his blue eyes looking at her, questioning, waiting for her answer.

"Yes, Mother." Janice put her fork down and placed her hands on her lap. She glanced quickly at her father, at his neatly combed hair, his freshly scrubbed, deep-brown arms extending beneath the rolled-up sleeves of his blue shirt. He looked at her, his eyes shocked, hurt, concerned.

"Wasn't he your classmate, Janice?" her mother prodded.

"We were in Geography Bee together. He was a seventh-grader," Janice spoke evenly, carefully. She had nothing to hide. She hoped her mother's questions would end once that had been established. The briefness of her relationship with Javier, she was unsure if it could be called that, had not quieted the turmoil in her mind, in her heart.

"John Pinchney says the boy's father worked on his place until a few months ago," her father contributed, speaking directly to his wife at the opposite end of the table. Janice hoped he was trying to direct the conversation away from her. "They lived in the old Nakamura place. That old house on Bonds Corner Road."

"How could anyone live there?" Janice heard her mother ask. "It's set empty since World War II. The Nakamuras never came back. It must have been in awful shape."

"Tom Greuter bought the land at a tax sale, and then the Pinchneys owned it these last few years. He's torn the place down and is going to plant on it."

"Good enough. Why, it was just a shack. Where did the boy's family move to?"

"John says they moved to El Centro. They live in Camp Tia Juana."

"That dump!" her mother exclaimed. She looked directly at Janice. "Nothing good ever came out of that place, all the stabbings and the fights. And drugs! The county should have burnt it down. But then where would the Mexicans live, I guess."

"Muriel Hinkle says that you danced with the boy at the Tea Dance," her mother continued, putting Janice once more on the spot. "Muriel was one of the chaperones."

"Yes, Mother." Janice's mind raced, but she did not know what to say. She had been stunned when the news swept through the hallway at Holtville High School, even before it had appeared in the El Centro paper. She could not believe it. How could the kind, gentle boy she knew be involved in a killing—and smuggling drugs?

From the first, she clung to the belief that Javier had been involved against his will, that he had been kidnapped and forced at gunpoint to participate. Why else would he surrender with his parents and a Catholic priest? If he were a hardened criminal, he would have run away, not run to his parents, wouldn't he?

But Janice had kept silent at school, even as her friends added garish embellishments to the little that was known. No one would believe her if she spoke up for him. And what would she say? She simply did not know.

Why was Javier in this awful mess, she asked herself through a long afternoon, unable to concentrate on her classes. What had she missed about him? Had she somehow been blinded? She did not think she had been wrong about Javier, but she could not come up with an answer.

Janice was heartbroken, her chest so tight it physically hurt. She wondered if she should try to get in touch with Javier. He might need her help, and if not, she needed to resolve the truth in her own mind. They had taken him to San Diego, but it was unreasonable for her to think that her parents would take her there so she could see him. Added to the torment she already felt, she wondered whether he would talk to her. Would he answer a letter? He had cut off contact with her, had not called after he moved, even though she had asked him to. She had never understood why. El Centro was not that far.

"Did your friends dance with Mexican boys?" her mother asked cannily.

That's it, Janice thought, and her back instinctively straightened. *Do I associate with the Mexicans, that's the real question.*

"Joe Christovich danced with Yolanda Gutierrez, but what's wrong with that?" she challenged, her voice rising. "Javier's not a Mexican. Not like you mean, Mother. He's ... just a boy!" Janice shouted. Her whole body quivered and tears flooded her eyes. She never had raised her voice at the table before.

Janice looked at her father. At times that she felt her mother was being unreasonably critical, she had been able to count on his quiet support, as if there was an unspoken pact between them. She regretted that she had not gone to him the minute he got home and talked out her thoughts. He would have listened and helped her sort things out, she thought. But her mother had sequestered him in their bedroom before she had a chance.

"Janice!" Her father's voice was stern, and his look surprised her. He stared straight at her, as if she had stolen from him. "What your mother is trying to get at—and I'll come right to the point and say it—if you're going to fly with crows, you're going to get shot down!"

As if she were fending off a slap, Janice's hand flew to her face. She gasped, but the sound was choked in her throat by convulsions rising from her chest. She jumped up, wide-eyed. A wail escaped her lips, and she fled to her bedroom. She slammed the door behind her, harder than she had intended. The full-length mirror on the back wrenched free and crashed to the floor. She threw herself on her bed and surrendered to huge, convulsive sobs.

Since her earliest memories, Janice had looked to her father for fairness, but he had abandoned her at this crucial moment. She lay curled up facing the wall. After a while, her sobbing subsided, but the hurt and disappointment coalesced, hardening her confusing thoughts about Javier into firm convictions of his innocence.

The fading evening light peeked between the slats of her blinds. She should have gone to the kitchen to do the dinner dishes, but she did not. She had homework, but she did not get up. She heard her door open. She did not turn. She heard her parents whispering as they picked up the broken pieces of glass and then the loud whine of the vacuum cleaner.

When the room quieted again, she felt her father's large, calloused hand on her shoulder. She did not know whether she welcomed it. Then his touch was gone, and the door gently closed. Janice lay awake. Something had changed in her life, and she could not entirely understand what or why. She cried softly into her pillow. Then she fell asleep.

25

"Marie C. Romero High School? Ain't that at the Youth Authority down in Paso Robles?" The owner of the truck stop where Javier was applying for a job pushed up the visor of his cap with the back of his grease-covered hand.

"Yes," Javier stammered. "But I graduated at the top of my diesel mechanics class. I can get a recommendation from the instructor."

"Nah, son, I just don't have anything for you right now."

Javier closed the folder that held his diploma, thankful at least that the man did not grab it and leave a smudgy print. He had walked to the truck stop on Highway 101 at the edge of town the same afternoon his father reported he had seen a help-wanted sign there. The sign was displayed in the front window just to the side of a red Coke machine, and Javier glanced at it again as he turned to leave. He was thirsty from the long walk, his throat still dry from anxiety over the interview, but he felt mocked by the sign and did not want to linger. He made his way between the busy gas islands back onto the frontage road.

Ohscar and Carolina had moved to Salinas to be nearer to Javier, and after his release on his twenty-second birthday, he rejoined his family in the small, wood frame house they occupied in a farmworker neighborhood. His parents had found plenty of work in the Salinas and Watsonville areas, enough to afford the rent.

Javier had been home for six weeks and had not found a job. Lettuce would be starting up soon, his father said, but Javier did not want to work in the fields. He feared that once he started, like his father, he would never get out. Life for a farmworker was just one continuous cycle of living hand-to-mouth, getting just enough money ahead to tide the family over to the next town, to the next field that needed harvesters.

"Things are improving," Ohscar promised. He had just returned from working in the grape harvest in Delano. "César Chavez has got the growers scared. All the grape growers have signed with him, and he's starting to organize in vegetables. We should be able to get forty cents a box in lettuce this year."

"Dad, that's only about $2.00 an hour. Peanuts. They're getting $3.50 in the cold storage, and drivers are getting $4.50."

"Well, you've got to be in one of those unions, and right now the Anglos and the Filipinos have those jobs sewed up."

"Dad, I don't want to be part of that anymore. It's all wrong. I want a chance at life. Be somebody. Settle down," Javier said. But when the lettuce started, he found himself standing on a street corner with his father in the pre-dawn *madrugada,* the daily ritual that determined what worker would board which labor bus and who would not go to the lettuce fields at all.

"Make a little money, have a little fun. That's what life is all about," his father's friend, Manny, quipped to the morose young man. Because Ohscar and Manny had worked lettuce for several years, a crew boss hired them right away. But it was only after nearly all the remaining workers had boarded buses that the crew boss finally motioned to Javier to get aboard the bus with his father and Manny.

Once in the field, Javier had to learn how to test the leafy heads for firmness. That part seemed easy, but it was not until the afternoon that he was handling his knife deftly enough to be able to cut the head free from the stalk with one stroke.

His back soon grew sore from stooping, and he tried kneeling, but that was slower and awkward. He could stand fully erect only after he filled a cardboard box with the leafy heads and stood to lift it to the waiting hands of the workers on the flatbed truck that followed closely behind the crew. The weight of the box pulled on Javier's unused back muscles. He had to race to keep abreast of the more experienced men and drew a rebuke from the watchful boss when he bypassed a few heads of lettuce to keep up.

Javier was more than ready to call it a day when the crew boss finally called a halt. The workers clambered back on board the bus that had sat at the side of the field all day absorbing heat from the sun. When they arrived back in town and spotted a white pickup, tubs of iced beer in the bed, parked next to the bus stop, cheers went up. Three Anglo men, they were organizers for the Teamsters Union, Manny said, passed the cold brews into the eager hands of the men filing off the bus. The Teamsters was a company union, Manny sneered to Javier, out of range of the beefy recruiter's hearing. But he, Ohscar, and Javier were soon quaffing a cold brew too.

On the opposite side of the street, a small flat-bed truck pulled up. Surrounded by flowers and lighted votive candles, a life-sized statue of the Virgin of Guadalupe was tethered on its bed. The red-and-black thunderbird flag of the National Farm Workers Association hung from a staff attached to the back of the cab, but the thirsty workers seemed to pay little attention.

As new lettuce fields came in and more pickers were hired, the madrugadas became less hectic. Most workers returned to familiar buses, rejoining crews that varied little day to day. The newly arrived scouted for vacancies, anxiously awaiting the wave of a crew boss's hand to jump aboard a departing bus. Still, each morning a few unlucky workers were left standing on the curb to shrug and walk back to their dwellings in the early light of dawn.

The soreness in Javier's back and legs soon gave way to new muscles, and his life became a daily routine. Up by four, father and son ate a breakfast of chorizo, eggs, and coffee prepared by Carolina, who then got the younger children up and off to school before going to her own job as a cleaning lady. Ohscar and Javier picked up Manny and then drove the short distance to the vacant lot at the edge of downtown where the labor buses parked.

Each day became the same, and as Javier worked, he counted: eight heads of lettuce per box, forty cents for each box, five boxes an hour, eight hours per day, sixteen dollars—less Social Security and tax. Living at home, his earnings began to accumulate, and at times, he thought about buying a car. Most men his age had one by now.

But no matter how often Javier counted, the life of a farmworker did not add up to what he wanted. Men got married and had children. After that, they and their wives, too, were compelled to work their way down long rows of lettuce for as many days as they could. Then they had to move on to harvest grapes, strawberries, or whatever else was available, if something was available, which often was not the case.

There had to be something more than scrapping for money, Javier thought. His junior high teacher, Mr. Hixson, and his teachers at CYA got more out of their lives than an endless cycle of grubbing for dollars to feed their kids. Javier knew what they had—a steady job, living in one place, a home, the chance to travel, respect—and he wanted that for himself, too. Most of all, he wanted respect.

The experience and skills he had worked hard to learn in CYA helped him rekindle his dream, but so far his diligence had not counted for much of anything. He still clung to his dreams, but achieving a life outside of farm work was harder to imagine now. His parents wanted to believe that somehow he could break free, but Javier understood that deep down they doubted it was possible. He stopped talking about it at the supper table, but once in the solitude of his bed, he refused to believe the life he aspired to since his adolescence was beyond reach.

But there was a part of Javier's dream that he tried hard to avoid, willing it away whenever it intruded. He wanted to be married to a wife who could understand and support his aspirations, like the girl he had once shared his dreams with at Holtville Junior High. He wanted a girl like Janice. So far in his heart, she had not been replaced. But thinking of her brought on an angry fit of self-denunciation.

Javier thought about joining the Army. Each time he looked at the formal picture of his father in his brown uniform, visored hat raised slightly to reveal his smiling face and eyes, stripes proudly displayed on his sleeves, Javier imagined himself in uniform too. His father said many times that he wished he had stayed in the service. The family would have gotten to travel, and the children would have had a chance at a good education, he said. Life would have been much easier for the family than the uncertainty of pursuing the crops.

The army might not be exactly the life he dreamed of, Javier concluded, but it was a way out of farm labor. At least he would have respect.

Ohscar and Carolina were not encouraging. "What about Viet Nam?" they asked. "You wouldn't want to go there." But there seemed to be something else his parents were afraid to say. Javier sensed it, as well. Because of his conviction, would he be able to join up?

Javier had worked in the lettuce harvest for six weeks when, one morning, the matter came to a head. As he started to climb aboard the bus with his father and Manny, the crew boss stopped him.

"I can't use you today, Javier," he said. "I'll give your check to your dad at the end of the week."

"Why?" Manny asked over Javier's shoulder.

"The boss told me to lay off six men. He hired some new guys who came by the ranch last night."

"Wetbacks!" Manny exclaimed. "He hired Mexicans!"

"He can hire who he wants, Manny," the crew boss said, not answering Manny's charge directly. "That's just the way it is. You know that."

Too shocked to protest on his own behalf, Javier joined the men on the sidewalk who were still hoping to be invited aboard one of the departing buses. Unsuccessful, dejected, he trudged home. The next morning, he did not get up with his father. After his mother left for her job, he walked downtown to the Armed Forces Recruiting office.

"Don't go in there! Stop!" implored a girl in hippie garb, a blue paisley bandana holding her blond hair back. She held a hand-printed sign that said, "Get the U.S. Out of Viet Nam!"

"Let us talk to you. You don't want to fight in a fascist war!" Her partner, a smaller brunette wearing blue jeans, put her hand on Javier's arm. "Cesar Chavez and Martin Luther King oppose the war."

Javier tried gently to remove the girl's hand, but she tightened her grip on his wrist and finally he was forced to use both hands to pry himself loose. He freed himself just enough to pull open the door of the storefront office and slip inside.

"They're persistent," a uniformed recruiter remarked. On his sleeves, Javier recognized the three yellow stripes of a sergeant, the same rank his father achieved in the Korean War. "Are you here to enlist? We're here to answer your questions."

"Yes … yes, I want to enlist," Miguel stammered. "But I do have some questions."

"Why don't you sit right here and fill out these forms first. Give us a little information about yourself. Then we'll be able to talk and answer your questions. The army runs on paperwork, and it starts right here."

The questionnaire was not long, but when he got to the line that asked whether he ever had been arrested, he paused. From the scuttlebutt at CYA, he learned he was not likely to be drafted because of his record, but he hoped enlisting, volunteering, would make a difference. He had wanted to ask the recruiter about it before he got to the point of filling out papers. He left the line blank and went on to other questions, finally signing his name. He walked over and laid it in on the recruiter's desk.

"Sit down," the sergeant said, motioning to a chair beside his desk. "Graduated from high school, I see."

"Yes, but I wanted to ask you about question seventeen."

"What were you arrested for?" the sergeant asked, looking at the empty space.

"Attempted smuggling."

"Drugs? Pot?"

"Yes," Javier replied. "But I've never done drugs. I've never smoked pot. I was fifteen at the time, and I was a witness for the prosecution. I was only involved because …," He stopped, not knowing how, or if he should try, to explain further.

"Do you have your records?"

"Yes, but they're juvenile records. They're supposed to be sealed. I'm still on probation, but I've completed my sentence."

"Hmm. Well, if you want to enlist in the Aarmy, you're going to have to let us see your records. And I'm not saying you'll be able to join. Someone else is going to have to decide that; someone above me. The lieutenant. Or maybe even the major."

After waiting well into the afternoon while the sergeant made phone calls and waited for a response, Javier was turned down.

Two nights later at the supper table, Javier announced he was leaving home. "I talked to my probation officer today," he explained. "He found me a job in LA. It's not much—cleaning out buses. But it's steady, and they'll hire me. It could lead to something."

26

Ohscar Romero sucked on a mentholated cough drop. His throat was not sore, but for weeks, he had been bothered by a metallic taste in his mouth. Food did not taste good anymore, and he was losing weight. The amber tablets were simply his latest strategy to overcome the distraction and permit him to concentrate on other matters, such as his duties as ranch committee president at Valley Fresh Growers.

On a backstreet near downtown Salinas, Ohscar pulled his pickup into an open parking space in front of the office of the United Farm Workers Union. The sidewalk, shaded from the early morning sunlight by a row of low buildings, was covered with dew.

Unpainted sheets of plywood shuttered the windows of the storefront building, but the door was propped open, a sign that his old friend, Manny Gomez, was already at work. During the recent garlic strike, someone had shot out the windows. Some of the members accused the growers. Others blamed goon rival Teamsters Union organizers, but Manny and Ohscar knew the shooter was a disgruntled member of their own, at times fractious, union. Manny felt that replacing the glass was an invitation to the culprit to do it again.

The open door let fresh air into the dim interior, and when Ohscar entered, Manny was still wearing his worn plaid jacket and was talking on the telephone. Smoke from his cigarette trailed to the door.

"That's not right, Robert. He's been very loyal to César—and to you," Manny pleaded, avoiding Ohscar's questioning gaze. "We were doing what we were supposed to do. We were telling the workers about the union. We were successful. They all joined up. We got hundreds of new members."

Ohscar assumed, almost correctly, that the call was another in the interminable post mortems with UFW headquarters at La Paz. The recent strike by garlic harvesters in Hollister had been a success; the workers had asked for the union's help and had gotten it in the form of hard work from Ohscar, Manny, and the other paid reps in Salinas. But, inexplicably, César had been opposed to the union's involvement. Ohscar was puzzled by Manny's failure to acknowledge him with so much as a nod, but with a sinking feeling, he slowly realized that the call was about him.

"You can't do that, Robert!" Manny sat up, the cheap plastic receiver pressed tightly to his ear, mouthpiece jutting forward angrily. "He doesn't work for you. He was elected by the ranch committee and gets paid by the ranch. You can't fire him!" He paused, muttering a series of short grunts while he listened to the voice on the other end of the line.

"Well, he's right here. Do you want to talk to him yourself? Yes … right here at my desk … yes, right now … But don't do this, Robert. You're making a mistake!" His dark eyes filled with alarm, Manny held out the receiver to Ohscar.

"It's Robert," he said with exasperation.

"Robert? Qué pasó?" Ohscar asked, pulling up a chair and bracing his elbows on the front of Manny's desk. Robert was César's in-law and, as a result of the interminable reorganizing at La Paz, was running field organizing this month.

"César doesn't want you to head the ranch committee anymore," Robert said, skipping a greeting. "You are no longer a paid rep. You are relieved as of this moment. You are to return your files and all union papers to the field office today."

"Why, Robert? What is the reason?"

"You have been disloyal to César. Disloyal to the union."

"How? When? I have never been disloyal. I have always promoted the union and supported César. I've been a member for over ten years!"

"Didn't you go to Hollister?" Robert accused. "Weren't you supporting the garlic strikers? And on union time?"

"Well, yes, but—"

"César did not authorize that strike. That was not a UFW strike." Deciding he had made his point, the official was curt. "You know that union phone calls must be limited to two minutes. I'm going to hang up now."

Speechless, Ohscar replaced the phone in the cradle. Manny watched him, his eyes wide with concern and dismay.

"We were organizing workers, promoting the union," Ohscar protested. "They all joined. It was a success. We got three hundred new UFW members. We weren't being disloyal to César, for Christ's sake."

"I know, 'mano."

During the lettuce strike in 1973, Manny and Ohscar joined the UFWA, and together they became volunteer field organizers. Ohscar had never forgotten meeting César Chavez in Delano and was thrilled when, after years of effort, the union broke the stiff backs of the grape growers, delivering contracts that increased worker's wages.

The '73 lettuce strike also was successful and resulted in union contracts with growers in the Salinas Valley. Field workers' wages doubled, and a system of fair hiring was established, ending the madrugadas. Paid for by the growers under the contracts, health care became available to workers at the clinic the union established in Salinas.

Ohscar organized his fellow workers at Valley Fresh, one of the largest vegetable growers in the valley. After another successful strike in 1979, Ohscar was elected to head the ranch committee. When Manny, his back crippled by arteriosclerosis, could not work in the fields anymore, César gave him a job at the Salinas field office. His pay, like that of all the union's paid volunteers, was ten dollars a week plus room and board. It was not much but sufficient for the disabled bachelor whose heart had always been for *la causa*.

"I want to talk to Cesar myself," Ohscar declared.

"Don't even try 'mano. He won't talk to you. Talking to Robert was as close as you're going to get. Right now, Robert is calling Valley Fresh, telling them that you no longer represent the union."

Ohscar knew Manny was right. Since UFW headquarters had moved from Delano to La Paz, an old TB hospital in the Tehachapi Mountains donated to the union by a Hollywood celebrity, César had become increasingly inaccessible. A daily presence during the years of the grape strike, he no longer was seen in the fields.

"We did right in the garlic strike, 'mano," Manny consoled. "The workers wanted to be organized—they had to be in order to take on the growers. We did our job. But, *chingao*, 'mano! What's happened to us? What's happened to the union? First Bert Sanchez got fired, and now you. Bert got it simply because he was the one to go to La Paz and try to convince César to support the strike. I didn't think he would fire you, too. Bert didn't do anything wrong, and neither did you. I don't imagine it will be long before I'm gone, too.

"Remember that César didn't want to do the lettuce strike in '79, either," Manny continued. "He wanted you and the other ranch committee reps to go around the country and organize a boycott instead."

"We couldn't have done that," Ohscar said. He stood and gazed for a moment out the open door. "We would have lost our jobs at the ranches and our seniority, just to stand around the door of a supermarket for months, and for what?"

"Anyway, the boycott never worked for lettuce like it did for grapes," Manny said. "How do you tell a housewife which head of lettuce to buy and which not to buy? There's no box in the produce bin so they can check the label."

"Well, we all decided not to go, and I know that made César mad," Ohscar said. "He kept saying a strike would cost the union money, but so did sending people off to boycott. And you don't sign up any new union members standing in the ice and snow in front of a grocery store in Brooklyn, New York."

"Yeah, that was the first time that I saw that César wasn't interested in organizing anymore," Manny said, leaning back in his swivel chair and turning toward Ohscar. "That was the turning point that I could see—1979."

"Do you remember the night that César came here and met with the reps?" Ohscar stopped pacing and leaned on his clenched fists on the top of Manny's desk. "You weren't in the meeting, but César argued for abandoning the strike. I asked him why he didn't want to organize anymore. He said it was no use; there were too many illegal aliens now. The growers could simply use them to break the strike."

"It's true the government is doing a lousy job of enforcing the border," Manny said.

"Well, I told César the answer," Ohscar said. "I told him we needed to organize each crop. When we've had contracts with all the growers, like in grapes or lettuce, the illegals had to join us if they wanted the work. At least that way the growers have to pay them the same wages they pay us, and the illegals aren't undercutting us anymore."

"What did César say?" Manny asked.

"He said, you can force a grower to sign a contract through a boycott, too. And I said how are you going to convince people to support a boycott if you don't have workers striking? In the end, he agreed to support the strike as well as a boycott, but he never liked it."

"Yeah, I know César didn't like it," Manny said derisively. "He never showed up for the contract signing at the Towne House."

"Well, it was a great victory anyway," Ohscar said. "We got five dollars an hour, good health benefits, and even paid reps. We got hundreds of new members. We couldn't have gotten that through a boycott."

"Yeah," Manny said. "And now it's the same thing with the garlic strike. He's just not interested in the farmworkers anymore. He wants to be the leader of all the Hispanic people, like Martin Luther King and the blacks. It's true there's always been racism in the way the growers have dealt with us, even when they have to negotiate with us. But why can't he fight racism and organize workers too? César can go off and deal with the politicians and the newspapers and celebrities and all that. But let us keep on organizing."

"César may be doing us good," Ohscar said. "But if we abandon organizing, it's going to hit us right in the belly—right at the supper table.

Already we're losing the gains we made in the seventies. Pretty soon, it's going to be all illegal aliens doing farm work because Americans can't afford to work that cheap."

On his way home, Ohscar worried about how to tell Carolina. She supported him and understood his passion to see farmworkers paid fair wages and treated with dignity. Even before it had become a paid job, his duties with the ranch committee and the union had kept him away from home many evenings and weekends. But she was as committed as he, and together they cherished the union's successes.

Ohscar thought about how things would have been different today for Javier. New crop cycles implemented in the years after the braceros were gone meant that farmworkers did not have to move as much, and hire-back clauses in union contracts eliminated much of the uncertainty. He and Carolina had been able to live most of each year in Salinas within a reasonable commute to work in the Salinas and Watsonville area. *Javier could have stayed in school,* Ohscar thought.

Oddly, Ohscar felt a sense of relief. He had watched warily over the last few years as César changed direction, as the union let contracts go uncontested to the hated Teamsters, a mere company union promoted by the growers. But fighting to maintain the direction of his own union had been stressful, and he wondered if there was a connection to the turmoil he felt in his stomach and bowels. Organizing the garlic workers cost him his job, but he felt a great satisfaction in the achievement. He had no regrets.

Ohscar pulled into the carport at the side of his home. The lettuce strike in 1973 raised wages to $3.90 an hour, he recalled with satisfaction, and using the UFW Credit Union, he and Carolina were able to buy the house. It had been a big step in their lives. Rita, Mirabelle, and Leopoldo graduated from Salinas High School. Javier lived in Los Angeles. After more than a year cleaning buses, he worked as a diesel mechanic and sometimes drove charters.

Ohscar thought the future would not be hard for him and Carolina. He still had a job at Valley Fresh, although no longer as the ranch committee president. Without the children, they could even return to the Imperial Valley for the winter vegetable harvest if they needed to, or to Delano for grapes. He was fifty-three, not too old to cut lettuce or thin sugar beets. They used a long-handle hoe to thin sugar beets now. The short-handle hoe, el cortito, the crippler of so many workers' backs, had been outlawed, another union victory.

Ohscar wondered for a moment about John Pinchney. He had heard that a large corporation had swallowed up the Pinchney ranch. But the best and the worst of the relationship between Ohscar and the grower were a distant memory. Workers no longer knew the men they worked for. Corporate executives, who did not deal directly with the workers, managed farms, orchards, and vineyards and relied on labor contractors to hire a crew and get in the crop. If field workers were to be protected, they had best have a contract enforced by a union.

César had been right. Ohscar shook his head sadly. *César knew it was coming to this,* Ohscar thought. *What had gone wrong? He had devoted his life to protecting farmworkers. Why had he given up?* It was clear to Ohscar that more than his job had been lost.

Before he went into the house, Ohscar thought he might try to get out of farm labor, try to find a job as a janitor or a mechanic, as Javier kept urging him to do. There was just the nagging matter of his erratic bowels and the metallic taste in his mouth. He was dosing himself with *epazote,* but it did not seem to help. Carolina had been after him to see a doctor, but after César closed the union health clinic in Salinas, it was no longer as convenient a matter.

27

"Javier?" The feminine voice, young, sexy, musical, drifted into his consciousness. An involuntary tingle shot through Javier's body. The intimate quality she affixed to his name in an instant activated an image hidden deep in the recesses of his heart, suddenly bringing to life a yearning he had fought against through long months and years of recriminations.

Caught in a throng of Sunday-afternoon mall shoppers, Javier turned and looked over his right shoulder. Janice's twinkling blue eyes met his in instant recognition, yet disbelief. Her light brown hair held in place by a banana comb, stylishly dressed in a frilly white blouse, bag-waisted denims, and espadrille sandals, she glided to Javier's side.

"Janice!" Overwhelmed with astonishment, jaw agape, eyes widened, Javier fought to control his reactions. "Janice," he repeated, unbelieving.

"How are you, Javier?" she said, grinning broadly.

"I'm incredulous," Javier stammered. Quickly remembering the elderly lady who was clutching his left arm, he said, "Mrs. Ahrens, this is Janice McDonald. Janice and I attended junior high together in Holtville."

The perfectly coiffed matron, her thin face powdered and rouged, held out a gloved hand to Janice. "How do you do? I'm very pleased to meet a friend of Javier's. Do you still live in Holtville?"

"No, I live in Pasadena now and teach school in Azusa," Janice said, taking Mrs. Ahren's hand.

"That must be hard, all those Mexican children."

"They're like any other children I teach. They're good, really."

"That's nice to hear. You hear so much of the other things. Javier is so good to take me shopping on these excursions," Mrs. Ahrens said.

The older lady quickly sized up the situation. "But do you know, I'm so glad you came along just now. Not many young men enjoy browsing through May Company with an old lady, and Javier I'm sure is no exception. Javier, I can do for myself this afternoon. Why don't we meet at Mrs. Fields later?"

Javier started to protest, but Mrs. Ahrens had disengaged her arm from his.

"Don't overdo it, Mrs. Ahrens," he said.

"This is such a fine young man," the old lady said, patting Javier on his forearm.

Janice smiled. "It was very nice to meet you, Mrs. Ahrens."

They found the Mrs. Fields nearby. Janice ordered a Diet Coke and a white-chocolate-chip-and-macadamia-nut cookie. Javier had coffee and a brownie.

"So, it's been a long time," Javier said.

"I see you're a bus driver now," Janice said approvingly, gesturing at the Southland Charters patch on the arm of his blue uniform shirt. "Is Mrs. Ahrens one of your passengers?"

"Yeah, I drive charters on weekends. During the week, I'm a diesel mechanic. This charter is a bunch of old folks going to Santa Anita, but Mrs. Ahrens doesn't care for horse racing. She likes to shop, so I bring her over here to the May Company. She rarely buys anything, but she likes to be out and around people who are doing things, people who are enjoying their lives, she told me once. I can relate to that, so I'm happy to accommodate her."

Janice smiled, leaning forward, her elbows on the table, playing with the straw in her Diet Coke.

"Yes, you would do that," she said.

"So, tell me about yourself. What have you been up to?" he asked.

"Well, after high school I went to USC. I got a teaching degree. I married Kent Armstrong. You might not have known him; he went to El Centro. His father had a lot of acreage up around Brawley. Kent was big man on campus, you know, top athlete, played football. He went to USC, too. The marriage didn't work, so here I am, teaching school and working out at Golds Gym. How about you, Javier?"

"Well," Javier started, "this is still hard. You're probably the last person in the world I ever wanted to have to admit this to, but I went to jail. You knew that, I guess."

"Yes, I knew," Janice said softly, her face reflecting concern. "I read about it, of course. It was all over the news. I just couldn't believe it. It just wasn't the person I knew, and I still believe that."

"I never used drugs. Going along with that petty smuggler was so stupid, and I've paid for it. Of course, you can never pay for another man's life, but I had no part in that. I was a witness. I told the FBI everything and testified for the prosecution. But I still had to serve time for the drug smuggling charge. How can I tell you how much I've regretted it?"

"I never believed that you were part of the killing. It was all such a shock, and I felt so bad for everything that happened to you. I felt bad when you left Holtville. I wished you had kept in touch."

"I was so mixed up over that. I'm much closer to my parents now, thanks to Father Jaime. Did you know him?"

"The Irish priest at Our Lady of Guadalupe in El Centro?"

"Yes, that's him. He was terrific. He came with my dad and me when I turned myself in. He was with me for all the trials and even came to see me while I was in California Youth Authority. At CYA, I learned diesel mechanics, and that's what I'm doing now—and drive charters."

"Are you married?"

"No, not even a serious girlfriend."

Janice smiled. "Afraid of commitments?"

"No, the right one just never came along." He blushed.

"I thought the marriage would work out, at least at first. My parents loved Kent, but he was more into himself than he was into me."

"People seem more self-centered these days, at least the girls I've met. You know, disco and all."

"Do you dance?"

"Yeah, I love to. Have you ever been salsa dancing?"

"No," she laughed, and then changed the subject. "You had a couple of younger sisters, didn't you? What are they doing these days?"

"Mirabelle is married. Her husband does farm work, like my dad did." Disappointed to be steered back to his past, Javier grew somber. "It was better for a while. Because of the union, for a while, they could make money, have healthcare and things. But because of all the illegals, things are getting bad again. They still have to move a lot to get work. My dad used to work for the union. He was the president of a ranch committee up in Salinas. Me, I'll never go back to farm work."

Sensing the unhappiness in his voice, Janice changed focus. "You know we used to talk a lot about travel. Remember the geography bees and Mr. Hixson? Here you are a bus driver now. Have you been to any interesting places?"

"I take a lot of charters to Las Vegas and to ski areas in the winter, but the ones I really like are the long-distance ones to New Orleans, even Washington, DC, and New York. I love to go cross-country. It's so diverse, and there are so many things to see. I'm trying to get on with Greyhound."

They talked through the afternoon and did not notice that Mrs. Ahrens had taken a seat at a table nearby, yet not so near as to intrude. When they noticed her, they quickly stood up and prepared to leave.

"Oh, you don't have to stop because of me," the older woman said.

Looking at his watch, Javier said, "Well, we really should get back to the track. It's almost time to load, and some of the people may be looking for the bus."

Janice smiled and squeezed his hand.

"Javier, have you asked Janice for her phone number?" Mrs. Ahrens asked archly.

"I guess I haven't," Javier stammered.

"Here, let me write it down for you," Janice said.

"I didn't know if you wanted me to call."

"I want you to very much."

28

"Farmworkers don't last very long," Manny said. "Their backs go, or they get hurt in an accident and wind up on the disability or the welfare. Or, like your father, they die from pesticides."

Manny sat in the rocking chair while Mirabelle served glasses of lemonade to the family and friends crowded into the small front room of the Romero's house. Standing beside the chair, Javier nodded agreement. Janice, seated beside Carolina on the couch, struggled to hear the conversation over the rush of wet air blowing into the room through a vent in the ceiling.

"Malathion was the worst," Manny continued. "They don't use it anymore; it's been outlawed, but they used it when Ohscar was working in the grapes."

"Didn't the growers furnish masks?" Janice asked.

"Yeah, but often they didn't fit very well, and your face gets sweaty, and they get loose. Sometimes the mask gets saturated, but when you're driving a tractor with all that spray gear, you don't want to stop."

"Dad always worked hard," Javier added.

"He did," Manny said. "That's for sure. And he never worked harder than when he was organizing with the union. That was a shameful story. He was the best."

"How's that going now?" Javier asked. "Dad said you were losing all your contracts."

"Yeah, we've lost pretty much everything to the Teamsters. I don't know how it is where you work, Javier, but here, they're just a company union the growers use to break us. Their contracts ain't no good, always involve rollbacks of the wages and benefits we fought for. There are more and more illegal aliens now, and they don't want the benefits. They'll work for peanuts."

"I'm a member of the United Transit Workers now. It's pretty good, but we have a strike vote coming up," Javier said.

"Good luck," Manny said. "Speaking of the union, your dad had a death benefit from the Farm Workers. I sent in his paperwork for your mother this morning. She should get a check in a couple weeks. It won't be much, but it'll help."

"That's good news. I know the union got out of the clinics. I didn't realize they still had a death benefit."

"It was the first benefit the union had. César organized the union around that before we started getting contracts. It was how he got members at first."

Janice had been at Javier's side over the months that his father's long undiagnosed colon cancer became increasingly debilitating, finally leading to his death. On the occasions she drove up from Pasadena with him to his parents' house in Salinas, she slept on the old couch in the front room. Although she was in love with Javier, short of marriage, it was as close as she would allow them to get to a shared living arrangement.

Janice and Carolina had become good friends. When Carolina had to visit the *farmacia* in Tijuana to replenish the supply of laetrile prescribed by the Mexican doctor Ohscar had visited at the *clínica* it was Janice who accompanied her across the border. Laetrile, made from crushed apricot pits, was illegal in the United States, and because of his conviction for smuggling, Javier feared being caught with it.

Janice thought the drug was useless, as did the majority of the medical community in the United States. Reliance on laetrile did not lead patients to forego more effective therapy. There simply was no cure for cancer as advanced as Ohscar's. Mostly, it gave Carolina hope, and what was the harm in that, Janice thought. After she witnessed the border inspectors simply smile and wave Carolina past, even when they could plainly see the farmacia bag, Janice quickly figured out that the officers were human too.

After Manny left and Carolina had gone to bed, Janice suggested to Javier that they take a walk. Once out onto the sidewalk in the warm night, she took Javier's arm. The air was pleasant, a welcome relief from the wet draft from the evaporative cooler. The houses along the street were dark, the Romero's neighbors having gone to bed in preparation for another day that for most started early.

Leafy oaks screened out the ambient light of the city, leaving the street in darkness, save for the single incandescent lamp that marked each intersection. Like violinists drawing their bows across the strings of their instruments, a thousand crickets rubbed their forewings together, filling the air with their nocturnal stridulation.

"I'm going to miss your father, too," Janice said.

"Yeah. I'm missing him already," Javier replied. "For a long time, I didn't understand him, but Manny put him in a perspective I didn't often think about. I guess when you're a kid and all wrapped up in yourself, you don't think about what your parents are going through."

"I think that's a universal truth. Mark Twain said that when he was fourteen he couldn't believe how stupid his dad was, but by the time he was twenty-one he was amazed at how much his father had learned in just seven years."

"That's pretty good. I guess that's the way I feel. When I was a kid, I couldn't understand why Dad had to be in farm labor, why we had to move all the time. My mom explained it to me in pretty plain terms one night. Wouldn't even let me back in the house. Even then, I wouldn't give him a chance. Now, I'm not sure I would have had the guts it took for him to stick it out."

"I think you would. Maybe not in farm work, but in something you choose. I know you would. We all have our life challenges. You've had yours, and look what you've done."

"Well, I haven't done much. I'm still just a bus driver. I haven't been responsible for a family like Dad was."

"No, but your horizons are far broader than what was possible for your father when you were a boy. That was the worst thing about farm labor, and I say that even though my family certainly benefited from that system."

"That's history, for our family at least. Although, how much of it is a thing of the past for others is still an open question."

"Do you know what attracted me to you, Javier? Back in Holtville Junior High?"

"I wasn't bashful, right?"

"You certainly weren't. Much to Mother's dismay."

"I was scared, walking up those steps. Do you know how many times I walked past your house before I got up the guts to knock on your door?"

"With Mother, you had a right to be scared. But it didn't stop you, and that's part of what attracted me to you. You weren't afraid of the future. You had those beautiful dreams. We talked about traveling to places. Countries like Egypt, and places like Paris and Rio."

"Mostly, I used to dream about you. About taking you to all those places. Back then, I didn't know how difficult life would be. I didn't know what you could afford on a bus driver's salary."

"Dreaming about going to those places is good enough for me, Javier. Perhaps we will make it there someday. Perhaps we won't. That's not as important to me as the fact that you can still dream about it."

They walked along in silence, each in his or her own thoughts, listening to the rhythm of the crickets. She held his hand loosely, almost indifferently.

"I wish Dad could have had those dreams," Javier said. "I wish he could simply have dreamed at all. He couldn't afford to have a dream, and I can't much either."

"But he did, Javier," Janice flashed. "Didn't you listen to Manny back at the house? Your father dreamed of improving the lives of all farmworkers, and he worked hard to see it happen."

"That's true. He did. I guess I didn't count that as a dream."

"But most of all, Javier, he had a dream for his family. He devoted himself to making sure that you and your brother and sisters had a future and a life better than his. Don't you see that you've achieved it?

It may not be the life that you've dreamed of … yet. But yours is the life your father dreamed for you and a far cry from the life he knew." She withdrew her hand. "Don't pity yourself, Javier."

They walked along in silence. Janice's sudden change of mood left Javier feeling glum. It had been that way recently, and he was afraid to think of why. He worried she might be giving up on him, only postponing it until after his father died. He knew what was on her mind, but he had not been able to push his own thoughts to the point of taking the next step, asking Janice to marry him.

There were so many obstacles. He wanted to marry Janice, but what sort of a future could they expect, she a schoolteacher and he a bus driver with a criminal record who had fallen short of his ambitions? And what about children? He was Hispanic; she was Anglo. She said those things did not matter, but would they not matter to her forever? How about her family? The one time he had accompanied her to her parents' home in Holtville had not gone well. Would they ever recognize that he truly loved their daughter, or would they continue to think he was just an opportunist trying to cross over? Or, was there a truth about himself that he was not acknowledging? In a way, his father's long illness had allowed him to put off thinking about it.

"Your father wasn't afraid to have a family, Javier," Janice said abruptly and fell silent again.

She's right, Dad wasn't afraid, and look at the world he faced, Javier thought. *Discrimination, prejudice. "Anglos Only" signs. A life of back-breaking labor with no way out. Poverty. I may not be making all the money in the world, but I'm not facing that. And still Dad and Mom had kids. They never dreamed about going to Paris. Or maybe they did. Why weren't they scared?*

"Let's go back," Janice said. "These shadows are starting to give me the creeps."

They had walked several blocks, but soon they were close enough to the house to see the light over the front door.

What am I doing? Desperation suddenly crowded into Javier's thoughts. *Don't let her just walk back into the house like this. She is the girl I've wanted all of my life—the only girl I've ever dreamed of. She is*

the one who inspires me and has kept me going, even through Dad dying.
Now, she's not even holding my hand. She's about to walk right out of my
life. What am I doing? I'm losing her!

Javier stopped in the darkness under a giant oak tree and grabbed
Janice's hand, pulling her around to face him. Looking up at him in the
weak light, her face appeared pale, questioning. He wrapped his arms
around her, pulling her body against his. He wanted to say something, to
explain about his father and courage and unfounded fears and the future.

"I don't know what to say," he stammered, "about those dreams and
things ... I guess I've been putting things off."

"I'm not going to wait for you forever, Javier!" Janice snapped.
Breaking his embrace, she went into the house leaving Javier standing
in the darkness.

29

Chill tule fog covered the San Joaquin Valley town of Lamont, and in the City Café, Lexie Hubble poured refills for the early-morning regulars seated at the counter. Two quick bursts of a siren from the street stopped her and silenced the chatter of the patrons.

Lexie peered out the front window in time to see the dilapidated, grey labor bus that had just boarded the workers waiting on the opposite side of the street pull back to the curb and ease to a stop. A green-and-white border patrol sedan, its rack of red and yellow lights flashing, pulled to the curb behind it. Her heart skipped a beat. Miguel was on the bus. He had left the café just moments before with the lunch bucket she had packed for him in hand.

"We haven't seen those fellows in a while," a ranch foreman at the counter remarked.

Without shedding the white apron she wore over her pink uniform, the plump blond woman rushed into the street. Two green-uniformed officers wearing tan Stetsons boarded the bus, pulling the doors closed behind them. Standing on tiptoes, peering in through the grubby windows, Lexie could see the officers working their way down the aisle checking IDs, but she could not make out Miguel. She worried if he had the fake green card and Social Security card he jokingly called his

"Mickey Mouse" papers with him. He had paid forty dollars for them, but she had little confidence that the officers would be fooled.

Presently, the doors of the bus sprang open, and the officers stepped off, followed by three workers. Miguel was not one of them, and Lexie's hopes rose.

"Are those the men you are arresting?" she asked the nearest officer, a tall, thin man with a mustache.

"No, ma'am," the officer replied. "These fellows have papers. It's the rest of 'em that don't."

"My friend is on the bus. Can I talk to him?"

"Does he live with you?"

"Yes, but we're not married."

"Well, I'll tell you what. If you can get his attention you can talk to him through the window. And if you wouldn't mind, we'd appreciate it, and I'm sure he would too, if you brought his personal belongings to our office in Bakersfield. Unless he asks for a hearing, we'll be sending him back to Mexico tomorrow."

Numbed, Lexie walked the length of the bus. As she neared the rear, a window scritched down, and Miguel's arm stuck through the narrow opening.

"Miguel!" she called, grabbing for his hand. "Are you all right?"

"Sí, sí. I'm sorry. *Ya me voy.* It's all right. I'm sorry."

With the border patrol car leading, the bus started to pull away.

"Call me, Miguel. Call me when you get there," Lexie yelled as the caravan disappeared down the street in the fog.

The previous year, Miguel had harvested wine grapes in Lamont and lingered into the late fall waiting for pruning to begin. When the work started, he had showed up at the café early each morning, taking a seat at the end of the counter and consuming a breakfast of chorizo and eggs before climbing aboard one of the rundown buses that lined up outside.

Lexie liked his Latin looks. Miguel liked the attention Lexie paid him—remembering his order, keeping his coffee cup full, making a joke of his taste for sweetened coffee by pretending to refill the sugar dispenser each time he eased onto his stool. When, by chance, they met at a local dance, he went home with Lexie and then stayed in her small trailer house in Lamont with her twelve-year-old son for nearly a year.

At first, Miguel told himself that living with a *gringa* woman was merely convenient. The grape season was over, most of the camps were closed, and he faced having to go home to spend the winter in Piedra Gorda. Living with a local, he could get work in the potato and onion harvests. However, his relationship with Lexie had grown into more than he had expected.

Miguel admired Lexie's self-assuredness and her ability to take care of herself and her son without a husband, traits he often had not credited to gringas. She had an aura of invincibility about her, a cheerfulness that countered his often morose and fatalistic nature. Lexie was confident of sunny days and food on the table; Miguel was certain only that life itself was uncertain, often fickle. She had cared for him from the start, content to feed, house, and make passionate love with him, despite his frequent bouts of guilt and machismo.

Like many older residents of Lamont, Lexie's parents arrived from Oklahoma in the Dust Bowl days. Starving, with nowhere else to go, the Okies faced bitter resentment from the locals, desperate themselves to hold onto their jobs. Lexie was concerned about the increasing numbers of Mexicans in the community. They moved into farm jobs, even packing-shed jobs, previously the domain of the locals. But living with Miguel forced her to view them in personal terms, and remembering the tales of her parents, she found a ready reason for sympathizing with the immigrants, despite knowing it was costing her a place in the divided town.

Although the income he brought to their small household helped, Lexie was careful that she and her son not depend on Miguel. He had been honest with her about Concha, and it did not bother her that he frequently bought money orders to send back to his family in Mexico. It did stir her conscience when the letters started to arrive from Mexico: small, flimsy envelopes, bordered with red and green hatches bearing a strange stamp, addressed in a neat, feminine hand ... to her home.

While Miguel was at work one day, Lexie tried to read one of the letters, phoneticizing the Spanish words. With Miguel's help, she had picked up a few phrases in Spanish, which she practiced with Mexican customers at the café. But matching her imperfect pronunciation to the words on the page proved impossible, and she quickly gave it up. Afterward, she felt ashamed.

Lexie did not press Miguel, but she wondered about his commitment to Concha. Lexie had been through love in the past, a marriage with the father of her son. The letters reminded her not to call this relationship love, although she wished she could.

In the hours after Miguel's arrest, Lexie tried to concentrate on her customers, but could not. Finally, after the lunch hour crowd had been served, she asked her boss if she could get off early. She was thankful her son was not home from school yet, and she set about washing and packing Miguel's clothes.

She thought about what she might put in the bag to remind Miguel of her. She paused for a moment when she picked up the teddy bear he had won for her at the Kern County Fair but decided to keep it herself as her memento of him. She briefly considered a black-and-white Polaroid photo she had let him take of her in their bedroom, but fearing that the officers would search the bag, she returned it to her underwear drawer. Leaving the matter of a memento unresolved, Lexie sat on the bed for a long time. She was not sure she was prepared to end things just yet.

When she heard her son come through the front door, Lexie quickly closed Miguel's duffel. After she explained to her son, she took it to the car and made the drive to Bakersfield.

Unable to sleep that night, Lexie lay alone in the bed she and Miguel had shared for over a year. She felt sad, but on another level, she felt relief. She had known all along that their relationship was not forever, that Miguel had a wife and had shown no inclination to abandon her. Lexie had known that the border patrol could pick Miguel up at any time and take him immediately out of her life as they had that morning. Perhaps that was the way it was fated to be, she rued—a convenient ending to a relationship that had to end somehow. It had lasted far longer than she had expected. This way, no one was to blame.

At the border at Calexico the second night after his arrest, Miguel stepped down from the large, green-and-white bus with windows covered with heavy metal screen and fell in line with dozens of other detainees. Uniformed officers watched as the deportees walked across the line to the Mexican aduana who awaited them.

"I'll be back," Miguel taunted as he filed past a patrullero. "I'll be back tonight."

"We'll be waiting," the officer grinned.

In the fifteen years since he had been arrested working on the Pinchney ranch, Miguel had returned to California numerous times, and he had been arrested by the border patrol on several occasions. Once, he had a formal deportation hearing before a judge who warned that if he returned again, he would face jail. But la migra no longer held illegales in the coralón waiting for fingerprint records. There were just too many of them. They no longer flew deportees to Leon, Guanajuato, as they had the first time he was arrested. The patrulleros just put the Mexicans back across the line to Mexicali or Tijuana the same night or the next. Rather than make the long trek home, it just made sense to the deportees to jump the line again as soon as possible.

Miguel had to feed the many mouths in Piedra Gorda who depended on him, and he faithfully sent giros home every payday. He and his family would do for a while if he did not work, he thought. He felt guilty about betraying Concha. He wanted to make some sort of amends, and he yearned to see his daughter, Lupe. He had not seen her since her *quinceañera*. A year later, she was the last of their children still remaining in the little adobe. In a letter, Concha said that Lupe had been writing to her childhood sweetheart who now lived in California. Concha suggested it might not be long before Lupe also was married and gone.

Miguel knew it was inevitable that he would return to el norte, but not just yet, he decided. He was not certain, when he did, that he would resume his life with Lexie. Still, he felt he owed Lexie an explanation. He had lived with her for a year, and she cared for him. He liked her; life with her was comfortable for him, and he did not want to hurt her feelings. But the relationship had to end at some point, if for no other reason than he was still married to Concha. It might be best for all to end it now, he reasoned. Despite his boast to la migra, Miguel decided he would call Lexie and then board the bus to Piedra Gorda.

In Lamont, after a long night of thinking the relationship was over, Lexie discovered she cared for Miguel more than she previously had admitted. Not seeing him in his usual place at the counter that morning made work at the café unbearable. At the end of her shift, she rushed home hoping he would call. He had become part of her life and depended on her, and she felt he probably needed her now more than ever. When, after two long days, he finally did phone from Mexicali, she found herself pleading with him to wait for her there, promising to drive the three hundred miles to be with him.

"Why do you want to do that? What's the use?" Miguel asked. "You can't live with me here in Mexico very long. You can't work here."

"Well, maybe not," Lexie responded. "But I miss you. Maybe we can figure out a way to get you back. I could hide you in the trunk of the car."

Although he had made up his mind not to, at least not right away, jumping the line was no longer a simple matter, and crossing with Lexie's help might be something to consider, he thought. The officers in Bakersfield had taken his documents, and without her, he would have to cross the border through the desert again. The routes had been taken over by thieves, thugs, and drug smugglers, and one stayed in as large a group as possible or risked being beaten and robbed. Paying a smuggler did not guarantee safety, and often as not, the coyotes demanded the pollos carry large bales of marijuana on their backs over treacherous trails through the mountains and canyons.

Many norteamericana housewives crossed the border to shop, Miguel thought, and a plain car like Lexie's probably would not draw suspicion. In the morning when many green-carders living on the Mexican side commuted across the border to work, the inspectors did not have time to open every trunk. Miguel wondered whether Lexie really was ready to do it. She would lose her car if they were caught. When he called her, he had not been prepared to talk about returning to Lamont. He needed time to think about it, he told Lexie. He would call her back.

Miguel weighed the pros and cons overnight. The year with Lexie had been a good one, giving him the opportunity to earn money and the comfort and companionship of a home. He had lived many years without such amenities, and without someone like Lexie, he faced many more. In the end, he found that he did not want to return to transient beds in stinking camps, uncertain food, and life among men who could turn brutal with the slightest unintended provocation.

His life with Lexie did not hurt his family, Miguel rationalized; it helped by cutting his expenses and getting him longer periods of work. On the other hand, his relationship with Concha, characterized by his long absences, had grown cold.

The next afternoon, Miguel called Lexie back. She packed her best dress, a blue taffeta with white lace trim, and arrived in Mexicali the following evening.

30

"Honey! There's the Gretna Green Wedding Chapel! That's where the movie stars get married." Lexie braked, pulling the steering wheel hard to the right and guiding her aging Ford onto a side street running the length of the mission-style edifice.

Nervous and in a hurry to get past Yuma, Miguel said nothing. As if having to keep a sharp lookout for la migra were not enough, he felt conspicuous riding in the front seat of a car driven by a blond woman. Lexie's untimely fascination with movie stars annoyed him, but for her sake, he cast an indifferent glance at the stucco building. He took no particular notice of the sign mounted between two blooming dogwoods that announced "Justice of the Peace."

A half-hour earlier, a few miles south, the couple had passed uneventfully through the port of entry at San Luis. Lexie drove while Miguel was concealed in the trunk.

"The officer was really nice," Lexie declared once they were out of sight of the border station and she had freed Miguel. "I kinda flirted with him, and he didn't even ask to see the trunk. He was really nice."

Sullen-faced, tensing his muscles as if he could somehow will the car forward, Miguel tried to ignore Lexie's teasing. Instead, the car slowed, and he heaved an audible sigh.

"Honey, let's stop," Lexie said, ignoring him. "I'll bet they have pictures."

Miguel wanted to shout no, but Lexie was not asking his consent. She slid the car into a vacant parking space at the curb marked "Visitors." From experience, he knew that despite what he wished, they would do what Lexie wanted. Already, she had the keys out of the ignition and her purse in her hand.

"Look, honey," Lexie gushed when they entered the quiet foyer. "Here's a picture of Stan Laurel. You've seen him. You know, Laurel and Hardy? And here's Rudolf Valentino. Oooh!"

Not sure why they had stopped to look at pictures in the hallway of a wedding chapel, Miguel followed silently. At least he would not be seen by la migra.

"Honey, I want to drop in here and ask a few questions," Lexie said as they reached an office at the end of the gallery.

Miguel waited in the empty hallway, vacantly gazing at the portraits mounted along the wall. Some of the grooms he knew from the movies, but he recognized few of the radiant brides. Like him, most of the men wore mustaches. He certainly was not rich and powerful as they were, he thought, but he identified with their machismo, feeling a kinship with the strength and ideals they portrayed.

Miguel was growing impatient when Lexie finally rejoined him. She had a serious look on her face and took his arm, pressing softly against him.

"Honey, do you love me?" she asked, looking at him gravely. She had never asked him such a question before.

"Well ... I-I ... sure," Miguel stammered.

"Do you love me enough to marry me?"

The question took Miguel aback. Their situation had been understood, he thought. "Well ... I can't. I'm already married."

"Didn't you tell me once that you had only been married in the church, not at the city offices?"

"Well ... yes." Miguel was suddenly defensive. *What was she getting at?* he wondered. He and Concha had been married by a padre in the church of San Pedro. That is the way campesinos did it, but the government did not recognize the padres' right to marry people. True, he had never taken Concha to the *presidencia* in Piedra Gorda to be married by the *registro civil*, but he never thought of himself as not married.

Alarmed, Miguel pulled his arm free and, with a quizzical look, turned toward the outer door at the end of the hallway. It was clear now why Lexie had stopped here, but he was totally unprepared for this turn of events. Lexie following, he walked slowly out into the sunlight. Her car was at the curb, but he did not know at first whether he would get in. Finally, worry about la migra caught up to him, and he slid back into the passenger seat.

Lexie was asking to marry him, he puzzled, and apparently she had been told in the office that they could do it legally although he already was married. In Mexico, it was common enough for a man to be married in *la iglesia* to one woman and married at the presidencia to another. It must be the same way in los Estados Unidos, he thought. Some men never thought anything about it. But he never had imagined he would do such a thing.

Lexie got in behind the wheel, but she did not start the motor.

"Miguel, I came down here for you. I broke the law for you by smuggling you across the border. I could have lost this car and been put in jail. I don't want to have to do it again. I care for you; I really do. If we get married, you can get a green card, and the border patrol will leave you alone. That may not be a good-enough reason for a marriage that will last forever, but it ought to be good enough for us for now."

Miguel put his hand against the dash, silently contemplating the strong veins that stood out like the roots of a giant oak. He could not turn his back on Concha, he thought. He could not wipe away twenty years of marriage and five children. What would she say if she knew he had married another woman? *What would she say if she knew I was living with a gringa?* he thought, dumbstruck at this sudden realization of the stark truth of his life with Lexie.

Miguel remained pensive for a long time, his conscience swept by unbearable guilt. He groped for rationalizations. He had lived a shadow life in el norte for over fifteen years, a life Concha was not a part of: hiding from la migra and phony names on phony papers, so many he could not remember them all, working for farmers who denied he even existed.

What would a marriage to Lexie be? he pondered. It would be for papers. That is all it need be. Concha would not know, and that was the point; between them, a paper marriage to Lexie would not be real. Many men, and even women, did that to stay in los Estados Unidos. That's all Lexie wanted, Miguel decided, just for him to have papers so he would not have to leave her again. Even she admitted it would not be forever.

It did not mean he was not married to Concha. Their marriage in the church of San Pedro was his real marriage. If Concha somehow found out and asked the padres, they would assure her that they were still married. Their children had their own lives now and need never know. It was just something he could to do to get by, to earn money to send home to his real family.

"Miguel," as if she were able to read his thoughts, Lexie interrupted. "I'm not asking you to leave Concha, even though in some ways you already have. I'm willing to wait and see what happens over time. This is for today. I love you, and I want to be with you now."

The arrangement would not hurt Lexie, Miguel told himself. After all, it was what she wanted. She understood that he was married to Concha in his heart. In the meantime, he and Lexie would continue as they had before; nothing would be different just because they had a piece of paper, except that no longer he would have to fear la migra. His relationship with Lexie would be over when it was time to be over, he thought, but not today.

"Okay," Miguel said and grinned at Lexie. What was the law? The law only told you what not to do, where not to go. It did not tell a man what he needed to do to get by, to feed his family. A civil marriage to Lexie would not break the law, not in Mexico, not in los Estados Unidos.

Lexie beamed and then leaned across the seat and hugged him.

31

 María Concepción Gutiérrez de Hernández—Concha—
waited impatiently on the concrete bench in front of La
Carnicería de Camacho. Behind her, a row of plucked headless chickens,
the skins yellowing in the open air, hung upended from a line stretched
across the front window of the whitewashed adobe butcher shop. The
bench was slightly higher than her short legs could accommodate, so
she perched on the front edge, her feet firmly on the ground.

Despite the warm midday sun, she kept her *rebozo* wrapped around
her head. The ends of the blue-and-white silk scarf draped her small
shoulders. A prominent nose and high cheekbones featured her narrow, dark-skinned face, and she sat turned so that her dark eyes could
keep the phone booth that stood at the end of the bench at least within
her peripheral vision. She was determined to deter anyone else from
stepping inside the *caseta* until after her call came through. She was
not quite sure how to prevent it—sometimes a cold stare worked—but
she did not want Lupe to have to place the call again. It was madden-
ing to wait while others gossiped interminably with a relative. Lupe
would not call midday, and on a weekday at that, if it were not about
something important, and while she waited, Concha's mind raced with
the possibilities.

When the butcher's son came to her door to say that Lupe had called from California and would call back in a half-hour, it had taken Concha but a second to don her best rebozo, a gift from Lupe, and hasten out into the rutted street for the short walk to the carnicería.

"Buenas dîas, Señora Hernandez," Sr. Camacho, a large man with a bushy mustache wearing a stained white apron, had greeted her when she arrived at the carnicería. "Your daughter hasn't called back yet. She sounded very excited. It must be good news."

Lupe was the youngest of their five children, born after Miguel set off to search for work in el norte, jumping the line illegally for the first time. She was the last to leave home, and it was natural that she would become the closest, Concha thought. When Genaro married, she and Miguel had given him half of their land. In his father's absence, he helped Concha tend the remaining hectares, and Lupe helped her mother plant and harvest corn also.

Concha had worried that Lupe would become an old maid. She was an attractive girl with a natural wave in her long dark hair, but she rejected any serious involvement with the young men of Piedra Gorda. Concha fretted that her daughter felt obligated to remain at home to take care of her in old age, and she sought subtle ways to convince the girl that, although she was getting older, she was by no means frail.

When Richard came back into Lupe's life, Concha was overjoyed. Ricardo Benavidez, Richard, had left for California with his parents when he and Lupe were in the fourth year of *la primaria*. Richard's father worked for a farmer who grew oranges, and the grower wrote a letter guaranteeing him employment so he could qualify for a green card. That was before 1965, the year los Estados Unidos kicked out the braceros and put a new quota on Mexicans who wanted to immigrate. Because they had not gone to California before the law changed, the family had to wait several years before they were able to join their father.

When the Benavidez family left, neighbors in San Pedro Piedra Gorda were scornful. Some said the parents were abandoning their culture and called them chicanos. But when the same neighbors realized that the family was going to live on a big farm near Los Angeles, near Hollywood, and they no longer would wear the *puebla* and huaraches worn in the village, but blue jeans and pretty blouses like Sr. Benavidez brought back for the family on his many visits, their sneers turned to envy.

In his first letter, Richard told Lupe about their journey by train to the border at Mexicali and then the trip to Oxnard by bus. Richard talked a lot about his school. In Piedra Gorda, boys and girls went to *la primaria*, and most attended school only until the fourth grade.

Because Miguel's giros enabled her to pay the tuition and for uniforms, after la primaria, Concha enrolled Lupe in *la técnica* and her correspondence with her former schoolmate increased. Ultimately, the letters were supplanted by phone calls, and Lupe became one of a covey of village señoritas who waited by the caseta each Saturday night for that special call from a suitor in el norte.

One day, when Lupe was twenty-one and Concha had long ceased thinking about her marrying a local boy, Richard came back to the pueblo driving a new Chevy pickup. He stayed for a month, long enough for the padre to announce the bans of matrimony between him and Lupe in the church three Sundays in a row.

On the fourth Sunday, Lupe and Richard were married. Lupe wore a white dress her mother made for her on the treadle sewing machine Miguel had brought back from California years before. A white-lace veil Lupe's sister brought from Puerta Vallarta covered the girl's long black hair. Miguel had come home for the event. Concha was ecstatic. A civil wedding at the presidencia followed.

After the wedding, Richard returned to California. It took several months for the paperwork to be completed so Lupe could get an immigrant visa to join him. Those were exciting months for Lupe as she prepared to leave the village and sad months for Concha who, despite her happiness for her daughter, dreaded the loneliness to come after she was gone.

When the phone rang, Concha waited impatiently for Sr. Camacho to step outside the carnicería and answer it. Even though it was a public phone and the telephone company paid him for the space it occupied, Sr. Camacho considered it an affront for anyone to answer it but himself.

"¡La Carnicería de Camacho!" he shouted, leaving the door of the caseta open so that Concha could hear. "*¡Sí! ¡Sí, Lupe! ¡Su mamá está aquí!*"

"*¡Bueno!*" Concha said formally into the receiver after Sr. Camacho handed her the phone. A telephone call, even from a loved one, required a measure of dignity.

"Mamá!" Lupe's excited voice sounded clear in Concha's ear. "Mamá, I'm pregnant! I'm going to have a baby!"

The news made Concha feel as if she were levitating. It must be how the angels feel, she thought. As she walked home, her feet felt so light she had to be careful to avoid stumbling in the rutted street. She was thrilled at the thought of another baby, gratified that Lupe's life had come together after so many anxious years. Her daughter had a fine husband, a good life in el norte, and soon a child.

Lupe wanted her mother to come to California, but Concha did not think such a thing was possible. The chance that she could be with Lupe and the new baby and not sit alone in the empty adobe day after day brightened her, but it was an idea she feared to entertain. Her life had been one of making way for others, her children, her husband, before herself. The talk of a reunion, but the seeming impossibility of it, made her feel lonely.

Two of Concha's children had died in childbirth. Of the others, only Genaro and his family remained in Piedra Gorda, living in their own home and scrambling for a living as she and Miguel had done. It was only a matter of time before he, too, would be off to el norte to work like his father. The young and able of most families in the pueblo were going to el norte, or to the *maquiladoras* along the border, leaving mostly the very young and the very old in Piedra Gorda. Their daughter in Puerta Vallarta worked in a large tourist hotel. Another son worked in Juarez and at times snuck across la frontera to find jobs.

Once, while home on a visit, Miguel casually mentioned he had gotten a green card. He had not explained very clearly how he had obtained the permit, but Concha did not think she would understand anyway, and it seemed to make little difference in her life. At the time, Lupe was still at home, and moving to los Estados Unidos did not seem that important. She did notice that her husband was starting to send more money, and travel was easier and safer for him. He did not have to sneak back across the border to return to his job after visiting.

Now with Lupe gone and she and Richard starting a family in California, things looked different. Concha had brought up the idea of joining him, maybe even living near Lupe and Richard. But, citing the Benavidez family's example, Miguel said there would be a very long wait before she would be eligible to come, and by that time, he might have enough money to stay in Piedra Gorda.

As Concha walked home, she began to think about the possibility of the visit Lupe offered. It would be wonderful being present for the birth of a new baby. Lupe seemed certain it was possible. *Would that include living with Miguel again, traveling with him to the various places in California where he worked? How would that be,* she wondered. *Would I want a job too, as most women seemed to have in el norte?*

Lupe had planted a seed in receptive soil.

Still overjoyed with the news she shared with her mother, Lupe hung up the phone. How wonderful it would be if her mother could be with her, she thought. Concha had sounded dubious when Lupe had broached the idea, but she thought that was only because her mother had not traveled before.

She would have to make her mother feel comfortable with the prospect of the trip, Lupe thought, maybe even find someone to travel with her. There were plenty of people who traveled regularly between Piedra Gorda and California these days. It seemed as if most of the men, and plenty of the women, of the village lived and worked in el norte. Lupe thought she could figure that out. Her mother was not old; she had just turned fifty and was strong.

First, her mother would have to get a passport, Lupe thought. That should not be hard. She had had to get one in order to immigrate. Her mother would need to get her birth certificate at the presidencia. She did not know whether there would be a marriage certificate available there or not, or whether one was required. Her parents had never been clear about a civil marriage. She would have to travel to the capitol, Zacatecas City, to *Relaciónes Exteriores* for the passport. There would be fees, little tips, but that would be easy.

Lupe was not certain about the visa. That was confusing. Some people had a *tarjeta local,* a local card, used to go across the border for a few days or so. Lupe did not know whether her mother could qualify for one, but many Mexicans were able to cross the border for short visits. She would ask the Catholic Migration Services lady who had helped Richard arrange her papers. She would know. Lupe was excited and thought Richard would be too.

32

When Concha stepped from the bright sunlight through the low doorway of Doña Graciela's front room, she was greeted by a myriad of candles flickering in the gloomy interior. Aromatic scents filled her nostrils. At first, she smelled citrus, or thought she did, but air eddying through the door and the lone open window changed the aroma to pine, then flowers, then incense, as if the capricious drafts were selecting each fragrance at random from a palette.

On an altar draped with white linen, a plaster statue of the Virgen de Guadalupe, haloed by a multi-colored sunburst, stood next to a silver crucifix. Red and blue votive lights shimmered in front of the icons, and a black-velvet painting of the Last Supper hung on the wall behind them. On one side was a life-sized statue of Saint Francis in brown-robes holding a fawn. The scene reminded Concha of church, but instead, the small, crowded chamber was Doña Graciela's *consultorio*.

Shelves and cabinets containing herbs and potions were crowded along the walls. Jars contained epazote to cure intestinal parasites, *taboache* for sleep, and dead hummingbirds for love. Open-topped boxes held antlers and lodestones for good luck. Alongside the religious icons on the altar cloth, the skull of an owl and the antlers of a small deer were arrayed among colored stones and amulets.

The *curandera* treated many maladies—depression, sorrow, nervousness, fright, infidelity, addiction—and offered advice for how to avoid them. She had potions and poultices for treating a wound or soothing the stomach, but serious illnesses sometimes required calling on spirits from the other side, the dark world that the padres feared. Some said Doña Graciela was a witch, but Concha thought that was a rumor spread by the padres.

Concha had come to see Doña Graciela because she had special insight into the psychic forces that controlled peoples' lives and could see into the future. Sitting alone in her casita, Concha had been able to do little other than think of Lupe's phone call. The older woman was elated at the news of Lupe's pregnancy, thrilled by Lupe's invitation to share a new life with her and Richard and Concha's soon-to-be-born grandchild. But she feared leaving her predictable life in Mexico for a life with so many unknowns in California. It was a dilemma she never expected to face.

It had been understood that Miguel would go to el norte to find work. Most of the men in Piedra Gorda did, even many of the women. Concha had never considered his sojourns permanent; it was la vida, a necessity of life. As the years went on, she had resigned herself to Miguel's long absences. The thought that one day she would leave their modest adobe and join her husband in California never occurred to her.

Their small plot of land and adobe house in San Pedro Piedra Gorda was a place of permanence, a primeval aspect of their being. It was the home that Miguel and their children always returned to. Miguel and Concha were born in the village. Their ancestors had lived on this arid plateau since the beginning of time. They believed that after Miguel no longer was able to work, they would live out the remainder of their lives in the same adobe casita in which their children were born.

On El Día de los Muertos, the Day of the Dead, they visited their ancestors in the *cementerio*. It was a duty, expected by the deceased, and only their son, Genaro, and his wife who still lived there, having received half of his parents' plot of land, would do it if she were not there. Concha could not bear the thought of leaving her two dead babies. She worried, would she ever have the chance to come back?

Concha was not happy living alone, but what if she went to California? Would Richard really be happy having her in their house with a new baby? What about Miguel? He had been distant lately, and during his last phone call when she told him the news about Lupe's pregnancy and her invitation, he did not seem happy about her coming. She began to wonder whether he had found another woman. On some nights, she was sleepless with worry over the possibilities. Finally, Concha decided she would visit the curandera. She had visited Doña Graciela in the past, most notably to cleanse the evil that had caused the deaths of two of her babies.

Doña Graciela clasped Concha's hand in both of hers and, after an effusive greeting, seated her in a low chair in front of a small table. The curandera passed a sprig of herbs in a circle over Concha's head, to ward off evil, Doña Graciela said. When she finished the benediction, she took her place sitting in an ornate, high-backed chair on the opposite side of the table. The room was warm from the lighted candles, and Concha slipped her rebozo from her head onto her shoulders.

Doña Graciela was a small, wiry woman who wore large silver hoops through her distended earlobes and covered her thin arms and neck with heavy silver and turquoise jewelry. Her grey hair was tugged back tightly from her temples, pulling her eyes, which were accented with eyeliner, into an almond shape. The bronze color of her skin and her prominent cheekbones and nose reminded Concha of a picture she had seen in one of Lupe's textbooks, a portrait of an Egyptian princess painted on the wall of a pharaoh's tomb.

After Concha explained the purpose for her visit and Doña Graciela ascertained that there was no need for her herbs or potions, the curandera produced a deck of tarot cards. She placed them face down on the black-and-white checkered oilcloth covering the table and instructed Concha to select ten. The curandera then arranged them, still face down, in a pyramid.

Doña Graciela turned over the cards one by one, pausing, studying, murmuring to herself as each esoteric figure was revealed, tapping the face of each card with the tip of her long, red fingernail. Concha sat on the edge of her chair, her hands clasped nervously in her lap. The frankincense was making her dizzy.

Doña Graciela turned over the Two of Cups. Concha gasped. The card had been revealed when she had visited the curandera after the loss of her two babies.

"But look," Doña Graciela exclaimed, quickly responding to her client's distress. "The cups are upright this time. The cups hold water, and water is the symbol of life. It's a good omen."

Concha smiled nervously and tried to relax. A vagrant air current brought the scent of frangipani to her nostrils, pushing away for a moment the frankincense. The next card was the Tower. Concha was unfamiliar with its meaning.

"The card shows that you are going through hard times, that you are unhappy with your present situation," Doña Graciela explained and passed quickly to the next. "Look! Here is the sun. It is the best of omens, and it is at the peak of the tableau, in the position that dominates all the other cards. It is certain that you will have success in the future."

Concha was relieved but watched anxiously as the next card was turned. The card depicted a young woman holding open the jaws of a lion.

"There is often a struggle between the two parts of us." Doña Graciela became pensive again. "We are often afraid of things that are not as bad as we make them out in our mind. Like the maiden who puts her fear of the lion aside, if we rely on our own strengths, we will achieve our dream."

Could this relate to my journey? Concha thought, admitting to herself that she had been fearful of a long trip to California. She drew up her shoulder, stretching a muscle in her back, and leaned forward, anxious to learn what the next card would say.

The card revealed a stooped old man holding up a lantern filled with stars. The figure was upside down. Doña Graciela clucked her tongue. "You must face the truth of your current circumstances," she said. "The hermit pursues enlightenment and truth. You can know the truth only if you do not try to fool yourself."

Next, Doña Graciela turned over a card showing the angel Raphael hovering over Adam and Eve in front of the rising sun. The curandera became very thoughtful. The only sound in the close room was the measured tap of her fingernail.

"There is a new beginning ahead of you," she said. "Perhaps a new life with your daughter, Lupe. But you need to make the correct choice. See, the angel has his eyes closed. Eve is looking up to him for guidance, but the angel does not give it. It must be you who makes the decision."

The last card was the Queen of Cups, forcing Concha to lean forward anxiously. The card was inverted, the cups pouring life out. The incense was again strong in her nostrils.

Doña Graciela brushed off the omen. "The queen of cups is of the minor arcana, and in this position not very important," she said quickly. "The fact that she is upside down could mean trouble, an infidelity possibly?" Doña Graciela looked up at Concha, arching her eyebrows.

"No, no," Concha replied, flustered. "I don't think that's true. Miguel is a good man—has been good to me always."

"It is probably nothing. It could mean many other things, and as I mentioned, it is not in an important position. Besides, you have had so many good cards today."

The consultation finished, Concha gave Doña Graciela her fee, which was large because Concha's husband and daughter were in el norte. Concha accepted that. How else could the curandera live?

As Concha was about to leave, Doña Graciela said, "If you decide to go to el norte, I can help you. I have contacts in Tijuana, and I also know of a traveling companion for you."

On the way back to her casita, Concha mulled over the omens that had been revealed to her. In general, she was pleased, but the presence of the Queen of Cups was troubling. Although she dismissed such thoughts, on occasion she did wonder whether Miguel had found another woman. Why else would he be reluctant to have her come to California?

The sun card had been an especially good omen. Clearly, the new life the cards promised was in California with Miguel, Lupe, Richard, and the soon-to-arrive baby. The cards could mean nothing else. Concha was particularly taken by the maiden holding open the lion's jaws. *What a lesson there!* she thought. Did she have the courage and strength of the young woman? As she walked in the bright sunlight and fresh air of the village street, her confidence grew until she was sure she did.

Concha was sure now that going to el norte was the right thing to do, and she began to make her plans.

33

Concha's eyes opened gradually, and it took a moment for her to realize that she was on a bus. Unable to get comfortable, despite the fact that the seat reclined, she had given up on sleep, but at some point during the night, as the heavy coach careened around the curves on the narrow mountain highway, her body had ceased fighting the momentum pulls, and she dozed. She did not know how long she had slept; it seemed brief. Looking out the window in the early dawn, she saw they were passing through a sparse pine forest.

The small body of her seatmate, who during most of the long evening had snuggled into her side, was turned away from her. The little girl's bare legs were drawn up on the seat. Her head, cushioned by a thick mass of auburn hair and a cloth doll, was propped against the armrest at an uncomfortable angle. Without waking her, Concha shifted the child so that her head lay on her lap.

Across the aisle, the child's young mother, whom Doña Graciela had introduced as her relative, Rosalinda, at the bus stop in Piedra Gorda, awakened and was again nursing her baby. Fearful that the infant might drop out of his slumbering mother's arms, Concha had fashioned a sling from her rebozo. Until she fell asleep, she checked it from time to time during the night to ensure that the infant remained upright.

Nevertheless, the baby fretted, probably because of the air conditioning, Concha thought.

Rosalinda was an attractive girl with a bright, open face and twinkling brown eyes. Her husband had worked in los Estados Unidos long enough to qualify for the recent amnistía and had gotten his green card. Now he wanted his wife and their children, Maria Elena and Carlos, to join him. She wore new clothing her husband had sent, stockings and high heels and a form-fitting cotton dress with a low neckline that she had to undo when she nursed baby Carlos.

Rosalinda already dressed like a *norteña*, Concha thought, but not smugly because she had received new clothing, too, in a package from Lupe. Self-conscious about wearing her new dress in the village, Concha packed it in a cheap cardboard suitcase she bought. She planned to wear it at Lupe's house, and chose a bright-embroidered dress she had made herself to wear for the trip.

Rubbing her eyes, her brown legs still folded beneath her, Maria Elena stirred and sat upright. Without interrupting her nursing, Rosalinda retrieved a small carton of juice from her bag and passed it and a straw across the aisle to her. Concha helped the child open the carton.

When Rosalinda had introduced her daughter the previous morning, Concha bent and asked the little girl how old she was. Maria Elena looked up with her big brown eyes and held up three fingers. While on the first leg of their trip to *la capital*, the child had gotten over her shyness enough to announce to Concha, "I've got a birthday coming up."

Rosalinda explained that Maria Elena had just had a birthday, but for the rest of the morning as they bounced along the dusty gravel road, the dignified middle-aged lady and the little girl discussed the precocious child's plans for her next birthday party.

When the group reached Zacatecas City, they transferred to a large, glass-and-steel Estrella Blanca motor coach. Doña Graciela had warned them that they would be on the coach a day and a half, and Concha had packed tamales to eat on the trip. In the late afternoon, they passed through Durango. The bus turned west and, after dark, began the long transit through the mountains.

Fully awake now, Concha gazed out the window at a never-before-seen landscape. The road clung to the high wall of a mountain, and as the bus rounded each turn, the pine forest opened out onto broad vistas. The rocky soil and nopal cactus of Zacatecas had been left far behind, and Concha was fascinated when the bus reached the coastal plain and she saw for the first time in her life the tall, bare trunks and broad fronds of palm trees.

In anticipation of crossing the border, as Lupe had instructed, Concha had obtained her passport at the Relaciónes Exteriores office in the state capitol. First, she had to obtain her birth certificate, and Doña Graciela had helped her complete the paperwork, passing along a gratuity to the *alcalde* of Piedra Gorda, who was one of her clients. She had done the same for Rosalinda, and both Concha and Rosalinda had given the curandera a substantial fee. But they were still uncertain about the papers they would be given when they arrived in Tijuana.

At first, Lupe had felt stymied when the caseworker at the Catholic Migration Services office in El Monte cautioned that her mother should wait until after Lupe became a US citizen and then apply for an immigrant visa. It would only be two more years, she said. But when Lupe pressed, the caseworker admitted that it was possible for her mother to get a temporary visitor's visa and helped prepare a letter explaining that Lupe was pregnant, which the caseworker said should be signed by her doctor. She also prepared a letter to be signed by Richard guaranteeing that Concha would be supported while in the United States. The caseworker cautioned Lupe that Concha was simply applying for a visitor's permit, and they often were denied.

When she next talked to her mother, Lupe passed along only the information about the visitor's permit, but when, in turn, Concha told Miguel, he was dubious. When Concha told Doña Graciela about her husband's concerns, the curandera scoffed. Her associate, she assured Concha, had powerful contacts at the border and would be able to get them a *permiso* from *la inmigración* with no problem. It was guaranteed, she said. They would be temporary papers, she admitted, but would suffice to get them into California where they could stay until they got their green cards.

When it became clear that Concha was determined to make the trip, Miguel sent her money and the extra fee for Doña Graciela and her accomplice in Tijuana. He said he would take time off from his job in Lamont to meet them but that August was the start of the grape harvest, and he would not have much time.

As they boarded the bus in Piedra Gorda, Doña Graciela promised Rosalinda and Concha that their journey would be uneventful, that her assistant would meet their bus and would competently handle arrangements for crossing la frontera.

In Sinaloa, the bus turned north again on a route parallel to the coast. As the morning passed, the bus rolled out of the tropical south of Mexico into the Gran Desierto of Sonora, the most desolate country Concha had seen. It was drier and sparser even than the high plateaus of Zacatecas.

Tiring of looking out the window, Maria Elena straightened back into her seat and retrieved her favorite book, pressing it into Concha's hands. "Will you read this to me again?" she asked.

Concha had read the story about a little bird that had fallen from its nest to Maria Elena several times the previous afternoon, and between them, they had developed a litany. Concha pointed to a picture of a hen.

"Are you my mamá?" Maria Elena pretended to ask the hen.

"No!" Concha responded, adding a cluck-cluck.

"I never want to lose my mamá," the little girl announced when they finished, hugging her cloth doll.

Late in the afternoon, approaching San Luis Rio Colorado, they passed through farmlands again, rich green fields, orchards, and small pueblos. An hour later, they passed through the large border city of Mexicali. As darkness fell, the bus journeyed through mountains that appeared to be huge jumbles of dry rock. Concha, Rosalinda, and the children were tired and relieved when the bus finally pulled into the busy station in Tijuana.

34

Miguel leaned against the tiled wall of the terminal watching as buses pulled in one by one and parked, leaving their diesel engines running on fast idle as they disgorged their passengers. The August evening was hot; little air circulated to dissipate the heat. The exhaust hung over the crowded platform, polluting the humid air and clinging to Miguel's perspiring body. It was past the posted arrival time for Concha's bus, but wanting to be present when it did arrive, Miguel resisted walking out into the street for a breath of fresh air.

The idling diesels deadened the voices of the people clustered against the railing in front of him, and he felt detached, as if he were in a cocoon. He did not feel part of the animated throng who were on the platform to greet relatives and friends arriving from the interior or to see family members off to destinations such as Guadalajara or la Capital.

At supper the night before, Miguel had told Lexie that Concha was coming.

"Is she coming here?" Lexie asked, surprised.

"No, no," he stammered, anxiously trying to gauge her reaction. "She is going to stay with my daughter in El Monte. She—my daughter, Lupe—is expecting a baby."

Lexie silently picked at the chicken enchilada on her plate with a tine of her fork. "Will you be going down to see her?" she asked evenly.

"Actually, I was planning to meet her in Tijuana tomorrow night and take her to El Monte."

"Will you be coming back here?"

"Well, yes, I have my job, but I think I'd better stay in the camp."

As Miguel finished his meal, Lexie sat silently, still poking at her enchilada. She did not come into the living room to watch TV with him after clearing the dishes, and she did not come to bed. In the morning when Miguel rose, Lexie already had left for her shift at the café. Next to the front door, she had placed his suitcase and a duffel bag packed with his freshly washed clothes.

The first-class Estrella Blanca bus from the interior was two hours late. Even as the gleaming green-and-white coach arrived, Miguel harbored misgivings about Concha's trip. It was not just the matter of Lexie, although he felt plenty of guilt and was truly sorry about the disappointment he had caused her. Despite Doña Graciela's assurances, he knew there was no guarantee Concha would be permitted to cross the border. If it were so easy, he had argued, why had not the curandera arranged a permiso for him and saved him dozens of risky trips through the mountains and deserts, sometimes being caught by la migra and being sent back to where he started?

Lupe argued that there was no reason her mother would not be given a visitor's permit. She had a legitimate excuse for the visit—the expected birth of a grandchild—and Richard had signed a letter promising support. It had been easy for Lupe, Miguel countered. She had gotten papers because she had married a US citizen. She did not know how hard it was for everyone else.

Concha dismissed Miguel's concern, citing the cards the curandera said promised success. Even though he himself had benefited from her potions and cures, Miguel scoffed at Concha's belief that Doña Graciela could predict the future.

Still, and not only because of his guilt over sleeping with Lexie, Miguel understood Concha's loneliness in Piedra Gorda and sympathized with her desire to be with Lupe. He knew that change had come to their lives:

the empty casita in Piedra Gorda and the soon-to-arrive grandchild in California. Events had crept up on him while he had dallied in Lamont with Lexie, but because of his transgression, he felt he no longer had the moral standing to ordain what Concha should do. He had not been a faithful husband; how could he expect her to be a subservient wife? In the end, he acquiesced.

Miguel spotted Concha as she emerged from the door of the gleaming coach, her head and shoulders wrapped in a rebozo, clutching the hand of a small child as she stepped down onto the platform. For an instant, he felt a bittersweet sense of loss over Lexie. Being with Concha again would be like stepping back into a time that did not exist for him anymore. Against the flitting memory of the blond woman who loved him and whom he had also wronged, he struggled to retain his resolve that his infidelity was a thing of the past. He wanted to feel honest and somehow reclaim the dignity that in his heart he had lost, to make amends before it would be too late for his family.

Miguel waited until Concha, her eyes searching for him among the many men wearing western shirts and straw tejanas, made her way through the crowd. When he finally stepped forward, he at first said nothing, even as she brushed against him, putting her hand on his arm by way of greeting.

Miguel smiled. "How was the journey?"

"*Bien*," she responded. "Long."

Concha turned to introduce her companions, Rosalinda, Maria Elena, and Carlos. When Miguel bent to offer Maria Elena his hand, she shyly backed against her mother's legs.

"Señora Hernandez? Rosalinda?" A lumpy woman in a too-tight, black dress bustled up. "I am Eliza. Doña Graciela has been in contact with me. I'm here to help you."

Concha seemed pleased and repeated to Miguel that the woman was Doña Graciela's assistant, just as she had promised.

"I have arranged a place for you to stay, but I did not know about señor." Eliza extended her hand to Miguel. "I'm very pleased to meet you. It will be extra, but you would be very welcome to stay there, too."

Miguel simply nodded and excused himself while he retrieved Concha's bag and then helped Rosalinda with her bulky valises. Concha and Eliza continued their conversation while Miguel followed them out of the station to Eliza's waiting car. They drove for several blocks and stopped at a four-story, cinder-block motel. Eliza conferred with the room clerk and then turned to Miguel.

"The cost for one night is eighty-four dollars," she announced.

Miguel, who had not known what to anticipate but knew money would be involved, reached for his wallet.

When she had gotten them into their rooms, Eliza asked for their passports. Concha gave her the packet of letters Lupe had sent as well. "I will take them to my office and prepare the applications for your visitors' permisos," Eliza explained. "Tomorrow morning, I will take you to the garita, the border."

Early the next day, Eliza gathered Miguel and Concha into Rosalinda's room while the mother nursed baby Carlos and helped Maria Elena dress. She explained the forms and the process they would go through. An official of the inmigración norteamericana would interview them, she said. The official wanted to be sure that they lived in Tijuana and would not stay in los Estados Unidos but return after a short visit.

"I've given you an address in Tijuana," Eliza said. "Be sure you memorize it because the *oficial* will ask you. Do not say that your husband is in los Estados Unidos," she warned the women. "The oficial will believe that you intend to stay there and not return to Mexico. Just say that you want to cross the border to shop."

"What about the letters from my daughter and her husband? The doctor's letter?" Miguel asked.

"Oh, you don't need those," Eliza responded breezily. "Having a daughter who is expecting will just complicate matters. It just gives the inmigración one more reason to believe that your wife simply wants to stay."

Miguel nodded. It was not unusual to have to fool la migra; at times, it had to be done. He had done it himself many times, including getting a green card. Still, he respected the fact that the US government had played fair with him, even though his marriage to Lexie had been a lie.

Eliza did not offer to give the letters back, and Miguel did not ask. Clearing their luggage out of their rooms, they loaded back into Eliza's car. Saying she did not want to get caught in the traffic lanes, the assistant to the curandera dropped them off two blocks before reaching the garita.

35

 Concha sat forward in her chair, grasping the edge of the grey-metal desk with one hand. She was awestruck by the confident young blond woman seated behind it.

The official, smartly dressed in a light-blue uniform, a brass badge displayed on her left shirt pocket, had greeted Concha and introduced herself as an *inspectora* of el Servicio de Inmigración de los Estados Unidos. Concha had never spoken to a gringa before, let alone a *guëra*, and she was struck by the woman's light-colored hair and surprised the young lady spoke Spanish. Eliza's instructions had been brief, and Concha did not know what to expect. Doña Graciela had promised that Eliza would take care of the matter of her papers, but Concha never imagined she would be questioned alone in an office by a norteamericana official.

The woman studied Concha's passport and the paperwork Eliza had prepared. "Where do you live, Señora Hernandez?" the officer asked, looking up from the papers.

"*Aquí*, here in Tijuana." Concha stammered.

"No, I mean where do you really live?"

Concha struggled to remember the address that Eliza had insisted she memorize. *Was it Calle Calderón or Calle Beltrán #136?* But it was useless. Nevertheless, she tried again. "Here, here in Tijuana. On the Calle Calderón," she repeated.

"It says on your application, Calle Beltrán #836." The officer paused, giving the older woman a long, but sympathetic, look.

Concha wished Miguel or Eliza were with her, but Eliza told them that she had another client to attend to, and she and Rosalinda would have to go into the port-of-entry office alone. "If the inmigración discovers that your husbands are in los Estados Unidos, they will believe you plan to stay forever with them and won't give you a permit," Eliza warned again just before parting.

Scared, but reliant on Eliza's assurances and Doña Graciela's guarantee of success, Concha struggled to remain calm. *What could be wrong with visiting my daughter who is going to have a baby?* she reasoned, forgetting that Eliza had not included Lupe's and Richard's letters in the papers she had handed the official and that she was claiming she only wanted to cross the border to shop. El gobierno *has given my husband and my daughter papers. Why not me?*

The official did not relent. "Where is your husband?" she asked.

"He's not here," Concha answered defensively. She had been forced to tell another lie, which increased her unease.

"Did your husband get his papers?"

"Sí, but he's not here." This time it was a half-lie.

"Señora, I have to consider your application, but I don't have to believe you. Unless you can tell me where you live, I will have to tell you, no."

"I live on Calle Beltrán, I just forgot."

"I'm sorry, señora. In order for me to give you a visitor's permit, you must prove that you have a residence in Tijuana that you will return to." The inspector marked something in the back of Concha's passport and handed it back to her. Then she rose from behind her desk and waited for Concha to do the same.

"But, señora, my daughter is going to have a baby," Concha blurted.

"It says nothing about that in your application," the officer said, picking up the form and looking at it again. "I think you meant to hide that.

"With your husband and your daughter here, it appears that you are an intending immigrant and need an immigrant visa. For that, your husband needs to file a petition for you. Today, I can do only what the law says I can do, and that is to decide whether or not to give you a temporary *permiso*. For an immigrant visa, you have to wait in line like everybody else, and that sometimes takes years. Go home and wait, señora. Your time will come."

"Gracias, señora," Concha mumbled. Defeated, she rose from her chair.

"Señora," the official called after her.

Concha paused by the door.

"Señora. Go home and wait. Your turn will come. Don't pay a coyote. Crossing the border is very dangerous. You could be hurt or even killed." The officer watched as Concha shuffled out of the room and prayed her advice would be heeded.

When Concha found Miguel waiting on the street, he tried to decipher the numbers and symbols the official had scribbled in the back of Concha's passport, but they held no meaning for him. Eliza was nowhere to be found, and they realized that it was she who had contacted them, and they had no idea how to find her. Rosalinda and the children had suffered a similar rejection, and Miguel found himself standing on a busy sidewalk in a strange city with two women, two infants, a pile of luggage, and nowhere to go.

Not far from the *garita*, they located a plaza and found a vacant bench. Miguel went to a *caseta* nearby and dialed Lupe's number. Lupe was incredulous. She and Richard had been prepared to drive down to the border to pick them up after Richard finished work.

"I don't understand it, *Papá*. How can it be that they won't let Mamá come? Did she show them the letters?"

"Well, she gave the *oficial* everything she had," Miguel equivocated. "But the lady didn't believe her." How could he explain to his daughter that they had ignored her careful preparations and acted on the advice of a woman they did not know and could no longer locate?

"Did you talk to the *oficial*? Did you explain to her?"

"No, the woman who was helping us said not to."

"Papá, that doesn't make any sense. There has to be a way. A lot of people are coming. I know other mothers who have been permitted to visit. Why can't Mamá come?"

"I don't know, Lupe. Maybe the others didn't have papers and just jumped the line."

"Well, in that case, Mamá should just come anyway. Lots of people do. You did. I understand there are places people can just walk across."

"Yes, yes, I know. But it is still dangerous and not easy for women."

"But, she can't just go home. She is alone down there in the village. She has to come sometime. We've got to figure out a way. Maybe Richard could bring her in his truck. Let me talk to him when he comes home. We can be down there in two or three hours. He should be home at five. Can you call me back?"

"Yes, yes, I'll call."

The dispirited group found shade on a bench in the shadow of a palm tree and waited the hour that Miguel was to call Lupe again. Attempting to lift their spirits, Miguel bought Sno Cones. Between attempts to catch pigeons that scavenged the pavement around the benches, Maria Elena played with her doll.

Twice during the seemingly endless afternoon, vendors offered to prepare fake green cards for them, pointing out a nearby shop where ID photos could be obtained for competitive prices. Another offered to rent them local border-crossing cards, substituting their photos for the pictures of the real cardholders. The cards were to be returned to an accomplice once they passed through the garita.

For one hundred dollars each, a Mexican-American woman, dressed in bright beach clothes, offered to drive them through the garita, hidden in the back of her camper. A wiry, dark-skinned youth wearing a Los Angeles Lakers T-shirt that hung to his knees offered to guide them through a hole in the fence and across a ravine to a shopping center on the other side. Miguel refused the offer, and the boy berated him, taunting his manhood and intelligence.

When the appointed hour came and Miguel called again, Lupe did not have encouraging news. She had suggested to Richard that he bring them across concealed in the bed of his landscaping truck, but he responded testily saying that he could not afford to lose his truck to the immigration if they were caught. He wanted Concha to return to Piedra Gorda and wait. His family had waited until his father had obtained the proper papers to bring them across the border, he pointed out. And, he reminded Lupe, she herself had waited until her papers were ready.

"Papá," Lupe pleaded, "can't you figure out a way to bring Mamá across? You've crossed so many times yourself." She was crying when they hung up. After he told the group that Lupe and Richard would be unable to help, Miguel glumly instructed Concha and Rosalinda to gather up their belongings.

Rosalinda had tried to call her husband during the afternoon, but without success. His crew had moved to Fresno in anticipation of the raisin harvest, and the crew boss's wife did not have a new phone number for her husband yet. The young mother and her children were now Miguel's responsibility, too.

Miguel gathered the suitcases, taking one in each hand and wedging the smallest of the three under his arm. Concha carried a bag, and took Maria Elena's hand. The solemn-eyed little girl was old enough to sense that the gay, holiday mood she had created for herself in the plaza had changed. She walked silently at Concha's side, clasping her doll.

They walked along the dusty street adjoining the border, past crumbling adobe and stucco dwellings. At each corner and across vacant lots, they caught glimpses of the grey chainlink border fence, topped with barbed wire, the base cluttered with brambles and trash. The structure was decrepit and had gaping holes. On the other side, the hard-packed dirt cliffs and ravines, dotted by clumps of dull-green brush and garbage, seemed a mere extension of the trash-littered streets of Tijuana. Yet, like millions of migrants, the party was drawn, and they saw beyond the ugliness to the order, cleanliness, and hope for themselves and their families that the country to the north promised. No one thought of turning back.

"Señor, I will take you to el otro lado. I know the route. La migra will never catch you." The boy wearing the Lakers T-shirt who had berated him hours before in the plaza appeared at Miguel's side. Barefooted, bareheaded, the dusty urchin attempted to take one of the suitcases, but Miguel shooed him away.

"I'm not going to rob you," the boy protested. "I want to help you. You want to go to Hollywood, live a good life, make a lot of money. I will take you. La migra will never catch you. Trust me."

Miguel ignored the boy, who dropped back and fell in step beside Rosalinda. She smiled at him.

"You want to have food for your baby, señora? You want to have many babies, find a handsome husband? I will take you to el otro lado."

Miguel turned threateningly, and the boy fell back several steps. But after a few minutes, he scurried to Concha's side and silently held out his hand. She stopped and, finding a few coins in her purse, put them in the boy's palm. Grateful, he scuttled ahead. Walking backward, he motioned for the group to follow him down a side street. It was only a short distance to the fence. After clearing away some old boxes and papers and pulling back some brush, the boy revealed a waist-high gap in the steel chain link.

The three adults duck-walked through the opening, Concha taking Maria Elena by the hand. Miguel made a second trip for their luggage. With a wave, the boy skipped off.

It was early evening, and they climbed down to a flat, open area that stretched along the decrepit barrier. They were north of the fence, but it was hard to tell that they had actually crossed the line into los Estados Unidos. Still, they were excited, apprehensive, but fearful that la migra would swoop down on them at any minute. The evening had begun to fade to darkness, and they were uncertain what to do next; they had no plan.

Around the edges of the clearing, small groups of people clustered: men, women, and several children. Some carrying luggage, small mochilas, or parcels. A few of the women started charcoal stoves, preparing to grill *carne asada* or heat up pots of pozole. Vendors sold cold drinks, beer, bags of chips, and even colorful toys. It was if Miguel and his dispirited charges had happened upon a carnival. They had eaten earlier in the day, tacos purchased from a vendor in the plaza, but the rich aromas and the apparent camaraderie of the assemblage raised the small group's spirits and sharpened their appetites.

A brushy ravine bordered the open field. Miguel spotted two green-and-white Jeeps sitting motionless on the dry bluffs on the opposite side. La migra patiently watched and waited. Just two of them would be no match for the scores of migrants, Miguel thought. Behind them, neat rows of roofs in housing subdivisions sketched geometric lines against the far horizon.

More people arrived in the clearing. The festive atmosphere promoted an air of excitement, expectation. Not wanting to make Concha and Rosalinda more apprehensive, Miguel did not point out the Jeeps, whose number had increased to three. As soon as it got dark, the migrants would surge through the canyon and attempt to make it across the bluffs. Miguel wondered how many patrulleros would be on duty after dark.

Manipulating a harness of sticks and strings, a vender danced a toy monkey, clothed in green and red satin, toward Maria Elena, but Rosalinda waved him away. Soon a soccer ball appeared, and after a few minutes of scrimmaging, the men formed themselves into teams. One of the teams was made up of men from Jalisco. The other called itself *los Zacatecanos,* and Miguel migrated to the cluster of men who appeared to be the team's supporters.

While cheering on los Zacatecanos, Miguel struck up a conversation with two men from Jerez. Yes, they were going to cross the ravine when it got dark; everyone was. La migra would be outnumbered—it happened every night—and so most of them would make it. Those that were caught would simply be put back across the border and would return here tomorrow night to try it again. If his party wanted to go too, he should talk to El Chaparrito who was mingling through the crowd just a few yards away.

"My wife and the woman with the children want to go," Miguel told the short, square-faced man in a dark, short-sleeved shirt when he located him. "I have a green card."

"Fifty dollars US for each," the stocky man replied without hesitation. The coyote was sweating in the warm evening air. "Cross with them if you want, but they'll take your green card away if you get caught."

"I only have a hundred in cash. Two of them are infants."

"Where are they?"

"Over there toward the fence … there!" In the gathering gloom, Miguel pointed out the two women. Rosalinda was sitting on a suitcase cradling Carlos, and Maria Elena was playing in the dirt. El Chaparrito looked a long moment.

"They can't take the bags. They will have to run for it. The children will have to be carried."

"Okay." Miguel reached into his wallet and carefully counted out five twenty-dollar bills. Although he had three uncashed paychecks, he noted that between paying Eliza's additional charges and El Chaparrito's fee, he had little cash left.

"On the other side, there is a lighted parking lot in front of a Burger King. You can see the lights from here after it gets dark. It is close by the garita. Just follow the trolley tracks. Wait for them there."

Miguel's eyes sought the landmark described by the coyote. It was not fully dark, and he was unsure if he saw the lights, but he was sure he could find the trolley tracks and follow them to the Burger King. That seemed easy enough. He returned to Concha and Rosalinda and explained what they would have to do.

36

 "You'll be able to see them when they come over that saddle," the stranger said. The man wearing a crisp white tejana had edged up to Miguel's side as he stood anxiously peering at the bluffs rising beyond the trolley tracks that ran along the opposite side of the busy street. The horizon was backlit by powerful lights used to illuminate the distant border fence, and at the stranger's prompting, Miguel could easily make out the dip between two rounded hilltops. But it gave him little comfort that la migra also would be able to spot Concha, Rosalinda, and the children as they made their way through the gap.

Miguel had found the Burger King easily enough. With the help of a countryman, he had located a place to store Concha and Rosalinda's luggage. Then, after walking through the garita, displaying his green card for the inspector, he followed the thoroughfare beside the trolley tracks, as El Chaparrito had instructed. He loitered in the paved parking lot, going inside once for a cold drink and to use the men's room. It had been nearly three hours since darkness had fallen, and the women had not appeared.

"They'll be here soon," the stranger said, confident that Miguel was waiting for friends or family who were at that moment attempting to scramble past the vigilant patrulleros. "There aren't many migra tonight so most of them should get through on the first try. If they don't make it, the night is still young enough that they'll be able to try it again. Even a third time."

Miguel cautiously eyed the man, who wore an expensive white silk shirt. His rolled-back cuffs revealed a jeweled gold watch on his wrist. Miguel first noticed him talking to another man in the parking lot who also seemed to be waiting for someone.

"My name is Dionisio—Nicho," the stranger said, extending his hand. "Where are you from?"

"Zacatecas," Miguel responded as he shook the man's hand.

"I'm from Fresnillo," the man responded heartily.

"Are you waiting for someone too?"

"Yes, *compañeros* from Lagos de Moreno. I have a van, and I am going to drive them to Los Angeles." Nicho waited for the information to sink in.

"Well, I'm waiting for my wife and her companion. The other woman has a baby and a small child."

The man drew in his breath. "*Ay-y*, that's tough. I hope they make it. I suppose you have a car?"

"Well, no," Miguel admitted. "I expect my daughter and her husband will come down from Los Angeles to pick us up."

"You know la migra will stop you on the freeway between here and Los Angeles?"

Expecting Concha to be given a visitor's permit, Miguel had not thought about the checkpoint the border patrol maintained on I-5 near the Marine base, stopping all traffic traveling north out of San Diego. His heart sank. "I guess I didn't think about that. Gracias, for reminding me."

"I know how to get past the checkpoint," the man volunteered. "I could take them, but they might have to carry the children on their laps."

Of course, there would be a price, Miguel thought, and he temporized. "Gracias, but I think I will wait to see if they make it here first."

"Don't wait too long. I go when my van fills up."

Although he could not see the border fence from where he stood, Miguel could hear the whirr of a helicopter and follow its progress as it patrolled the fence. At times, it veered off to probe the brushy ravine with its spotlight. Once, it passed noisily over the parking lot. He wondered how people in neighboring houses slept.

From time to time, men and women in groups of two or three appeared from the shadows on the other side of the tracks, then scurried across the busy street and slipped away again through darkened corridors between the gleaming steel roofs of parked cars. A group of short, stocky men clutching plastic suitcases appeared. They were hatless, and Miguel speculated they were Chinese. He did not see any of the Zacatecanos from the soccer field. He asked a group of out-of-breath migrants if they had seen two women carrying two children. They had not.

Pedestrians disappeared in the shadows along the dimly lit sidewalks to be picked up by cruising cars and pickup trucks that quickly disappeared into traffic. Nicho met his group and was off without so much as a nod in Miguel's direction.

Occasionally, a green-and-white border patrol van circled the parking lot. On one turn, the patrulleros stopped a car that had just picked up six migrants. In the glow of flashing lights, they frisked each of the Mexicans, including the driver, and loaded them into the rear of the van. The van drove off, leaving the coyote's car parked at the curb.

Two patrulleros on foot questioned Miguel. "What are you doing here?" the shorter one asked.

"*Nada, nada*," Miguel responded, rattling the few chunks of ice remaining in his Burger King cup. "I just stopped for a *refresco*."

The officers examined his green card in the beam of their flashlights and moved on.

Miguel thought maybe Concha and Rosalinda were afraid to come into the parking lot and were hiding in the dark on the other side of the tracks. He crossed the street and walked along the trolley line, checking in the shadows behind darkened buildings and even walking a short distance toward the bluffs. He called their names, but there was no response. Returning to the street, he walked several blocks in each direction, thinking they might have gotten confused and gone to the wrong place. Maybe there was another Burger King nearby, he thought. But he did not find them.

Miguel regretted not staying with the women, but the coyote had warned him that if he were caught, la migra would punish him for smuggling and take his green card away. It was best to let him take the risk, El Chaparrito said, promising he would take good care of Concha, Rosalinda, and the children.

Dawn came and there was still no sign of Concha and Rosalinda. Unsure what to do, Miguel walked back to the garita. Afraid he might be accused of being complicit in their illegal crossing, he ruled out asking the inspectors on the US side whether the two women had been caught. Crossing an overpass to the Mexican side, he approached an official on duty in the pedestrian lane. "Señor, where do the people go who are sent back from los Estados Unidos?"

"¿Quién sabe?" The official replied indifferently.

"Señor, por favor, I'm looking for my wife and her companion. A young woman with a baby and a child."

The official abruptly paid attention. "There is a *refugio* on Avenida Padre Kino that looks after the women and children, señor. It is the second street to the left. It's not far. Just ask."

"Gracias, oficial."

When Miguel arrived at the two-story, white stucco *dormitorio*, he was overjoyed to find his charges. Rosalinda and the children were asleep on a single bed, and Concha explained what had happened. In the darkness, the group had been following El Chaparrito single file along a trail through the brushy canyon when suddenly everyone started running. Rosalinda was carrying Carlos, and Concha was carrying Maria Elena, but they could not keep up and quickly found themselves separated from the group. In the darkness, they hid in the brush until they were spotted by la migra and taken to a coralón. After the patrulleros fingerprinted them and finished their questions, the group was taken to the garita and put back across la frontera.

Miguel was relieved, but now what would they do?

37

"Hola, señor!" A small man wearing a snap-brim fedora pulled low over his left ear stepped out from the shadows of the building next door to the dormitorio and accosted Miguel as he started up the street. "Do you have relatives in there? Children? Perhaps I can help?"

Annoyed, Miguel stared curiously at the intruder. Half of the man's ear appeared to be missing, leaving a gnarled remnant that could not be completely hidden under the brim of his hat. Intent on reclaiming Rosalinda and Concha's bags, Miguel held his hand to his tejana and brushed on by, pushing on along the crowded sidewalk.

Chuy Gallegos decided to bide his time. From long practice, he easily had spotted Miguel as a potential client. No doubt an *esposa*, and probably *niños* also, were in the shelter, and the mark was bound to return. A family needing to cross the border could be shaken down for a lot of money, particularly if there were other relatives already in the United States who could pay.

In the twenty-five years, since the patrullero was slain in Davies Valley and that asshole kid, as Chuy bitterly referred to Javier Romero, had ratted him out, Chuy had not dared to cross la frontera. Born in the United States to Mexican immigrant parents, he was recognized as a citizen by the laws of both countries. That was fortunate for Chuy.

Before the murder, border crossing had been easy, but he hated Mexico and the United States with equal passion.

The United States wanted Chuy for his part in the murder of Patrol Inspector Garner, and were it not for a dispute over the saline content of the Colorado River water, Mexico gladly would have given him up. But because Mexico deemed the United States had not honored its treaty obligations, the government had decided not to repatriate any of its citizens accused of assaulting, or even murdering, a US Border Patrol officer.

Despite refusing to repatriate Chuy, Mexico had not welcomed him. He had been jailed in Mexicali while the federal governments of both countries exchanged diplomatic notes. After his release, fearing capture by vigilante migra, he fled to an *ejido* in Aguas Calientes where his grandmother still lived. Not surprisingly, he did not fit in. Fieldwork was too hard and paid so little he was forced to get drunk on peasant liquor instead of the expensive Scotch he had acquired a taste for in border cantinas.

Chuy next went to Guadalajara and tried to support himself by petty theft and working cheap cons on tourists. But even though he was not the one actually to pull the trigger on the unfortunate patrullero, Chuy had obtained a reputation. Upon learning his identity—the gnarled ear was always a giveaway—the *policía* demanded increasingly large amounts of mordida. Worse, he was a mark for petty thugs who wanted to prove their own machismo, and most succeeded. His nerves frazzled, Chuy returned to la frontera. For once in his life, his timing was perfect.

Mexican farmworkers facing hunger in Mexico were returning illegally to fill jobs they once held as braceros or to seek new work from employers eager for cheap labor. Mexican families, barred by new limits on legal immigration, were jumping the line to join husbands and fathers who had departed for el norte. Hundreds of thousands of migrants thronging to la frontera, afforded rich opportunities for coyotes like Chuy, who for a price guided the pollos through the mountains and deserts, rafted them across the All American Canal, or simply boosted them over the border fence. La migra was overwhelmed by their numbers.

Not being able to cross the border himself proved only a minor inconvenience. Chuy knew la frontera, and being a wanted fugitive in los Estados Unidos gave him cachet. He got enough for his services that he was able to hire *guías* to escort the migrants he recruited across the line. He developed a network of accomplices to meet pollos on the US side and transport them to places like Los Angeles, the San Joaquin Valley, Oregon, or even the apple-picking region of Washington State.

Adding to his opportunities, hippie kids in el norte wanted pot. Often, Chuy would demand that the pollos he recruited mule bales of marijuana. Cocaine and heroin were easy to smuggle across trampled border fences and past the outnumbered patrulleros.

The money Chuy demanded from pollos and the fees collected from the farmers when the workers were delivered earned him a double windfall. His proceeds were immense, but so were his expenses: shakedowns from powerful gangsters and mordida paid to local oficiales.

Chuy had been loitering near the garita early that morning and saw Miguel pass through the pedestrian lanes. Mexicans, El Salvadorians, and people from other countries who were caught by la migra during the night and were being put back across the line were all potential clients. But Miguel had a different look. He was obviously a norteño, but he carried no luggage, and for some reason, the aduana had helped him, pointing out a direction. Curious, Chuy followed Miguel as he walked away from the garita and then turned onto Avenida Padre Kino to the children's shelter.

When Miguel returned to the dormitorio, his arms loaded with cumbersome luggage, Chuy tried again. "I know a place your family can cross safely. A place where there are no migra," he said, certain now that he understood Miguel's situation.

Miguel pushed past, wrestling the bags through the door of the shelter, but he returned a few minutes later. "We have two infants," he said to Chuy.

"It doesn't matter, in fact all the better for you. I will take the babies two for the price of one."

"But, I don't want to cross here anymore. With the children, the women can't run, and there are too many migra. And they still have to get past the highway checkpoint."

"Then how about Mexicali? I know a route north of La Rumorosa."

"No, not there either. I know that route too, and it is too hard for women and children."

"I know—Arizona. It's easy, and there are few migra."

"Through the desert?" Miguel asked dubiously.

"Yes, but they won't have to walk very far. They will be picked up on the other side, and I will have them taken wherever you want me to."

"To El Monte?"

"Yes, that's in Los Angeles. That's easy," Chuy said.

"How will they get to Arizona?"

"I have a van. I will take them myself."

"What do you charge?"

"Five hundred each for the women, and five hundred for the two children."

Miguel opened his wallet. "Well, I only have three paychecks," he said.

Chuy did a quick estimation. "In that case, I will only charge for the adults. The children will go free." He could shake them down for more money on the other side. Fathers always paid.

Miguel was relieved that he would be left with a few dollars. "When will we leave?"

"Tomorrow. I've got clients coming in this evening. First, I've gotta contact another guy in Arizona who works for me. I'll pick up your group here tomorrow afternoon."

"Good. We'll be ready." Miguel did not offer to shake hands. He wondered again about the gnarled ear.

Concha did not like the idea. She had seen Miguel talking to the devious little man on the street, and she did not like his looks. She thought that taking the children through the desert would be risky. They were too young. The desert heat and the rattlesnakes were a danger to them all.

Miguel tried to reassure her. "You'll only be in the desert at night," he said. "Snakes scurry away when they hear footsteps. A car will pick you up on the other side, and there won't be any migra. You can carry the children. Besides, there will be other men along to help, so you won't be alone. The coyote is going to pick up the others tonight."

The thought of other men accompanying them comforted Concha somewhat, but she remembered that no one came back to help them when they became separated on their last attempt. And that coyote, *yi!* But the alternative was to return to Piedra Gorda, and she was not ready to do that.

True, Miguel thought, the coyote had the way of evil people. There was something peculiarly familiar about the man that he could not quite place. He thought he had heard the man's voice before but could not be sure. The man was no different from any other coyote, though, and he had dealt with them before. They all wanted money. Some were treacherous and cheated pollos. But, they wanted to outwit la migra as did he, Miguel thought.

Miguel had heard crossing la frontera into Arizona was easier, and they would not have to get past the checkpoint on I-5 as they would if they crossed at Tijuana. He was suspicious that extra fees might be charged once they got to el otro lado. He would feel better when they got across, he decided. He could deal with what was to come from there.

At length, Concha's fears were assuaged, and those of Rosalinda, who, after the night of hiding in the brushy ravine, also was apprehensive. Rosalinda still had not been able to contact her husband, and she was grateful that Miguel had taken her and the children under his wing. But she felt awkward knowing he had to pay so much money to the coyote for them. She wanted to do her best to make it easy for him. He had not complained, and if crossing through the desert was the way he wanted to resolve their situation, she felt obligated to go along with his plan.

The patrulleros had been fair and respectful of her and the children, Rosalinda thought. If la migra were all they had to fear when crossing the border, it would be all right. With Concha accompanying her and helping with the children, a short walk in the desert could not be all that bad, particularly in the cool of the night.

38

When Chuy returned in the early afternoon of the following day, he parked his van down the street from the dormitorio. The nun who was the director of the facility had previously chased him away and called the authorities. He sent a boy to summon Miguel.

At Miguel's insistence, Chuy grudgingly produced a map from the glove box of his white van. Two orange lines crossed the tattered page from left to right. Interstate Highway 8 in Arizona was almost a straight line east and west. On the Sonora side, Mexico Federal Highway, Ruta 2, angled southeast so closely paralleling the border that Miguel at first mistook it for the international boundary. Miguel could not judge how far apart the two highways were: near Yuma, the lines were close to touching, but they diverged towards the east.

"The women will cross through here," Chuy said, thrusting his middle finger across an area partially obscured under a brownish semi-circle where a coffee cup once rested. "It's only an hour or two of walking. They'll have a guide."

The distance between the highways could be five or six miles as the coyote claimed, Miguel concluded, or twenty or thirty. Concha could easily walk five or six miles; it was part of life in rural Zacatecas. She could walk twenty miles easily if need be, he thought, although it might be harder since she had gotten older. When he had talked to Lupe the previous night, she worried about the arrangements but agreed that her mother was capable of making the journey.

Miguel would have closed the deal by now, but he was nagged by concerns about Rosalinda and the children. She still had not been able to contact her husband. He felt confident he would be reimbursed the money he was about to pay the coyote, but if Rosalinda had to stop or turn back, Concha would be obligated to remain with her. Certainly, she must, he concluded. The two women had been companions since leaving Piedra Gorda, and the young mother could not care for two children in the desert by herself.

When Miguel had talked it over with the women the previous evening, Rosalinda was confident she would be able to make the trek. She was after all, a young, healthy woman, Concha pointed out, and there were bound to be men in the group who would help with the children if need be. It was not as if the travelers themselves were coyotes, Concha reassured him.

"Look, hombre," Chuy said impatiently, "it's all flat walking. They'll do it at night when it's cool. My partner will meet them at the pickup point on the interstate in Arizona and drive them to Los Angeles. There are no migra checkpoints along the way."

"My wife is going to our daughter's house in El Monte," Miguel reminded him.

"All right, sure. No problem."

On top of his concerns about Concha, Rosalinda, and the children, Miguel was finding it hard to trust the coyote. His attention kept gravitating to the man's mangled ear, to his whiny voice. He thought that he had met the man before, but try as he might, the circumstance would not come to mind.

He knew at some point he must trust Chuy or search for some other way for Concha to cross the border, and he could think of no practical options. People paid coyotes all the time, he rationalized, thousands of them. He had hired smugglers himself; it was a business arrangement. Although many times the danger came from the coyotes themselves, with all the perils migrants faced these days, it was a necessary risk.

Despite his doubts, Miguel had cashed his three paychecks at a *casa de cambio*, and now he counted out ten one-hundred-dollar bills into Chuy's waiting hand.

Miguel stepped back into the dormitorio to retrieve his charges. When they arrived at the van and he opened the side door for them, they found that behind the vehicle's dark-tinted windows eight men already had arranged themselves on the three rows of seats. The men watched silently as Concha and Rosalinda squeezed onto the middle seat, causing the two men already seated there to slide together and place their packs at their feet. Rosalinda was wearing a stylish embroidered top and new jeans and held Carlos. Concha held Maria Elena on her lap. The close interior was heavy with the scent of sweating, unwashed men. Carlos began to fuss.

Miguel pushed a cloth shoulder bag containing twelve pint-bottles of water into the space at Concha's feet. He made sure that she had the slip of paper with Lupe's address and phone number and then reached in and hugged her. He promised to see them all at Lupe's house the next day.

Standing at the still open door, Miguel crossed himself three times and asked God to be with Concha and Rosalinda and her children on their perilous journey. Concha joined in the benediction, offering a prayer to Saint Martin de Porras for protection. With that, Miguel slammed the door shut and stepped back as Chuy backed away from the curb and drove off down the street.

Rosalinda had dressed Maria Elena in green shorts and the Mickey Mouse top her father had sent from California. The little girl was quiet at first, clasping her cloth doll tightly to her chest, but Concha soon got her to smile by playing itsy-bitsy spider. Her giggles caught the attention of the smooth-shaven young man with a dark mustache sitting beside her. He introduced himself as Guillermo. He was from Jalisco, he said, and told Maria Elena that he had a little girl just like her.

"Are you going to Disneylandia?" Guillermo asked Maria Elena.

"No, señor," the little girl responded. "We're going to live with my papá."

"Well, maybe your papá will take you to meet El Ratón Miguelito," he said, poking his finger at the figure of Mickey on the front of her T-shirt, "and El Pato Donald."

"My papá will take us everywhere. He does lots of things."

"Is your papá handsome?"

"He's very handsome, and he's big and strong. He's going to take care of my mamá and me and baby Carlos."

As the van rattled through the crowded streets toward the outskirts of Tijuana, the men, who had remained quiet since Concha and Rosalinda boarded, gradually resumed their banter. Guillermo and Maria Elena struck up a conversation about one of her favorite topics, plans for her next birthday party.

"We had a big piñata. It was green and red, and it was this big," the child said, arcing her arms above her head. "I got to hit it, and it broke, and do you know what was in it, Yermo? There was lots of candy and presents for everyone. When we get to California and Mamá and Papá get a big house, I'm going to have another birthday party, and we're going to have another big piñata, and it will be even bigger."

Even baby Carlos seemed to relax, smiling and gooing at his mother as she laid him lengthwise on her knees and loosened some of his clothing to better cope with the oppressive heat in the unairconditioned van. Clearing the outskirts of the city, the aging vehicle struggled up the winding highway into the barren, rock-strewn mountains east of Tijuana. Bent over the wheel, Chuy was silent.

By the time they reached the border town of Tecate, everybody had been introduced. Two of the men from Guanajuato said a judge had ordered them deported because they had been caught too many times, and if they got caught again, they could face jail time. It was too risky for them to cross again at Tijuana, they said, but they had to have work. Guillermo and two brothers, also from Jalisco, had been put back across the line, what the patrulleros called voluntary departure, after they were caught working near Bakersfield.

Three young men from Guerrero in the back row had been caught several times trying to enter at Tijuana and, like Concha and Rosalinda, were looking for a place to cross where the odds were better. Their relatives had gathered the money to pay the sum Chuy demanded, and they were excited about their improved prospects in this new attempt. Having failed, no one considered it an option to return to his village.

After an hour of cresting successive grades, they reached La Rumorosa. The highway split into uphill and downhill lanes and dropped precipitously—over four thousand feet—through dry, rocky canyons to the desert floor. Chuy, who had remained silently aloof from his clients, took the opportunity to demonstrate his machismo. Careening around curves at high speed, tires screaming, the heavily loaded van swerved unnervingly to the left and then the right, passing other vehicles in a mad plunge to the valley floor. The tightly packed passengers stiffened. Concha and Rosalinda tightened their arms around the children on their laps. Welcoming the change of mood in the van and determined to match Chuy's bravado, the men whistled and shouted at each turn.

At the bottom of the grade, the road leveled out onto the desert. One of the brothers from Jalisco continued to mimic Chuy, bending forward with a maniacal look and twisting a mock steering wheel inches in front of his face. Chuy caught the performance in the rearview mirror and responded sharply with a crude rebuke. Chastened, the passengers fell silent.

When they reached Mexicali, two of the men asked to stop at a *servicio* to relieve themselves. Chuy grudgingly complied but ordered the rest to remain in the vehicle until they reached San Luis Rio Colorado, sixty miles further east. Maria Elena had been squirming, and without asking permission, Concha got out and led the little girl into the excusado. Needing to change Carlos, Rosalinda followed. Chuy glowered but kept his mouth shut.

An hour later, they crossed the Rio Colorado, and Chuy pulled into a *gasolinera*. While he gassed up the van, the passengers got out and stretched their legs. Concha was glad to get Maria Elena off her lap and stood and smoothed her blouse and skirt. The trio from Guerrero, confident that on this attempt they would finally make it to el otro lado, bought bottles of beer and toasted farewell to Mexico. Some of the men bought tacos at an adjoining taqueria, and Rosalinda and Concha followed their lead. Concha shared hers with Maria Elena. They each drank a bottle of the water Miguel had insisted they take along.

Rosalinda passed Carlos to Concha and loitered a few feet away while she finished her taco. Guillermo, who had been watching the trim young woman out of the corner of his eye, took the opportunity to start a conversation.

"Are you anxious to see your husband again?" he asked.

"Sí, it has been a long journey for us, particularly for the children."

"I really like Maria Elena. She reminds me so much of my little girl, Guillermina."

"Guillermina? She was named after you?"

"Yes." Guillermo smiled. "My wife insisted."

"Your wife must be a special woman to love you so much."

"She is, and I miss her. She is young and pretty like you."

Rosalinda blushed. "I miss my husband, too."

"Yes, but you are journeying toward him. I am journeying away from my family."

"I am sorry, Guillermo," she said, touching his arm softly with her hand.

Just then, Chuy whistled and jumped into the van. A slender youth with long bleached hair piled into the front beside him, crouching on his heels between the two front seats, steadying himself with one hand on the dash, the other around the back of Chuy's seat. Chuy called him Guërito. The two talked in low voices as the van rolled along the desert highway through a series of dusty little settlements with high-sounding names: Rancho Las Delicias, Ejido Reforma Agraria, Aquiles Serdán.

Although it was early evening, the air was still oppressively hot. The sun at its back, the van cast an elongated shadow on the vacant blacktop road ahead. The long straight highway passed from the cultivated farms, irrigated by the Rio Colorado, into a monotonous sea of low dunes, capped by grey-green clumps of greasewood and saguaro cactus. Shadows cast by the late afternoon sun highlighted every gully, fault, and ridge in the range of dry mountains looming ahead of them. The features stood out like veins on a dried leaf.

Presently, in the gathering dusk, the packed vehicle slowed and pulled across the empty oncoming traffic lane onto the desert hard-pan. Anticipating the final night of their journey, uncertain whether la migra, or something worse, awaited them in the empty landscape, the migrants fell silent.

39

 Shadows crept across the wide plain, sprinkled with scrag-
gly grey-green greasewood thickets, and up the slopes of
the rocky peaks. Angling off to the northwest, the lifeless pinnacles pro-
cessed in single file, a ghostly metaphor of the migrants' lonely journey.

Hushed by the emptiness of the desert, the migrants clambered out
of the van and tried their cramped legs on the hard ground. Guillermo
helped Rosalinda, giving her his arm and holding the soft-vinyl shoulder bag filled with baby supplies while she clutched Carlos against her
breast. Concha carried the cloth bag Miguel had given her, which now
held ten bottles of water.

As if la migra were about to swoop down from the peaks, Chuy
backed the empty van between the low dunes, careful to keep the vehicle
only on the hard pan, and then shot forward onto the pavement. The
rear wheels spewed dirt and rock as he sped off toward San Luis. He
did not look back.

Alone, the migrants clustered together as if each feared being
swallowed alive by the vast emptiness. Between the tiny group and the
nearby mountains stretched a decrepit barbed-wire fence: la frontera.
Far to the west, the sun dropped below the horizon, lighting the sky in
waves of reds and pinks.

"*¡Mira!* We have to walk north toward the mountains," Guërito said, gesturing toward the uneven row of peaks. In the silence of the open desert, the sound of his voice dissipated quickly.

"We're not going to cross the mountains," he continued, satisfied that he had everyone's attention. "There is a trail that runs along the west side that we will follow. It goes right up to the interstate and comes out at the pick-up point. We have to be there before dawn. After daylight, *la migra* patrols with airplanes, and it will be too dangerous for the driver. We'll get picked up only if it is still dark.

"We have to hurry. If you fall behind, just follow the trail," Guërito said looking directly at Concha and Rosalinda.

Falling in behind their new leader, the men shouldered their mochilas and clambered over the trampled remnants of the fence. Quickly distancing themselves from the women, they moved off in a cluster toward the mountains. Guillermo hung back.

"I will help you," Guillermo said to Rosalinda and Concha. "I will make sure that we don't lose track of the group." He stepped on the rusted wire, pushing it down so they could step over. Concha carried Maria Elena.

Skirting thickets of greasewood, they walked only a short distance before Maria Elena squirmed in Concha's arms and reached for Rosalinda. Concha put her down, and the child grabbed her mother's hand, talking as they walked in the still evening air.

"Mamá? Does Papá live here?"

"No, mija. Papá lives a long way away yet. We will be there tomorrow."

"Are there trees where Papá lives?"

"Yes, mija. Lots of trees and grass and water."

"And people?"

"Yes, people too. Nice people. Papá says there are schools that you will go to. And we will live in a house. And there will be children to play with, little girls like you."

"I hope we see Papá soon."

Then even Maria Elena grew silent; the empty desert seemed to swallow up all sound.

"Guillermo," Concha said presently. "The boy said we would have to hurry to be at the highway by dawn. That means we will be walking all night."

"Yes, I suppose."

"But the coyote told my husband that the walk was easy and would only take an hour or two."

"Well … I'm not too sure what he told us. Three or four hours, I think."

"This is going to be hard for Rosalinda and the babies."

"Not too hard, I believe. We're not going up into the mountains. It should be level all the way."

"Guillermo," Rosalinda said anxiously. "We don't want to be left behind."

"You won't be. I'll be here with you and the children. I won't leave you."

As dusk settled in, they walked in silence. The desert fauna having rested through the heat of the day began to emerge. Maria Elena moved to Concha's side and took her hand. Concha pointed out birds darting over their heads that seemed to come out of nowhere, swallow-tailed birds whose names Concha did not know. Watching for them kept the little girl occupied.

The warm, dry air evaporated the moisture from their bodies. Without the direct rays of the sun, the evening was pleasant. Venus appeared in the lingering light of the western sky. As it grew darker, the big constellations appeared. Concha pointed out Orion's belt and sword to Maria Elena. Then the big dipper appeared, and as if to reassure the walkers, the North Star took its place high in the heavens to their front. As Concha identified each new wonder for the child, Rosalinda listened too. The women traveled back in time to evenings spent sitting on stoops in front of their casitas in Piedra Gorda as their own mothers pointed out the marvels of the night sky.

Presently, Guillermo called a halt. They had not seen the rest of the group in some time, and he thought he should run ahead and try to reestablish contact with Guërito.

"What about us?" Rosalinda asked. "How will you find us again?"

"Just keep walking past the mountains," he said, gesturing to the dark hulks that loomed in the ambient light of the heavens to their right front. "I'll come right back to you. If you're tired, stop. I'll find you."

"I'm afraid of snakes," Concha said, confessing a fear that had nagged her since Miguel had explained they would be walking through the desert. "I don't want to sit down."

"Here," Guillermo said, handing her an unopened pack of cigarettes and a small box of matches. "Snakes don't like smoke. Just light a couple of these and lay them on the ground around you. Snakes won't bother you."

After Guillermo disappeared into the darkness ahead, the women walked only a short distance. Losing confidence, they stopped. After standing in the same place for what seemed a long time, Concha lit one of the cigarettes and dropped it on the ground. After a pause while the women speculated which direction the smoke was drifting and whether it actually would keep snakes away, they sat down next to the glowing red ember.

Concha took out two bottles of water, sharing hers with Maria Elena. The child was hungry, and Rosalinda took a packet of saltines out of her bag and gave them to her. She ate three and then slept cuddled in Concha's lap. Rosalinda nursed Carlos.

Guillermo did not return. Feeling anxious, the women struggled to their feet and pressed on. Carrying the slumbering children, they walked toward the dark hulk of the mountains, which they could just make out in the light of a late-rising half-moon. The ground sloped upward, and they found themselves trudging through loose sand. The muscles in their hips and thighs burned from the effort. They stumbled into the prickly branches of creosote bushes. It was tough going, and they stopped often, trying to find their way. A high haze had crept across the sky, and they no longer could find the North Star. They stopped and drank two more bottles of water.

When the pre-dawn light began to brighten the Eastern sky and Guillermo still had not returned, the women puzzled at the landscape. Instead of appearing to their right, as they should if they had walked far enough, the mountains were to their left, the higher peaks already lit by the rising sun. A single rocky promontory stood to their right where the pinnacles were supposed to be. There was no sign of a trail, only indentations in the soft sand behind them made by their own feet. In despair, they dropped to the ground at the foot of a towering saguaro cactus, its prickly arms pointed straight up like a silent green sentry.

Near panic at finding themselves alone, they sank to the ground. Exhausted, they dozed fretfully, Concha waking to set out lighted cigarettes. Through the night, they had walked toward the sunrise, and now the orb appeared ominously above the eastern horizon. They slept until it had a good start up into the cloudless sky.

"¡Hola! Rosalinda! Concha!"

Concha thought it must be a dream; the voice seemed so small in the oppressive silence surrounding them.

"¡Hola!" Guillermo dropped down beside them. Concha and Rosalinda sat upright, disturbing Carlos from his sleep and awakening Maria Elena.

"I couldn't find you on the trail, and it was only after dawn that I could find your tracks."

Rosalinda was overwhelmed with relief. "Thank God that you are back. I prayed to the Virgencita all night that we would not get left behind. She has answered me."

"Do you have any water?"

"Sí," Concha said, passing Guillermo one of the plastic bottles. She passed another to Rosalinda, and after she took one, she noted they now had only three bottles left. Maria Elena was thirsty too and hungry. Rosalinda gave her the last of the water from her bottle and allowed her to eat more of the saltines. Already they could feel the heat of the advancing day.

"Do you know where we are?" Concha asked as soon as Guillermo had some water. "What happened to the others?"

"I caught up to them, but they didn't want to wait. When I returned on the trail I couldn't find you."

"But we couldn't find any trail in the dark," Rosalinda interjected.

"It's very faint. Like Guërito said, it does run along the base of the mountains. It's on the other side from where we are now. You passed to the south of the mountains, across a low ridge. I know where we are.

I can get us back to the trail. We'll be all right, but we have to go back quite a distance."

"But what about our ride?" Rosalinda asked. "How will we get to Los Angeles?"

"I don't know. Maybe we'll find a ride with someone else, another coyote, a friendly gringo. Norteños generally help, if you can get one to stop."

"We have just three bottles of water," Concha said. "Will that be enough?"

"I've had enough and won't need any more," Guillermo said. "But I suggest we walk a little ways now and try to find some shade to spend the day. Then we can walk again in the evening. Once we get back to the trail, it will be easy. We can make it."

Concha did not think she would drink any more water either. In order for Rosalinda to continue nursing Carlos, the young mother would need it. And poor little Maria Elena would be thirsty, too. They got up and followed Guillermo, backtracking toward the low ridge they had unwittingly crossed during the night. The sun was hot, and Guillermo gave Rosalinda his tejana. From the crest of the ridge, they searched the desolate landscape before them for shade, but there was nothing but greasewood brambles, scraggly mesquite, and occasional lone saguaros.

It was close to noon when they stopped. Guillermo had insisted on backtracking until he found the footprints of the others, confirming they had indeed found the trail. But there was no shade. The blazing sun was directly above them, and there was no place to hide from its relentless rays. Guillermo's lips were swollen. Bareheaded, his face and neck were sunburned. Yet he kept to his word not to consume any more water.

They sat at the base of a greasewood bramble. Concha tried to improvise a shelter by draping her rebozo over the scraggly branches, but it had little effect. The best they could do was try to keep the children and their heads under the meager shelter. Rosalinda draped Carlos's blanket across her shoulder making a tent over the child, but it was hot under it and the infant cried constantly. She nursed him, but worried about how long her milk would last. Concha and Guillermo encouraged her to drink one of the remaining bottles of water.

Rosalina shared some of the water with Maria Elena, who through the morning had remained somber. Guillermo had fashioned a headscarf for the child from his blue bandana, and after they were seated in the sparse shade, Rosalinda took it off and fluffed out the child's curls by running her fingers through her matted hair like a comb.

"Mamá, are we ever going to see Papá?" Maria Elena asked.

Rosalinda paused. She was uncertain of the answer herself. "Yes, mija. We'll see him soon."

"Mamá, are we lost?"

"We were, mija, but Guillermo knows the way, and we're going to be all right."

"Is Yermo taking care of us like Papá?"

"Yes, mija. Just like Papá would if he were here."

"I promise, my pretty," Guillermo joined in, his voice raspy, "I'm never going to let you go until I can put you in your papá's arms."

"You won't leave us again, will you, Yermo?"

"Never."

40

 Guillermo no longer could endure huddling in the thin shade afforded by Concha's rebozo and the scraggly branches and tiny leaves of the greasewood bush. The late afternoon sun beat down on his bare head as he tried to get to his feet, and he fell to his hands and knees. His clumsiness surprised him. He had not had any water since rejoining the group in the early morning, and the grueling walk in the sun with no hat had left him dizzy and sick to his stomach by the time they stopped. As he dozed through the afternoon, he hallucinated, and now he was having trouble thinking straight.

Concha nudged Rosalinda, and the two women struggled to their feet. Carlos seemed to be feverish, but his skin was cold, and they debated whether to cover him or take off his clothing. Despite consuming the last bottle of water, Rosalinda's milk had dried up. Still, she held Carlos to her breast for, when she did not, he cried in a low, rasping sound that worried them and upset Maria Elena.

"Is baby Carlos going to die?" the child asked.

No one answered.

Praying that this march would bring them to the promised highway and rescue, they trudged north along the trail, following the footsteps of the others of their party that had passed this way the night before.

Mostly, they wanted the trek to be over and to find relief from the merciless heat and thirst of the desert. As they walked, their hope grew. This had to be end of their torture. This had to be the way to the highway. Never mind if they were met by coyotes or arrested by la migra. Only a few more hours, and they would be free from the desert.

Throughout the long afternoon, the dry desert air sucked molecules of moisture from their skin. The relentless sun had burned into every part of their bodies not shielded under the makeshift shelter. Grasping the beads one by one, the women prayed on their rosaries, silently, mouths and tongues too dry to repeat the prayers aloud. *Ave María, full of grace. The Lord is with thee. Blessed art thou among women, and blessed is the fruit of thy womb, Jesus. Santa Maria, Madre de Dios, pray for us sinners now and at the hour of our death. Amén.*

As they struggled north on the indistinct trail, the hot sand burning their feet through the thin soles of their shoes, they beseeched the Virgen de Guadalupe, patroness of campesinos; San Cristóbal, patron of travelers; and San Martín de Porres, worker of miracles for the poor. They prayed that Jesus would be merciful to little Carlos, who lapsed into short periods of fretful sleep, only to awaken and resume his dry, at times soundless, cry.

Guillermo and Concha switched off carrying Maria Elena. They had done their best through the afternoon to keep her bare legs and shoulders from being exposed to the sun, but she had suffered burns during the morning's hike that made her miserable.

"I'm thirsty, Mamá," she said, before they had gone very far.

During the afternoon, Rosalinda had shared the last bottle of water with Maria Elena and the last of the saltines. "We don't have any more water, mija," she explained. "None of us have water, not even baby Carlos."

"Does baby Carlos have milk?"

"No, mija, I gave him all I had. I have no more."

"Is baby Carlos going to get well?"

"When we get there, mija, then we will all be better."

"When will we get to where Papá lives?"

"Soon, I hope. That's up to Jesus."

As darkness fell, Guillermo felt they were making good progress. The trail ran northwest, parallel to the base of the mountains, as Guërito had promised. Guillermo was confident that by keeping the dim outline of the mountains to his right, they could continue to follow the trail through the night to the highway and rescue. He did not expect the moon to rise for several more hours, but the stars provided sufficient light for him to make out the mass of the mountain.

After it became fully dark, the route seemed to get easier. It became obvious they were on some sort of cleared road, perhaps a Jeep trail. Instead of struggling through patches of ankle-deep sand, they were walking on a firm surface, and it was easier to follow. They stumbled less into greasewood thickets. Their spirits lifted, but the night air was still and hot and continued to pull moisture from their tired bodies. Guillermo felt it could not be much further and kept the group on their feet, insisting on carrying Maria Elena when Concha expected the child should be traded off to her.

Rosalinda started to lag behind, and Concha, who had been trying to bridge the distance between her and Guillermo, dropped back to her side. The young mother walked in silence, her top opened and Carlos at her breast. Concha could not hear Carlos sucking. Nor could she hear the infant's rasping cry. The two women walked side by side in silence. Concha put her arm around Rosalinda's shoulder. She could feel the younger woman's soft sobs as they trudged through the silent night.

The exhausted walkers did not see the quarter-moon rise behind them and then hang, silver and useless, in the pre-dawn light. They stumbled along until dawn gradually came, and they could see the surface of the desert road. Rosalinda clutched the still body of her infant to her bare breast, fearing to take it away, afraid to acknowledge the awful truth.

Ahead, Guillermo carried Maria Elena, the fitful toddler still clutching her cloth doll. They had walked for hours through the night and still had not come upon the highway. They ached with fatigue, their mouths too dry to talk. They passed in and out of dreams, dozing even as they shuffled one foot ahead of the other. Guillermo dreamed he was home in Jalisco, waking in bed in a soft dawn, the cool, pliant body of his wife at his side, and their young daughter cuddled to his chest.

As he trudged down the dirt road, Guillermo strained to see the end of their journey, to catch a glimpse of the promised highway where they hoped to find rescue. Instead, he saw they were on a road graded through the desert sand, fulfilling some unknown purpose, stretching endlessly before them to the horizon. His vision was blurry; it was as if he were looking through a tunnel. He turned his head, suddenly remembering that the mountain should be to his right. Seeing nothing rising above the flat plain of dunes and greasewood, he wondered why he thought there would be a mountain there.

Confused, Guillermo stopped. Turning slowly around, he saw the dark shapes of Concha and Rosalinda standing in the middle of the dirt road fifty steps behind him. In the distance, far behind them, were the mountains, their slopes still in dark shadow. His head ached. He had trouble with his vision. He looked in the dirt. There were no tracks. He tried to remember why there should be tracks.

Guillermo took several more slow steps and stopped. The women stopped behind him. They had walked all night *away* from the mountains—*toward the west.* Away from the trail that was supposed to lead to the freeway. He squatted on the sandy surface, set the sleepy child on her feet, and cried. But his eyes were dry, his eyelids like sandpaper. His dehydrated body could provide no tears.

The women stood silently as Guillermo came back to them and explained that they had been walking the wrong way. Somehow during the night they had gotten on the wrong trail and were no closer to the highway than before, maybe now further away. Rosalinda did not seem to hear. She still cradled Carlos. She sat down where she stood, in the middle of the dusty road, and gently rocked her dead infant. Concha bent down, touched the little head, and asked God to have mercy. Then she sat in the dirt beside the grieving mother.

41

It was clear now to Concha that the Queen of Cups had indeed been an omen, a sign of death, as had been the Two of Cups at the time of the death of her infants. And more death was to come. In the matter of her own life, she knew there was little she could do. She felt bad for Lupe and Miguel, but Lupe had her own life now, and Miguel had long lived on his own.

Concha had been successful in the life ordained for her in the village by her religion and her family. She had been a good wife and a good mother. The new life she had expected to embark upon at the end of this journey was not as important. True, she would miss her grandchildren. She would miss beginning a new life with Miguel in California. But it was not to be. Despite what Doña Graciela said about the cards, it had not been fated. The Queen of Cups had become her nemesis, clearly trumping the Sun card that had promised success. As had Eve beneath the closed eyes of the Archangel Raphael, Concha had made the wrong choice, and there was not going to be a new beginning for her.

Guillermo and Rosalinda were another matter. They were fine young people who had their whole lives ahead of them. If they died, they would leave halves of families. It was such a shame they could not have met at an earlier time, courted, had a family, and led a full and happy life.

What a father Guillermo had been to Maria Elena. *Lord Jesus, please let the child live*, Concha prayed.

Unable to comprehend the changes in their lives, Maria Elena stood looking at the small body of her dead baby brother, still clutched at her mother's breast. Concha reached for Maria Elena's hand and drew her close.

"Baby Carlos has gone to heaven to live with Jesus," she said in a rasping voice. "He will be all right there. He will be happy."

Tears cut long streaks through the layers of dust caked on the child's face. Her small body heaved with sobs. Concha pulled her into her bosom.

Guillermo squatted on his heels in front of the women. "Our only hope is to go back and follow the tracks of the others," he rasped in a voice so dry and low the women could barely hear him. "But we have to do it in daylight while we can see the tracks."

Rosalinda, grieving her lost child, sat with her head down and was silent.

"Guillermo, we can't go any further," Concha said. "We will never make it walking through the day. You go. You're young, strong. You have a family waiting for you. If you make it, send somebody back for us. We will be here, alongside this trail. We will never survive walking through the day. We would only hold you back. Our only chance is you."

Guillermo silently poked his finger in the dirt.

Rosalinda lifted her head until her feverish eyes met his. "Guillermo, go! Take Maria Elena with you. Don't leave her in this terrible place!"

Concha and Rosalinda did not watch as Guillermo, the child in his arms, started back along the road. After a while, as the sun began its merciless arc into the heavens, Concha struggled to her feet and once again fashioned a lean-to from a thicket of greasewood and her rebozo. She coaxed Rosalinda, still cradling the body of her infant, to sit in its meager shade. Concha took her place beside her.

The two women sat facing south, peering across miles of low dunes and gray-green greasewood toward their homeland, their vision compressed by trauma into a narrow corridor extending directly to their front. They dozed, their minds transposing a thousand miles of empty space, and dreamed of their families. Had they looked up, they would have seen the harbingers of death, buzzards, circling in the sky above them.

They shifted occasionally through the blistering hot day, trying to stay within the slender band of shade afforded by the rebozo, draped across the scraggily grey branches of the greasewood bush. The relentless thirst of the dry desert air sucked the little remaining moisture within their bodies through their skin and the membranes of their nostrils, eyes, mouths, and throats. In the harsh heat, their hearts and lungs struggled to get more blood to the surface of their skin to substitute for the cooling effect of perspiration. They panted despite their inactivity.

Between periods of half-consciousness, the women dreamt, but their dreams were interlaced with hallucinations. They prayed on their rosaries—*Madre de Dios, deliver us from evil now and at the hour of our death.* Darkness came, but there was little relief from the oppressive heat.

In the morning, Concha awoke to the sound of chirping birds. She saw a quail and a pair of doves. Then she saw a lake with sparkling blue water surrounded by palm trees as she had seen from the window of the bus coming down from the mountains in Nayarit. Miguel was standing on the shore with Lupe and Richard. Guillermo was there, smiling and handsome, holding Maria Elena by her hand. The Queen of Cups sat on her throne, floating on the water out from the shore, smiling and waving to her. They called to her, and Concha got up and walked down to the edge of the water. She took off her clothes, no one minded, and folding her skirt, her blouse, and her petticoat, laid them carefully in a pile on the sand. She placed her underwear on top, weighting the pile down with her shoes, carefully turning the soles up. She stood for a moment looking down at her depleted breasts and at her weathered hands resting on the taught, light-colored skin of her round belly. Then she waded into the lake and felt the cool, soothing water rise on her torso. She lunged forward, splashing and rolling over in the water, laughing in pleasure as the cool water soothed her tormented body.

42

By midmorning, Lupe and Miguel had long finished the breakfast of huevos rancheros she had fixed, and they sat at the Formica table in her kitchen drinking coffee. Four days had passed since Miguel had helped Concha and her companions into the coyote's van in Tijuana, and they still had heard nothing. Concha had not appeared at Lupe's house on Saturday afternoon as the coyote had promised. There had been no phone call explaining a delay, not even a call from the coyote demanding more money as Richard suggested might happen.

It was now Wednesday, and they knew they must do something, but whom could they call? Richard had called the sheriff's office in Yuma Monday morning but had been referred to the border patrol. Lupe and Miguel urged him not to make more calls. How would they explain? A call to law enforcement might endanger Concha; she was in the hands of smugglers. But the border patrol might be the only ones able to help if Concha were in trouble, Richard urged.

There were so many possibilities, so many unknowns. Lupe and Miguel had gone to Mass each morning and prayed for Concha's safe return, and Lupe had kept a votive candle lit in front of the statue of the Virgen de Guadalupe on the side table in their living room. They were at their wit's end, filled with doubts. Hidden beneath their worry was the guilt neither dared express for fear it would lead to recrimination from the other.

Richard had left the house early in the morning to pick up his landscaping crew, but unexpectedly, they heard his truck pull into the driveway. The kitchen door opened and Richard, grim faced, pushed into the kitchen clutching a newspaper.

Lupe gasped. "Richard, something bad has happened!"

Still standing, Richard unfolded the front page and haltingly translated the English words into Spanish. Lupe leapt to his side and tried to follow the story over his shoulder.

> *TODDLER SURVIVES DESERT HORROR*
>
> *A child was found alive near the dead body of a man in the desert east of Yuma, Ariz., by U.S. Border Patrol agents Monday afternoon, less than a mile from Interstate 8. After a further search, on Tuesday morning, the bodies of two women and an infant were found on a desert trail eight miles away. Authorities believe they were members of the same party and were illegal migrants attempting to cross the U.S. border from Mexico. Temperatures in the area exceeded 120 degrees on Monday.*
>
> *The child was taken to the Yuma Medical Center where she was listed in critical condition. A medical center spokesperson said the child was able to give her name and tell nurses that she was 3 years old.*

Sobbing, convulsing, Lupe collapsed against Richard crushing the newspaper between them.

Seated at the table, Miguel stiffened, his face stony.

43

Lexie was not surprised when, out of the corner of her eye, she spotted Miguel climb onto his stool at the far end of the crowded counter. She kept her back turned while she refreshed the coffee in the cup of a local grower she knew as Jake and then methodically topped off the half-empty cups of the other diners at the counter.

She had seen her husband early one morning as he walked to one of the labor buses that loaded at the curb on the opposite side of the street, his eyes avoiding the café. On the mornings that followed, although she tried not to, she kept an eye out for him. At supper one evening, her son mentioned he had passed Miguel on the street on his way home from the high school. Neither had spoken.

It had been two months since Miguel had left her, and Lexie had not gotten past his sudden departure. She had hoped their marriage would lead to happiness for them both, but she was forced to admit that Miguel had never considered himself married to her. She tried to ascribe the loftiest of motives to their union, but such thoughts were mocked by the memory of their hasty ceremony at the wedding chapel in Yuma and the knowledge that he married her to get immigration papers.

Still, she had missed him, and despite her efforts to suppress such feelings, each of the sightings had rekindled hope that he would come back. He was living in the camp, apparently, which meant that Concha was not with him. She must be staying with their daughter in El Monte, Lexie reasoned. She could not bring herself to concede that the woman, until recently so far away in Mexico, was his real wife. She preferred to think of Concha as a long-abandoned common-law wife.

But the jolt of Miguel's leaving made her cautious about resuming their relationship. Lexie allowed her pragmatism to take the upper hand, the same practical sense of survival that had enabled her to walk away from her first husband, a man who had, in every way but his sporadic visits to her bed for sex, abandoned her and their infant son.

She had no reason to hope that, if Miguel came back, there would not be a next time. When it happened again, her suffering could only be worse. *How many times could the tree be bent before it would break?* Lexie asked herself, exasperated with the side of her that sought to catch a glimpse of him each morning.

Unable to ignore Miguel any longer, Lexie walked the length of the counter and poured the lukewarm remains from her coffee pot into his empty cup. He did not look up, and she was surprised to see his haunted look. He was unshaven, unwashed, and smelled of alcohol. Working in the café, she was used to men who did not shave before they went to the field and inebriates who, at any hour of the day or night, reeked of drink. But, Miguel had been neither. Something was clearly wrong.

"Would you like to order?" she asked, steeling herself to treat her former lover like any of the other diners but knowing that her relationship with Miguel was no secret to the regulars at the counter. She prayed there would be no banter about it today.

Without looking up, Miguel shook his head, no.

During the next half-hour, Lexie refilled his cup twice. Busy with other customers, she had ample excuse not to stop and ask him how he was or what he was up to. At 7:00 a.m., the labor buses across the street pulled away. She was surprised he remained on his stool, but she filled his cup again. Then, about eight thirty, after the farmers left and the local merchants started to arrive, she turned around, and he was gone.

That evening, Miguel appeared at her door.

He is still my husband, Lexie tried to assure herself as she held open the door, and the man she had slept with for over five years stepped across the threshold into the small white bungalow. Neither spoke.

"Would you like to sit down?" Lexie asked, pulling back a chair at the kitchen table. She was shocked at his dirty clothes. He looked as if he had been sleeping in the fields. "Are you hungry?"

Miguel nodded.

Days and nights of self-doubts and recriminations faded from Lexie's memory, eclipsed by concern for the disheveled man who once was, perhaps still was, her lover. She heated up the leftover stew from the meal she had served her son and herself earlier in the evening.

"Are you working?" she asked.

"No."

"Are you staying at the camp?"

"The boss won't let me."

"When is the last time you worked?" she asked cautiously.

"Last week."

"What happened?"

Bit by bit, through the long evening, during which neither moved from their place at the Formica table, Lexie patiently coaxed Miguel through the painful recollection of his reunion with Concha; her inability to get the permiso promised by the fixer, the failed attempt to cross the border that night, his bargain with the coyote with the gnarled ear, and finally, tragically, the deaths of Concha, Rosalinda, and the infant in the Arizona desert, deaths that he blamed on himself. Late in the night, numbed by the pathos of the story and the extent of his hurt, Lexie put Miguel to bed on her couch.

Two days later, Lexie ran into Joe Rodriguez on the street. "I haven't seen you, Joe. Why don't you come in for breakfast anymore?"

"Well, Alice has been feeding me at home these last couple weeks."

"Joe, do you suppose Miguel could come back to work?"

"That depends, Lexie," the crew boss said. "Where is he now? Is he back with you?"

"Yes, he's home," she said. "Joe, I know why you laid him off. And I'm not asking you to take him back if you don't want to. But he's had an awful hard knock, and I'm trying to get him back on his feet."

"God bless you, Lexie. I'd like to help. He was a good worker before. It is a little slow right now though, and with all that drinking, I can't."

"I think it's just temporary, Joe. I don't know how much you know, but he lost a relative out in the desert who was trying to cross the border. He isn't going to get it out of himself lying around on my couch all day."

"Lexie, work might help, but I got pruning coming up, and we'll be doing Thompsons at that. You've got to select the best canes, well-browned wood with plump buds about three inches or so apart. He's got to be sober."

"I can't promise you that, Joe. So I guess I'd better leave it go for now," she said, starting to turn on down the street.

"Lexie!" Joe caught her arm. "One other thing you might not know. I had to kick him out of the camp because he kept pickin' fights. He gets mean when he's drunk. I think you ought to be aware."

When Lexie arrived home that afternoon, Miguel was on the couch watching a *telenovela*. He made no effort to hide the pint bottle of tequila on his lap. She wanted to tell him about her conversation with Joe, that if he were sober he could go back to work, but the sight of the bottle stopped her. Before she left for work that morning, she had been careful to remove all the liquor from the house.

"Did you go out today, Miguel?"

"I went down to the store."

Lexie wondered where he got the money. It was pretty obvious he had come back because he was broke, had no place to stay and nothing to eat. But now Lexie feared there was something else. He needed money for booze. She went into the bedroom and retrieved her purse from the closet, the large black one where she kept her extra cash between paydays. She thought twenty dollars was missing. Her first thought was to confront him, ask if he had taken money, but the bottle in his lap answered that. She sat down on the bed for a moment. Perhaps it was best just to let it go for now, see what he was going to do, what effect being back in her life would have.

As days went by, Lexie continued to discover money missing from her purse. She emptied it, carrying the money in her wallet, but the next night her son complained that money was missing from his desk drawer. Thinking she could at least help Miguel preserve a small part of his self-esteem, she started leaving a five-dollar bill on the table when she left for work in the morning. But she wondered how long she could keep that up.

Miguel spent most of the day on the couch or sitting alone out in the backyard. Some evenings, he simply passed out, too drunk to eat dinner. His drunkenness began to annoy Lexie. Her son started going over to friends' houses instead of working on his homework in the kitchen or watching TV with her in the living room in the evenings. Lexie could not blame him, and she decided she had to try to bring matters with Miguel to a head.

"Miguel, let's talk," she said one morning as she set out his breakfast on her day off. "I know why you're drinking, but you can't keep on like this. Being drunk all day solves nothing. It's not going to bring anybody back to life."

Miguel shoved his plate away and, in his stocking feet, stormed out of the house. He spent the rest of the day sitting in the plastic lawn chair in the backyard, his back turned to the house.

Lexie began to think that maybe she was part of the problem. She hated drunks and resented Miguel's drinking, making it hard for them to communicate even on the chance occasions during the week that she found him lucid. She wanted him to come to church with her, talk to Father McDermott at Sacred Heart. She thought maybe the priest could assist, but to get Miguel there, persuade him that it was in his interest to get help, she had to be able to talk to him.

It occurred to Lexie that maybe she was the one holding back. She had not taken him back into her bed yet. He continued to sleep on the couch where he spent most of the day slouched down with a pint bottle of tequila in his hand, finally slumping over unconscious in the flickering blue-grey light of the TV. Maybe if she reached out to Miguel completely, slept with him, he would respond to her. It would be a chance, she thought, perhaps her last chance.

That evening while Miguel still was awake, she sat down beside him. He was watching *Hill Street Blues*. After her son came home and she saw the light go out under his door, she went to her bedroom and took her black negligee from her underwear drawer—the one Miguel liked. Fearing his eyes would be closed before she got back, she hurriedly undressed and slipped the smooth nylon garment over her naked body.

As she stepped back into the living room, Lexie whistled a bar from *The Stripper*, a movie they had watched together the previous spring. Recognizing the notes, Miguel turned his head and stared at her in the flickering light. He grinned. It was the first smile she had seen since he had come back. She took his hand and helped him as he rose unsteadily from the couch.

In the darkness of the bedroom, standing at the side of her bed, Lexie unbuttoned Miguel's shirt and let it fall to the floor. Then she unbuckled his belt and opened his zipper, kneeling to slide his jeans and jockey shorts down over his lean hips. His penis was limp. It must be the effect of all that alcohol, she thought. Hoping to bring it to life, she caressed him, but to no avail. She felt his body tense, and he started to back away.

"Relax, honey," Lexie murmured. "I know just what to do."

The first blow caught Lexie on her temple. Her head snapped to the side, enough so that the second landed squarely on the center of her face. Lexie screamed as she slumped to the floor, her nose and mouth filling with warm blood. Before she lost consciousness, she heard the bedroom door crash open and her son's outraged curse.

"I'm sorry for calling you so late at night. Is this Lupe Benavidez?" Lexie said pausing to permit the sleepy voice on the other end to respond. "I don't know how to tell you this—I'm a friend of your father—and I wish there was some other way. But you need to come and get him." Again a pause. "No, he's not hurt—at least not physically—but if you don't come and get him tonight, the sheriff will, and then he's going to go to jail."

44

"Papá, listen to me," Lupe pleaded. She clung to the edge of the half-opened bedroom door, fearful that what she had to say would trigger another bout of his rage. "Richard says you can't stay here anymore. You have to leave in the morning. The police have come twice now. If they have to come again, they'll put you in jail. Just like the officer told you tonight."

Miguel sat on the edge of his bed. Sitting up made him dizzy, and he resented being awakened. Peering into the light flooding in from the hallway, he could make out only the outline of Lupe's head and shoulders. He was unsure what she was saying. Did she say he'd have to leave? *No! Richard shouldn't have pushed me*, he told himself self-righteously. *He shouldn't have tried to grab my bottle. It's none of Richard's business if I drink.*

The events earlier in the night shifted in the fog that gripped Miguel's mind. Of course, Lupe would take her husband's side, but how fair was that? *Just like that cow Lexie had to listen to her stupid son and put me out of her house.* Miguel did not want to think, let alone sort anything out, right now. Why could not people leave him alone? He just wanted Lupe to close the door and let him sleep. He would deal with leaving later. She would see his side of it in the morning.

It had been two weeks since Lupe and Richard had collected Miguel from Lexie's house in Lamont. The two women stood a polite distance apart under the light above Lexie's front door—Lupe, her belly swollen with her soon-to-arrive child, Lexie, her face covered by a bandage after her nose had been set at the emergency room in Bakersfield; Lupe wiping away tears, Lexie, her arms crossed. Each woman fearful that touching the other—an embrace was out of the question—would somehow mean approval and make real what to each was a nightmare.

In the cab of Richard's truck on the two-hour drive back over the Grapevine Pass to El Monte, Miguel sat slumped between Lupe and Richard. No one spoke. Lupe, dabbed at her eyes with the damp, crumpled handkerchief she alternatively twisted around her fingers. Turned low, the radio played *banda* from a far-away all-night station. They arrived home at dawn.

In the days following, Richard tried to put Miguel to work in his landscaping crew, but by midmorning, Miguel would start searching for a drink. Once, while pruning a rhododendron out of Richard's view, Miguel slipped away to a nearby liquor store and bought a pint of tequila. Richard and Lupe got rid of all the alcohol in their house and tried keeping him away from booze by not giving him money. Their efforts simply provoked his rage.

Miguel could not control the anger that welled within him, ready to explode without warning. The picture of Concha, Rosalinda, the baby, and the little girl, squeezed together on the seat, innocent, trusting him, flashed through his mind. Day and night, the grating metallic thump as he had slammed the side door of the coyote's van shut rang through his head. He had even tested the latch to make sure it would hold. It was as if he had slammed the lid closed on their coffins.

It was not enough for Miguel to admit that he had been a fool. He probed dark questions about his character and his manhood. He had known the dangers the women would face in the desert; he had faced them himself. It was no place for women, especially for women with children. He knew the venality of the coyotes; they were in it simply for the money and did not care whether people died. He knew the likes of Eliza, the arranger. He had let Concha be swayed by Doña Graciela, whom he knew was a *bruja*, a witch.

Miguel reminded himself repeatedly that he had chosen the coyote, he had arranged for the party to cross through the desert in Arizona. He could have prevented the tragedy by reversing course at any number of points, but he had not. Trusting him, Concha and Rosalinda had simply gone along. *What sort of man would recklessly send women and children to their deaths?* he asked himself. Miguel could not live with the answer.

Miguel's remorse prevented him from thinking clearly enough to make a solid connection, but an instinct for the truth sparked guilt over his adultery with Lexie. He had been unfaithful to Concha, who had been steadfastly loyal to him. He had wanted to make amends, but he had been too weak to do what was called for, honor Concha again as his wife. Instead, she had been provoked to make the journey to California alone because of his absence, a journey he had known she had little chance of completing.

After Concha's death, Miguel had at first resisted going to Lexie, but in the end, physical and emotional survival drove him back to his former lover. It was as if it had been foreordained and he could not prevent it. He was cold, hungry, craving alcohol on the evening he stood on Lexie's doorstep and knocked. Although he tried hard to deny it, he was desperate for her to help him with his guilt and console his anguish.

Miguel had been thankful Lexie had taken him back, but in the end, he resented her for it. His guilt overpowered the pleasant memories of the years she had cared for him. His returning forced him to admit that he had become dependent on her, and he hated himself for being needy. Living in Lexie's house, beholden to her for even his green card, reminded him of how little he was in charge of his life, and he felt emasculated. It served him right that he no longer could get it up, he thought, but he should not have hit Lexie. His impotency was his own fault.

Lexie's final rejection of him simply added to Miguel's self-hate, and at Lupe's house, he continued to attempt to shelter himself in a drunken stupor. When Richard stopped paying him, he cobbled pocket change from the other workers on the crew until he had enough to sneak away and buy a half-pint. But despite the palliative, the volcano within him could not be held in check.

In the morning after his latest blowup in Lupe's house, she served her father breakfast. Neither spoke. Finally, she said, "I'll help you pack your things."

Miguel did not respond. What could he say? Lupe was his daughter, but this was not his house. What could he do now but go back to Mexico? He was still angry with Richard. Miguel was not hurting anybody by drinking.

"Papá, I love you, and I've tried to help you," Lupe said when she dropped him off at the bus terminal in downtown El Monte. "Richard has tried to help. But I can't have you bringing tequila into the house. I'm afraid for what will happen when my baby arrives."

Early in the morning on El Dia de los Muertos in Piedra Gorda, Miguel, Genaro, and Genaro's wife, Magdalena, went to the cementerio. They set up a small altar, a folding tray table they brought from their casita, and lit two candles, one for each of Miguel and Concha's two children who died as infants. They decorated the altar with white flowers and set out a breakfast for the children of porridge, fruit, and glasses of water. Miguel arranged toys made of wood and clay, including the little carved dog that had been in the family for generations. Then they sat and waited for the children to come.

As the morning progressed, they remembered what they could of the infants and told stories they thought the children would enjoy. Magdalena and Genaro sang "De Colores." Miguel mostly hummed along.

> *Canta el gallo, canta el gallo* with his kiri, kiri, kiri, kiri, kiri
> And the cluck hen with her cara, cara, cara, cara, cara,
> And the baby chicks
> And the baby chicks with their *pio pio pio pio pio de colores*
> And so must love be of many bright colors
> To make my heart cry

De muchos colores
Me gustan a mi.

The verse, which Miguel had heard Concha sing to their children many times, made him melancholy. He had vowed not to drink that day—Concha would not like to see him drunk—but without alcohol, his head ached. He wanted to believe her spirit was happy, as their culture and religion said, but missing her and his guilt left him feeling quite a different way. He could not decide whether he felt morose because he had not had a drink that morning or because of anxiety over Concha's imminent visit.

At noontime, they cleared away the meal and the toys for the children, who were leaving to return to their place, and prepared for the arrival of the adults. They covered the graves and the headstones with marigolds and replaced the white candles with black. They placed grinning skull-masks of the dead, made of sugar, on the altar, and put out *calabaza,* pumpkin cooked in brown sugar, *Torta de Muertos* with red frosting, and chicken with mole.

Throughout their preparations, Miguel's anxiety grew. He expected the souls of his parents to be present, but they did not worry him. What happened in life was simply la vida and of no concern to the dead. The expected visit by Concha was quite a different matter, however, and although he missed her greatly, he was frightened by the thought of being in her presence again. From her vantage point in the spirit world, she would know about his infidelity, how it had affected every decision he made and led to her death. Fears about what she must think consumed him.

At midafternoon, Genaro and Magdalena left, promising to return for the all-night vigil. Miguel remained, sitting alone beside Concha's grave. After a while, he took off his hat. The late autumn sun felt good, and the breeze played with loose strands of his graying hair, which had gone uncut since Concha's death.

"Concha," Miguel called tentatively, grown anxious after what seemed to be a long time. "Concha!" he called, louder this time. The air was silent except for the murmur of voices carried on the wind from families gathered at other gravesites.

"Concha. Are you here?" he asked. "Can you hear me?

"Concha, how can you forgive me?" He decided to forge ahead. "Concha, I've been unfaithful to you. I have been the cause of all your suffering—the cause of your death. I've been worse than a fool. How can you forgive me?"

Water began to well in Miguel's eyes, and a tear escaped running in a rivulet down his weather-burnt cheek.

"I was not there for you, Concha. I could have helped you with the truth from Doña Graciela. We could have found a better way. Maybe not have tried to go to el norte but stayed in Piedra Gorda. I could have stayed home. Lupe and her baby could have come to us—as it should be. She could have visited us in our casita here. I was such a fool to abandon you."

Miguel took a deep breath. "Concha, I am so ashamed of my infidelity to you. All my time in el norte, I thought of you, missed you. I never meant to leave you—the marriage was only to fool la migra. I never meant to leave you."

There was no answer, just the breeze and the muted laughter of families celebrating on nearby gravesites. He suspected they were mocking him, and he felt alone and overwhelmed. If Concha had come, she was choosing to ignore him, he thought. It was worse than if she were merely angry with him. In despair, Miguel slumped forward, holding his head in his hands while the sun continued its journey to the west and began to sink below the far horizon. He wished for a drink, but he feared quitting his vigil and offending Concha further.

Miguel's mind was preoccupied with yet another list of his sins when at last Concha spoke to him.

I know all these things, Miguel. The voice came from nowhere, but everywhere, as if it were in his head.

"Concha!" Miguel gasped, straightening up.

I can see everything that has happened to us—the good things and the bad. There is nothing we can do about what has occurred, Miguel.

But I am happy in my new place. One day, you will be here too, and we will both be happy.

Do you remember Lupe's baptism? We waited until you came back from el norte, and then we had the feast. It is like that now, Miguel. You have to be where you are because that's what life has ordained. But, one day, you will join me, and we will feast again.

"Concha! Concha! How can you forgive me?" The words came in a rush. Miguel did not want her to leave before he had a chance to make amends. "I am so sorry for all the awful things I've done. How can you forgive me for leaving you alone with the coyote? Letting you go into the desert to die? How horrible that must have been. How can I atone? I can't work. I've become a drunkard, and Lupe won't let me stay in her house. Concha, what can I do?"

If you want to find solace on earth, it can only be through what the living do, and you might not find peace at all. Only a few do. When you get here, Miguel, in the place of the dead, you will find that all is forgiven. What a wonderful place this is.

"But, I can't go on living like this."

You must. Ask the Virgencita to help you, Miguel. Make a peregrinación *to her* basílica.

45

"Miss Janice?" Maria Elena waited at the side of Janice's desk in the third-grade classroom that had emptied for the day, a pink Minnie Mouse backpack dangling at her feet. The child wore a frilly white dress, tied in the back with a bow, and black patent-leather shoes, attire she had worn on all the days she had come to school. Her short, dark hair was held neatly in place by two pink barrettes.

"Miss Janice, I'm not going to come to this school anymore."

Janice had grown attached to the child, and she felt her shoulders slump. Maria Elena was unusually bright, and her love of books and reading quickly endeared her to the teacher. She discovered that Maria Elena was able to read far above the third-grade level and advanced her to a sixth-grade anthology of children's classics.

Janice had little reason to expect that the child would remain in her classroom for the full year. Many students in her bilingual education classroom stayed only a few months, leaving when their parents moved on to other jobs or returned to homes in Mexico for a winter or a season. She sought to conceal her disappointment by continuing to shuffle the stack of turned-in work she was readying to take home that evening.

Beyond her lyrical name, Janice had known very little about her new third-grader. One morning soon after school started in the fall, Maria

Elena had simply appeared in her classroom. The child did not chat about herself, her family, or her past as most children her age did, and Janice asked no probing questions of her. Far too often with students at Mountain View Elementary, the answers contained troubling details she could do nothing about.

Maria Elena was quick to pick up the English words and phrases Janice taught in the classroom's bilingual setting, but it seemed to Janice that the child's lack of socialization was holding her back from fluency in spoken English. The little girl was shy about making friends, although, with Janice's encouragement, several of her classmates had tried.

On the days she came to school—some weeks, she appeared in the classroom only once or twice—Maria Elena stayed in during recess and lunch. With Janice's permission, she went to the school library or browsed through books on the classroom's bookshelves. She liked to talk with Janice about books she had read.

"Miss Janice, do you think Jonas and Gabriel get released?" Maria Elena had asked one day, hoping to start up a conversation with her teacher about *The Giver*, a book by Lois Lowery that recently had been translated into Spanish.

"They might," Janice had replied. The novel's ambiguous ending prompted speculation. "They had rules, and Jonas and Gabriel were no longer fitting in. Do you think being released always meant a bad thing?"

"It could mean like going to heaven," the little girl had replied. "Or, it could be like they wouldn't be little kids anymore and could choose what they wanted to be."

The child's frequent absences, however, had drawn Janice's concern, and she wondered about the little girl's parents. She was always well groomed when she came to school, but Janice could tell in little ways that she did not have the help of a mother. She discovered that Maria Elena did not come to school on the bus. Attempting to catch a glimpse of a parent on afternoons she was out front on bus duty, Janice kept watch on the vehicle turn-in. Occasionally, she spotted Maria Elena climbing into a small, candy-apple green car. Loud Mexican rock music throbbed from the car's hyper-loud speakers, causing Janice to worry about the child's hearing.

Janice enlisted the aid of Henrietta Sanchez, one of the school's two community liaisons. Herself a teacher, Henrietta worked with parents of Mountain View Elementary pupils. Many of them were from rural Mexico and never had the opportunity to attend school beyond the fourth grade.

"Maria Elena lives with an aunt and uncle," Henrietta told Janice after class one afternoon a week later. "Both are young, and they don't have children of their own yet. The uncle works in construction, and his wife at a fast-food restaurant."

"What do they say about her absences?" Janice enquired of the caseworker.

"They don't live near a bus stop, and they are only able to bring her when the uncle is not working that day or the aunt is not on shift. They're young, immigrants, neither of them high school graduates and, I took it, not too happy to be burdened with someone else's child."

"Where are Maria Elena's parents?"

"The mother is dead. The father, the young man's brother, works farm labor and is up in the Delano area pruning grapevines. The couple is taking care of Maria Elena because the father can't while he's living in a farm labor camp. They were pretty close-mouthed, but I took it the mother died traumatically."

"Maybe the mother was illegal?"

"Maybe, but they say the child has a green card. The uncle says her father got his in the amnesty in 1987."

"So what does Maria Elena do home alone while her aunt and uncle are at work?"

"She watches TV and reads a lot. The father sends her books. That is unusual, but perhaps it's the one bright spot in the picture. They say she watches *Plaza Sésamo* every morning."

"So why can't they make arrangements to get her to school?"

"I tried to work through some suggestions with them, but there wasn't a lot of interest. Two things, I think. They're young, don't want a lot of responsibility, and feel that they are already burdened just housing the child. The other, they see Maria Elena reading and watching educational TV programs; possibly, the child is already reading at a level better than they can. They may believe the child is already doing better than they did and doesn't need school. I explained the law to them, and it just led to more resentment of their situation. So, I don't know what you can expect, Janice."

The following week, Maria Elena was in Janice's classroom four days.

Janice looked into the girl's serious brown eyes. "Why won't you be coming to school anymore, Maria Elena?" Janice asked.

"Because my papá is coming to get me, and I'm going to live with him."

"Where will you live?"

"We're going to go to El Centro. My papá says there is a lot of work there. He's going to pick carrots and lettuce."

Janice's mind raced back to her youth. Her father grew vegetables in the Imperial Valley and hired crews of itinerant farmworkers to harvest them—Mexicans, Filipinos, faceless people wearing large straw hats and multiple layers of clothing, bent over long green rows of lettuce or carrots, strangers whose lives she never thought about, until she met Javier.

Then, one sunny afternoon sitting with Javier on the front steps of her house, Janice listened, enthralled, as the handsome, brown-skinned boy, the son of farmworker parents, told her of his dreams. Her world suddenly opened. The people who harvested her father's crops and their children had dreams, she discovered, aspirations for lives of their own. The realization ignited in her a desire to work with the children of migrants and led her to finish degrees in Spanish and education at the University of Southern California.

In a time of great social shift in the country, Janice wanted to be part of bringing about change. She settled on a career as a bilingual elementary school teacher. Some of the children who came to her classroom were not fluent readers in either English or Spanish, and learning to read in one language or the other by the end of third grade was vital. But Janice sought to do even more for her highly transient students. A love of reading, she knew, could be the spark that kept her pupils learning even after they left Mountain View school, and she did her best to instill it in them.

Farmworkers had a natural right to live, work, and raise children knowing they could partake of the wealth that they helped create, she earnestly felt. But by the mid-eighties, improvements in the lives of the migrants seemed to have stopped.

César Chavez was no longer organizing them. Agriculture had become corporate owned and profit driven, enabled by the constant waves of new immigrants. Farmworkers could experience the American dream only vicariously—on TV if they had one.

It troubled Janice that most were illegal immigrants, as if that were some sort of justification for denying migrant families a decent livelihood and the opportunity to educate their children. For the children of farmworkers in America, having and achieving a dream were concepts far removed from one another. Beyond farm work, the jobs available to an under-educated young adult were low pay and dead end, not the better manufacturing jobs that earlier generations had moved into. Many youths simply stopped trying to find work and joined gangs.

Janice worried about what Maria Elena's future would hold. *There are some kids you want to help because they try so much to help themselves,* she thought, *and she is one of those.*

"I hope you'll have the chance to continue in school, Maria Elena. Have you talked to your father about that? You're a very good student and a very strong reader. The best in the class."

"I want to go to school. I hope someone will be able to take me."

"Soon, you'll be old enough to go by yourself, and you must. Please promise me you will."

"I will. I want to be a teacher when I grow up. Like you, Miss Janice."

46

"Hello, Javier."

Javier stared at the receiver. He had not heard from Janice in months. In the six years since his father had died, their contact, which was usually initiated by him, had been sporadic, occasional, just enough to keep in touch. He carried a flame for Janice, but she had kept him at arm's length, leaving him at times morose and heartbroken. He had finally decided he had to get over her. He wondered what was up with her call, and he could not fully suppress his hope.

"Janice! What's happening?"

"Well, of course I want to know how you are. But I have a favor to ask of you, too."

"First the favor," Javier laughed, thankful to avoid, at least for a moment, the sometimes painful introspection their talks often triggered.

"Javier, I had this very bright little girl in my class, Maria Elena. She was a wonderful reader, but very alone. Her mother is dead, and she was taken out of school to go live with her father who is a Mexican farmworker. He's supposed to be down in the Imperial Valley picking winter vegetables. I'm really worried about her. Mountain View hasn't gotten a request for a transcript from the new school as they normally would when a child transfers.

"Javier, I just can't bear the thought that she's not in school—she's such a bright child, and she's special to me. I want to find her. Is there any way you can help me?"

"Oh! And because I'm a Mexican, I'd know exactly where to find her?" He flashed. Javier was astonished that he had delivered the rebuke, but at the same time, he felt an odd sense of satisfaction. There was silence on the other end of the line.

"Javier ...?"

"Janice, I didn't mean that."

"No, perhaps you did. Maybe that's what's been between us, what is keeping us apart."

Again there was a long silence.

"Javier?"

"Yes ..."

"Let's open this up. Let's not run from this; let's talk about it."

"Yes ..." Javier paused. "That's probably a good idea."

Javier believed ethnicity should not be an issue in his relationship with Janice, denied that it was, and his outburst surprised him. During their long courtship, they often talked about their attraction for each other, and clearly, they were in love. But suddenly, Javier was forced to admit the thought that each might be different was in his mind—like a bothersome fly in the living room.

Javier was never entirely sure why he had not proposed to the girl of his dreams. What was he afraid of? She had chided him for lacking his father's courage. Was it true? After lengthy self-interrogations, he had concluded that it was. But, why?

Certainly, his being a Latino was not an issue with Janice. But was it with him, he wondered. And if so, how? It seemed to be about children. How would Janice feel about a mixed-race child? He admired her dedication to educating Spanish-speaking children, but how would she feel about one of her own—his child?

His deep-down fear was rooted in how he felt about himself, Javier concluded. Certainly enough had happened in his life—his incarceration, his lack of education, his blue-collar job—to justify his harsh self-evaluation. Nothing about his background seemed to bother Janice, but

Javier was convinced an inequality existed that could be exacerbated by marrying an Anglo and having mixed-race children.

Javier had toyed with discussing his fears with Father Jaime—they had kept in touch over the years, and he was just a few hours' drive away—but he had never acted on it. Suddenly, it occurred to him that now might be the time, and the priest might be able to help locate Janice's student as well.

"Janice, I think we can talk about us and get help finding Maria Elena, too. Do you remember Father Jaime at Our Lady of Guadalupe in El Centro? I think he can help—all of us."

Father Jim Fogarty hung up the phone. He had been Javier's pastor and friend for over twenty years, ever since his parents had brought the troubled youth to the rectory one summer night and asked for help. He was with Javier during the lengthy trials as he testified as a witness. The priest remained in contact, visiting Javier at the youth facility in Paso Robles on every trip north. He said the funeral mass for Javier's father, Ohscar, and at the funeral he had met Janice. The priest mused at how efficiently God's ministry propagated. The troubled boy he helped years ago now was seeking to help others, a child and her father.

Over the years, as increasing numbers of migrants and their families came to the Imperial Valley, the priest had come to think of his calling as a ministry without borders. In truth, it was. Concerned primarily with saving souls, it did not matter to Father Jaime whether or not the person was in the United States legally. A border did not bar a soul from heaven. From his upbringing in a poor neighborhood in Ireland, he knew that his flock had needs in this world, too, and he did what he could to help.

During the winter months, large numbers of migrants, like Maria Elena's father, moved into the valley to harvest vegetables and melons. Father Jaime was at his busiest, but it was also a time that stoked his energy. He knew Janice's quest to find Maria Elena would be fraught with problems, but he took on the task eagerly, anxious to help old friends and concerned because it involved a child.

The children of migrant families often lived in a twilight zone between the law and reality, he had explained to Janice and Javier during the call. Births invariably were recorded, their parents known, but the children often were raised in informal arrangements, dictated by a birth family's economic situation and the child's physical presence north or south of the border. As much as possible, informal "parents," *padrinos,* avoided dealing with authorities.

From what Janice had said, it appeared that Maria Elena's real father was raising the child. That also presented problems. It was difficult enough for a farmworker couple to raise children, feed them, house them, and keep them in school, let alone a single father. If the child were not in school, the father would want to keep her out of sight of county social workers. He likely would try to conceal the child from Janice, as well, he told them.

Then there was the question of what to do once the girl was found. Even within families, solutions could be complicated. Father Jaime had little doubt that Janice and Javier would want to do what was best for Maria Elena, but it remained to be seen what that would be. If they tried to force the father to put her in school, the father might simply move on, taking the child with him.

Taking Maria Elena from the father was almost out of the question, Father Jaime cautioned them. It was difficult enough in any circumstance, but nearly impossible in the highly mobile existence of migratory laborers who never were around to be served papers and could not be counted upon to appear in court if they were. The border was simply too close, too convenient a barrier to legal process.

Still, it sounded to Father Jaime, and Janice agreed, that the father cared for his daughter, and he had at least nurtured her by buying books and clothing. He had tried to keep her in school by putting her up with the brother, but the arrangement apparently had not lasted for long. The father might be willing to work something out, Father Jaime suggested. Janice said that Maria Elena was welcome to stay with her, but the priest cautioned that such a plan was premature. He would do his best to find the girl, he promised.

Father Jaime had not seen a single father with a nine-year-old daughter attending Sunday Mass at Our Lady of Guadalupe or the mission churches in Holtville and Brawley. Janice had given him the name of Maria Elena's father. That would be a start, the priest thought. He picked up the phone again and dialed Joe Rodriquez, a board member of his congregation who had been a labor contractor in the valley for over forty years.

"Joe, I'm looking for a father who has his young daughter with him, a single guy," the priest said after the usual small talk. "He's supposed to have come down here about a month ago to harvest winter vegetables. Have you heard of him in any of your crews? His name is Hector Gomez."

"No, I can't say that I have," the contractor said. "A single father wouldn't bring his daughter along unless he had no other choice. And, he probably wants to be pretty private about it. I got four crews going, two in lettuce and two in melons. I'd know it if he was in my camp, but not all the men stay with me these days. A lot of them with families stay up there in Duroville. I'll keep my ears open, Father. Even if he's workin' for me under another name, someone will say something about the little girl sooner or later."

"It could be that they are in Duroville," Father Jaime conceded. "If a family is having real hard times, that's generally where they end up. But Roy Henderson has always been pretty close-mouthed with me."

"He's gotta' be. The last thing Roy wants is people asking questions, including you, Father. The county is trying to shut him down. Lots of stuff happens there that he keeps hushed up. He don't want the law of any kind coming into that place and lookin' around."

"Is that serious now?" Father Jaime asked. "People have been trying to close Duroville for years."

"Well, before it was about the sanitation and stuff. But, lately, the sheriff has been concerned about all the fights and crime. Roy lets things go on until they get out of hand, until it leads to a stabbing or something. He has control over everything in there. The only telephone is at his store. The people have to go to him first, and he warns them not to call the sheriff. He says his place is private property, and the sheriff has no business there when there aren't no crimes being committed. He's one of those libertarians—don't believe in government and don't want to pay taxes that might help someone else. At any rate, the other night, the supervisors said they're going to try and get an abatement order and make him shut the place down."

"That's interesting to know, Joe," Father Jaime said, thinking. "I believe I'll drive up there in the morning."

47

"Mornin', Padre," Roy Henderson said from behind the counter as Father Jim Fogarty entered his store. Bald, Henderson wore a soiled white T-shirt, his huge belly slung over the waistband of his trousers, which were held up by a straining pair of sweat-stained suspenders. His raspy, whiskey voice conveyed not so much a greeting as a warning. But it also carried a note of wariness, recognition that if a contest were about to begin, the proprietor of Duroville might not win against the tall, redheaded priest.

"Good morning, Roy," Father Jaime replied. The priest had on many occasions called upon Roy Henderson, usually over the settlement of a debt, which for the tenants was easy to run up in Duroville. In glass cases behind the proprietor, a large stock of alcohol and cigarettes was displayed, all at inflated prices. Less prominently displayed, the store carried necessities such as bread and milk, canned goods and dry cereals for tenants lacking transportation to Westmoreland.

At the end of a rutted road, Duroville squatted on land too alkaline to till between the Alamo River and the New River near where they drained their brackish water into the Salton Sea. The rivers carried raw sewage from Mexicali and excess fertilizer, insecticides, and alkali leached from the farmland of the Imperial Valley. At times when the temperature of the putrid water was warmer than the air above it, a malodorous fog settled on Duroville.

The unincorporated settlement comprised of a collection of worn-out trailer homes and wooden squad-huts, surplused from the El Centro Naval Air Station at the end of World War II. When viewed at a distance by travelers on Route 111, the decrepit shacks baking in the desert sun looked forlorn and abandoned. Dubbed "Hard Times Town" by early residents, the Spanish-speaking farmworkers in turn called it "Duroville," but no road sign announced it. At the dusty turnoff from the highway, a hand-lettered sign read, "Residents Only."

The inhabitants were a mixture of welfare recipients, retirees, and migrant farmworkers who had few other options. The pleasant weather in the Imperial Valley during the winter months brought thousands of snowbirds at the same time vegetable crops required thousands of harvesters. Few places were available at a reasonable rate. The rents in Duroville were extortive, but it was the last resort for residents whose credit was no good elsewhere.

The sole advantage Duroville offered to its residents was anonymity, and Father Jaime knew that to ask Henderson directly about Maria Elena and her father was to invite a quick denial that they were there. He would have to find them himself.

"Roy, we've talked about this before, but I'd like to try you again on the idea. Many of your tenants are migrants from Mexico and would like to attend Mass on Sundays. I'd like to be able to come out here and give them the sacraments."

"You know the answer to that one, Padre," the proprietor said. "What makes you think I'll change my mind?"

"Because you need my help right now," the priest said, looking Roy Henderson directly in the eye.

Henderson looked away for a second and then turned back to Father Jaime, his expression quizzical. "Does that mean you'd say something to the board of supervisors?"

"No, but you'll be able to say that a priest visits and Mass is being said in Duroville every Sunday."

Roy Henderson stroked his unshaven chin. "Let me get this straight. You'll come out here every Sunday and hold a service?"

"Yes."

"I don't have a place to have it in."

"I'll use the hood of my car for an altar."

"All right … all right," he said, still stroking his chin. "I guess that'll be okay with me."

Father Jaime did not see the child on the first two Sundays, but a satisfying number of farmworkers attended the Mass. Many were Mixtecs and Zapotecs from the southern states of Mexico and Guatemalans, the newest groups of migrants to arrive to harvest California crops. They had all but displaced the Mestizos from the central Mexican states who had dominated farm labor in California for a generation.

The poorest of God's poor, Father Jaime thought, but he had long given up on challenging the rapaciousness of corporate agriculture for ever-cheaper labor in favor of ministering to the needs of its victims. Corporations did not have souls, he often said, but farmworkers did. He had been working to learn the new dialects to add to the Spanish he already used for the Mass.

The third Sunday, he spotted a young girl among the throng of worshippers. She appeared to be by herself. She wore a red-checked shirt over her jeans, her dark hair held neatly in place by a pair of pink barrettes, but he did not get a chance to speak to her. She slipped off while he was putting away his chalice and folding the altar linen, and he did not see which of the shacks she returned to.

On the following Sunday, Father Jaime asked the children to come up and squat in a circle for a children's sermon. It was the second Sunday of Advent, and he talked about the coming birthday of Jesus. He gave the children multi-colored booklets illustrating the story of Jesus, Mary, and Joseph.

"I like the story in Luke best," the little girl said when he asked her whether she had read the story of Jesus's birth.

This time, the priest paid careful attention and noticed the child disappear into a rusty blue-and-white trailer.

"That's Maria Elena!" Janice said excitedly when Father Jaime called her that evening. "That's exactly what she would say."

The following afternoon, Javier and Janice met Father Jaime at the turnoff to Duroville. The priest thought a straightforward approach was best but cautioned the couple against expecting too much.

"She might not be living in conditions that you would find acceptable for a child, Janice," he said. "But, they are probably the best her father can provide."

They walked along a litter-strewn driveway until they spotted the trailer. Three men lounged in front of the steps, amber liquid visible through the clear-glass bottles each held. Father Jaime was wearing a Roman collar, and the men eyed the group as they approached.

"*Buenas tardes, señores,*" the priest greeted them.

"*Buenas tardes, Padre,*" a man with grey in his hair and mustache replied.

"*¡Es el Miller time, Padre!*" a man with short, curly hair, the youngest of the three, joked, raising his bottle of beer.

"*Sí!* I can see that," the priest replied. "Perhaps another time I would join you."

When it became apparent that the priest had some business he wanted to discuss with them, the two men who had spoken got to their feet.

"Señores, we're looking for Hector Gomez. This is Señora McDonald, who was his daughter's teacher in El Monte, and her friend, Javier. Is Hector here?" Father Jaime asked.

No one answered. The older man started to edge away. The young man with curly hair looked down uneasily at the man still seated on the ground.

"No, there's no one named that around here," the seated man said. He tried to appear nonchalant, but after a moment of awkward silence, he rose sullenly to his feet, leaving his partly consumed bottle of beer on the ground. The vein in the side of his neck throbbed.

"Do you know of Hector?" Father Jaime pressed. "His daughter lives with him."

"*No ...no,*" the man said. But as he spoke, a girl appeared at the screen door of the trailer.

Father Jaime spotted her immediately, as did Janice, who let out a cry. The man glanced over his shoulder at his daughter, and turning back to Father Jaime, gave him a sharp shove in the chest.

"Where were you, Padre, when my wife, Rosalinda, died?" His voice rose to a scream. "Where were you when my baby son, Carlos, died in the desert? Where was God? Padre!"

This time, the man's fist landed squarely in Father Jaime's solar plexus, staggering him. The priest stumbled forward against the enraged father.

"He was there!" the priest managed, grasping at the man's arms before he could be struck again. "God welcomed them into his kingdom that day, Hector!"

The shorter man's rage turned to sobs, but he continued to struggle against Father Jaime's encircling arms.

"They did not die alone, Hector!" the priest consoled. "God did not forsake Rosalinda and Carlos. He was with them. What happens on Earth is the fault of men, not God!"

Hector stopped struggling. The priest's voice calmed but remained ardent. "God was there, Hector. He welcomed your wife and your son into heaven. He does not forsake those who believe in him, Hector. He will not forsake you."

Breathing heavily, the two men stood in a tangle of arms. Maria Elena had disappeared into the dark interior of the trailer. Janice started toward the screen door, but Father Jaime shook his head, warning her back. Wresting himself free, Hector sat down on the step. The priest sat down beside him, his arm resting around Hector's shoulder. The other two men moved off around the end of the trailer.

Javier touched Janice's arm, and they turned and walked silently back to their car, leaving the priest and the distraught father by themselves. They waited in the car for over an hour before Father Jaime came back to get them.

"You can come and talk to Maria Elena now," the priest said. "As you may have gathered, her mother was Rosalinda. When Maria Elena was three years old, she, her baby brother, Carlos, and her mother, were apparently abandoned in the desert by a smuggler. Maria Elena was the only one who survived."

"My God!" Janice gasped.

"Hector does not want to be separated from his daughter," Father Jaime continued. "Maria Elena is the only one of his family he has left. He knows he can't continue living like this—the other two men live in that trailer also—and he has to do something for her education. He is willing to talk to you, but he says he is going to take Maria Elena back to Mexico where she'll be raised by his parents."

"But she deserves a chance," Janice said. "She's a bright girl. What chance will she have down there?"

"Well, she has to have a chance to grow up, too," Father Jaime said. "And a big part of growing up is being raised within the love and support of a family. She can have that in her grandparents' home."

"What about school?"

"Maybe it won't be as good as here. They come from a small town, San Pedro Piedra Gorda, but Hector says there is a *secundaria* there. He says he'll be able to send money to support her and pay for the school."

Janice bit her lip. Javier put his arm around her shoulder.

"Janice," Father Jaime said, "the big problem he has is letting his daughter go, but he says that for Maria Elena's sake, he is willing to do that now. I know it's not the solution that you want, but it is the solution that he accepts as the best for his daughter. And frankly, I don't think you can come up with a better one."

"I can't, Father. Not even if I adopted her. I know it wouldn't be right for her."

After leaving Duroville, they had followed Father Jaime to El Centro and in the quiet of his office reviewed the day's events. Janice was sad. It was as if a part of her had been taken away, she said, a dream denied. For dinner, they sent out for pizza, and Father Jaime gently switched the conversation to the two of them. Janice was comfortable with the give and take, but to Javier it seemed like a pre-nuptial counseling. It was dark when Javier and Janice left the rectory to begin their long drive back to Pasadena.

In Javier's car, they kept the conversation light. They drove on a long stretch of highway paralleling the Salton Sea, passing the turnoff to Duroville. It was late at night when they finally turned onto I-10 at Indio and began the last leg of their trip up the Banning Grade, through San Bernardino, and then home.

In the soft glow of the dash lights, Janice seemed dreamy. As they passed Palm Springs, Maria Maldaur crooned from the radio, "Midnight at the oasis/ Send your camel to bed/Shadows paintin' our faces/Traces of romance in our heads."

"Would you really have adopted Maria Elena?" Javier asked without a preamble.

"If I could have, I certainly would," Janice said.

"It wouldn't have bothered you that she was Mexican?"

"It never bothered me that I was with you."

"Is that the same as dating a Mexican, I mean a Mexican-American? I mean adoption is so permanent, commitment-wise, I mean."

"So is marriage, Javier."

"I guess I have to ask because we never really talked about it—and I guess this is maybe what you were getting at when you said we had to talk. But, would you rather have an all-white baby than a half-Mexican baby?"

Janice sat up straight. "It wouldn't matter, Javier. Why is this an issue?"

"I have to know. Maybe you don't have doubts, but I do. Not about you, but how it would be for a child."

"Javier, you know dozens of couples, Anglos and Latinos, and nothing has ever come because of it except happy wives and happy children."

Yes, he had many friends in biracial relationships, black and white as well as Latino and Anglo. There were jokes, friendly, good-natured, but he had sometimes wondered if the humor hid a deeper truth, resentment, or regret. Were they confronting the secret, special problems he feared? Probably they were, he concluded, because as Janice said, nothing bad ever seemed to come of the relationships. They were happy. Their children were no different from any others.

Couples dealt with it, Javier concluded, probably because they could communicate with each other, as Father Jaime had pointed out earlier that evening. Could he voice out his fears with Janice? Tonight he was trying, he thought.

They drove in silence. On the radio, Pat Benatar followed Natalie Cole. Javier's mind was in a quandary. The familiar litany of his fears was still in his head, but they appeared no longer important. Janice seemed to whisk them away as if they were smoke from a cigarette.

Javier felt something had changed. Could it be that simple, he wondered, a fear so hidden, but when it hits the atmosphere, when a couple talks about it, it simply goes poof? Indeed, that was what seemed to have happened. He felt a sudden sense of relief, as if he had conquered Mt. Everest.

"Janice, first of all, I love you. I always have, and I always will."

Slumped back in her seat, Janice did not respond.

"I've had some nutty thoughts," Javier explained. "And, I guess I've allowed them to prevent me from asking you to marry me. I can see that now. I saw in you and Maria Elena today how inconsequential those fears were. Now they just seem to have evaporated.

"Janice, I want you to marry me. I want us to build a life together. I want us to have children like Maria Elena. And some day, we will go to Paris and see the Eifel Tower."

Janice turned her face to Javier and smiled. She reached for his hand and held it to her lips.

"Yes," she said.

✸✸✸

In January, a letter arrived for Janice at Mountain View Elementary School, a small envelope addressed in a neat hand to "Mrs. Romero." Inside was a photo of Maria Elena, dressed in a school uniform: plaid skirt, white blouse, and dark-blue sweater. The letter said:

Dear Mrs. Romero,

How are you? I am fine.

I am very happy that you got married. I hope you and your husband have a good life.

I am enrolled in the secundaria. I was supposed to wait until next year when I'll be ten, but the principal said I read good enough and can spell.

Thank you very much for the books you sent at Christmas time. I enjoy them. Especially Goosebumps.

My abuelos take good care of me, and my father pays for my school and sends clothes.

Your friend,
Maria Elena

48

 Staccato trumpet blasts and vigorous guitar strumming announced the arrival of the mariachis on the sunlit lawn of Lupe and Richard's small stucco house. The musicians wore tight-fitting black *charro* suits and huge black sombreros, trimmed with silver spangles. As the orchestra launched into "La Bamba," Lupe rushed out of the kitchen. Richard, who had been fretting over getting the huge cake that occupied the greater part of the dining table out the door and to the church hall, joined her at the front window.

When Lupita's *damas* had begun to arrive earlier that morning, Miguel had retreated to his cot in the family room where he sat on the bright, green-and-red serape that was used as a day cover. He was struggling to pull on his new, black charro boots. Despite the stiffness in his joints and his hands, he succeeded with the left boot and rested a moment before attempting the other. He had already put on a white shirt and string tie and the black suit Lupe had rented for him for the occasion. The attire was unaccustomed—the suit coat seemed too big for his spare frame, the sleeves too long, but nonetheless, it made him feel significant and a part of this important day.

Suddenly, Lupita, burst into the room and posed in front of him, one hand on her hip, the other behind the lace and pearl tiara on her head. Her long black curls, arranged at the hairdresser's earlier in the morning, cascaded over her bare shoulders and down the back of her shimmering white-satin dress.

"*Abuelito, abuelito*, am I beautiful?" she demanded excitedly.

"¡Sí, si, mi princesa!" Miguel responded, playing the role they had created together when she was a child. "You are the most beautiful princess in the entire world!" Surprised by her entrance, still struggling with the stiff boot, he could not get off the cot quickly enough to stand as required by their ritual, but he bowed from his waist and raised his hand as if to salute.

The girl was off in an instant, her sequined, high-heeled shoes clacking on the tiled hallway as she joined her damas, clustered at the front door. The moment she stepped into the sunlight, the mariachis launched into "Las Mañanitas."

> *Éstas son las mañanitas*
> *Que cantaba el Rey David,*
> *A las muchachas bonitas*
> *Se las cantaba así.*

Left alone, the rest of the household's attention commanded by the mariachis on the front lawn, Miguel hummed softly to himself.

> *Despierta, mi bien, despierta.*
> *Mira que ya amaneció.*
> *Ya los pajaritos cantan.*
> *La luna ya se metió.*
>
> *Wake up, my darling, wake up.*
> *Look the dawn has broken.*
> *Now the little birds are singing.*
> *The moon has gone down.*

Lupe came into the room and sat beside him. She wore a black cocktail dress. Petite, with prominent cheekbones and large, brown eyes that offset the deep caramel of her skin, she reminded Miguel of her mother. The mariachis had paused for a moment, but she softly repeated the refrain.

> *These are the morning verses*
> *That King David used to sing.*
> *Today because it's your birthday,*
> *We're singing them to you.*

"Lupita's wearing high-heeled shoes," Miguel accused. "She should wait until after she has taken her vows, after she leaves the church."

The customs to be observed on his granddaughter's quinceañera had been an issue for many weeks. Although she had not directly said so to him, Lupita wanted to skip the church ceremony and go directly to the lavish party that was being organized to celebrate her fifteenth birthday. In the end, there had been compromise; there would be a Mass, but a mariachi Mass, and Lupita would be allowed to wear a white dress. Still, the shoes were a surprise to Miguel.

"I know, *Papá*," Lupe said softly, gently rubbing his shoulder. "That's not the way we did it at home in Mexico. But we are here now, in El Monte. Lupita wants to have her celebration like her friends do it."

Miguel was quiet. With age, he had grown impatient, and change unnerved him. Although he could not remember events in the house in the past few days or weeks, memories from his youth in the village of San Pedro Piedra Gorda were vivid and precise. Internally, he railed at the seeming triviality of his daily existence. The decline of his strength and energy no longer permitted him to work in the fields, or with Richard, and left him confined to the bland routines of a house emptied for most of the day by the work and school schedules of the younger members of the family.

In the early mornings, Miguel tended the garden he and Lupe had planted, weeding and watering the sweet corn, peppers, and tomatoes, tasks he completed with patience and care. By midmorning, he was back in the house to watch telenovelas, sharing the couch with Lupe if she was off work for the day. Enduring the family's occasional teasing, he refused to concede he was hooked on the daily TV dramas. He was inside because of the midday sun, he claimed. The remainder of his day was spent napping.

Discussions at the dinner table were hard for Miguel to follow, and he often felt left out. He had no knowledge of MP3 players, cell phones, or the latest clothing styles, which seemed to dominate the conversation between Lupita and her mother and sometimes her older brother, Ricky, when he also was at the table. Miguel coveted the chance to speak from his memories, to interject a moral lesson from his youth, but such opportunities were infrequent.

Miguel read Spanish-language *revistas* and watched the news on Telemundo, but he did not understand enough about current events in the United States and California to hold a satisfactory conversation with Richard, who watched the network news in English. "The ilegales should not be a problem at all," he declared at the dinner table on evenings when the conversation turned to the subject he felt confident he understood. "The farmers need workers; the Mexicans need work. Let them come in."

"But, Papá," Lupe protested. "There are so many of them now, from all over, even Guatemala, and there aren't enough jobs. That's Ricky's problem; he can't get a good job."

"It's not just that farmers need workers," Richard interjected in an attempt to support both sides. "The farms are all owned by big corporations now, and they bring in the cheapest labor they can get. They don't want to be responsible for the people they bring here and won't support them when there's no work."

"They're even bringing in people on visas to work, European kids," Lupe protested, picking up on her point about the lack of employment prospects for her son. "They're working in the fast-food places. Our kids don't have a chance these days."

Privately, Miguel did not think the boy would work even if he were offered a job. That was the unspoken part of his point, but he never pressed it with Lupe. Norteamericanos did not want the jobs, he believed.

Parents, Richard and Lupe included, supported their sons and daughters too well and would not admit it. He was tired of the argument and often wished he was in Piedra Gorda where he could find conversation with men who had to work to live and experienced life as he had.

"At my quinceañera, I was carried to the church on a donkey cart, remember?" Lupe continued. "You and Mamá, my damas and *chambelánes,* and three mariachis all walked behind the cart, remember? I was so proud and happy. Mamá made me a new pink dress. Today, Lupita and all her attendants will travel to the church in a big white limousine."

"You mean everyone will fit into one car?" Miguel asked. There were seven girls and seven boys, all dancing on the lawn as the mariachis broke into a Beach Boys tune, "Kokomo." "Is Richard paying for such a thing?"

Lupe looked down momentarily. Her father, never sure of the source of it, disapproved of the money Ricky flashed around the house. But he would find out sooner or later, she decided, and drew a breath. "It is a gift from Ricky, Papá," she said.

Miguel and Ricky did not get along. The boy avoided talking to his grandfather unless he was compelled to. Miguel did not like the insolence the boy at times displayed to his mother and father, and he considered the baggy clothes the boy wore gang attire.

Lupe had been carrying Ricky when her mother died, and Concha had wanted to be there for the boy's birth. That she could not be, that because of him she had died a horrible death in the desert, still filled Miguel with guilt. Ricky seemed to sense his grandfather's blameworthiness, and Miguel had tried to make it up to the boy over the years, but nothing worked. With each failure, Miguel's feelings grew more deeply inward.

Miguel knew the distress Ricky caused his mother, and he vowed to be helpful on Lupita's coming-of-age day. Like the other young men dancing on the front lawn, the boy was dressed in a light-blue tuxedo with a lacy shirt.

"It's good that Ricky is one of Lupita's chambelánes," he said. "In Piedra Gorda, all of your chambelánes and all of your damas were relatives: uncles, cousins."

"Yes," Lupe replied, grateful that for today at least she would not have to defend her son. "We don't have as many relatives here, but Lupita has a lot of friends."

"Yes, she has many friends, beautiful friends, and you have every right to be proud of her. She has very good manners. She is very lovely," Miguel said.

"Lupita does well at school, too," Lupe countered. "She told me the other day that she wants to go to community college and learn to keep the books for her father."

Miguel laughed. "You and Richard have much to be thankful for with her," he said. "And Lupita has very much to be thankful for with you. I'm sure she will make good thank-you speeches at the altar today and that you and Richard will be very proud."

Lupe's voice became serious. "Papá, quinceañeras don't do that here. Lupita won't be making a speech or taking vows like they do in Mexico. It's no longer the custom."

"But the vows are important," Miguel protested, taken aback by the revelation. "The quinceañera is celebrated to remind her of the importance of fidelity to God, to teach her about our Church, about love and respect to her family, about our morals and our culture—principles that guide us through our lives. Life is filled with difficulties and hard choices. She must prepare herself."

"Papá, you have been her teacher as much as any of us. Because she was born in this country, she will never have the tests that challenged you. You came to California without papers to feed us; you lived in hardship, without dignity, so that we could survive, so that we could live in the way you could not. But you never gave up the truths you believed in. You never lost your faith in God. You always loved us. These are the examples your children and grandchildren see.

"For sure, Lupita will face challenges," Lupe continued. "There will be tests in her future that you and I cannot comprehend. But it is not the taking of vows that will guide Lupita; it is how you, and Richard and I, have raised her. And, we have followed your example. You have taught us and her."

"But she must thank you," Miguel interrupted. "She must learn humility. It is important for her to acknowledge you and Richard for bringing her to this day."

"Yes, Papá," Lupe replied. "I know it is important for children to honor their parents, and I'm sure she does. I'm sure she's thankful. But it is different here in los Estados Unidos. Kids don't tell their parents thank you in a public ceremony. In this country, kids are encouraged to make up their own minds and not be so dependent on their parents." Lupe paused, struggling to keep a sudden rush of emotion from stopping what she wanted to say next.

"Papá, on my quinceañera, I stood before you and Mamá in the church and told you how I thanked you for everything you had done for me. I renewed my vows to God and pledged to honor and respect you and Mamá forever. I still thank you for everything we have. I say that again to you today. We have a better life because of you. You wanted a better life for Mamá too, and you tried to bring her here. I grieve for Mamá every single day, as do you. You did your best for her, for us, but God, not you, took her from us. You were a true father and spouse."

Miguel leaned forward, his elbows on his knees, and studied his knobby, weathered hands. Twenty years had passed since Concha's death, but mention of her still brought painful memories: the hours and then days he and Lupe had waited for word of her, the searing guilt he had felt, still felt, as if a hot branding iron had been pressed to his temple. He had sought atonement, carrying a heavy, framed portrait of the Mother of Christ pressed to his chest as he trudged the last fifty miles to the basílica and crawling across the stone plaza while his knees bled, calling out to the Virgen.

The Virgencita had answered him. He had stopped drinking. But despite having his life back under control, he could not talk comfortably with Lupe about her mother. Thinking she was respecting his grief, Lupe had allowed her father to dwell alone with his conscience, and Miguel continued to insist on his guilt. At her mention, in his mind, he repeated *soy culpable,* I am quilty, as if saying Hail Marys on a rosary. The preparations for the quinceañera had brought them as close to the subject as both felt they dared.

"Papá," Lupe continued, no longer trying to stop the tears that smeared her eyeliner and cut through the makeup on her cheeks. She took her father's hand. "I wanted Mamá to come to California. I didn't want to wait until she got her papers. When you got your green card, I wanted Mamá to come right away. It didn't matter to me that the law didn't permit her to. All the families were coming. Everybody was doing it. It was so easy to cross the border. Nobody else was waiting. I didn't want to wait."

The petite woman shifted her weight on the cot.

"Papá, I wanted her to be here when Ricky was born. That's why I urged her to come. The guilt is not yours alone, Papá. It's mine too. How foolish I was, and now Mamá is dead."

Until this moment, Miguel had been unsure how his daughter felt about his role in her mother's death. Surely, she must hate him, he had thought for so long, the more so because Lupe knew about his infidelity. His need for reassurance had become a dependency.

"Mija ...," he started, but words were not there. Lupe's arm was around his shoulder as she dabbed with a handkerchief at her eyes.

"Papá, I know you want to go back to Mexico," Lupe interjected before he could compose himself, putting into words what had been so long on his mind. "I understand. I love you. This is not the life you want or deserve. We will miss you terribly. And I want you to know that I don't blame you for Mamá's death."

The hubbub on the front lawn had subsided as the mariachis, singing "Cielito Lindo," accompanied the damas and chambelánes to the waiting limo. The front door of the house burst open.

"Mamá! Abuelito!" Lupita called. "The limo is here. Are you ready? It's time to go!"

49

 At seven in the morning on the last day he was to drive the El Monte-Los Angeles-San Ysidro run, Javier Romero found his rig amidst a long row of shiny motor coaches and swung open the rear engine compartment door. He flipped a toggle switch to check the water level warning light, fingered the belts for tautness, looked for any sign of oil leakage, and pulled out the dipstick. In the bright morning sunlight, a sheen of oil glistened just under the full mark.

Then, taking care not to soil his light-blue uniform shirt and his neatly pressed trousers, he struck each of the rear tires with a mallet and listened for the characteristic thump, or thud, that would tell him whether the tire was properly inflated. For an instant, he considered letting the air out of the inside duals when he returned the bus at the end of his run that afternoon. *A Mexican ought to know how to change a tire,* he thought bitterly, but he quickly put the idea aside.

Javier edged his way to the front of the bus through the narrow aisle between the parked behemoths. He was startled to notice that the company logo already had been removed from the side of his coach. On other mornings, he patted the image of the sprinting grey dog as he passed, wishing himself, and it, good luck. But since the day the company announced it was turning his run over to its newly formed

Mexican subsidiary and replacing him with a Mexican driver, for Javier, the world's most recognizable corporate symbol had become a spirit-draining totem of betrayal.

Javier jammed the door release button with the heel of his hand, then climbed the steps, and eased into the driver's seat. He had gained weight over the years but still wore fitted shirts and kept his mustache small and neatly trimmed. He flipped the master switch and hit the starter button, listening as the engine rumbled to life. Satisfied with its steady throb, he flipped on the fast-idle switch, then got out of his seat, and walked to the back to check the restroom. Passengers liked a spotless interior, and even on his last day, he took care to see that they had a clean bus.

Returning to the driver's seat, Javier adjusted the mirrors. The air pressure gauge read 90 psi; the motor coach was ready. As he pushed down on the parking-brake release, he noted the satisfying *tssssssssh* of escaping air. He shifted the gear selector to drive, and for the last time, rolled the heavy coach forward and out the exit gate.

Morning commute traffic on the San Bernardino Freeway was sluggish but moving. After a few minutes, Javier threaded the coach expertly through the long lines of cars to the exit lane and off onto El Monte Boulevard. Exactly on time, he pulled into the parking lot at the new central transit station, past the neat rows of commuter cars and SUVs, shaded at each end by recently planted decorative trees. From his elevated seat, the roofs of the parked autos looked like polished rocks, bordered by rows of glistening, round-top shrubs in a giant's sunlit garden. But after today, Javier reflected, he would no longer be that giant. He pulled the coach to the curb just short of the multi-lane exit that led back onto the freeway.

Javier set the parking brake, opened the door, and hopped down to the sidewalk. In an orderly line, morning commuters—men carrying folded suit-coats over their arms, women smartly dressed in business attire—shuffled forward. Clutching briefcases and folded *LA Times* in one hand, they held out their ticket to Javier in the other.

"Are you going to be with us tomorrow, Javier?" a man wearing an Oxford-cloth shirt with an open collar asked loudly enough to be heard over the idling engine. The creation of the Mexican subsidiary and its authorization to operate bus routes in the United States had been reported in the business pages, touted as an example of the new opportunities afforded American business under the North American Free Trade Act, NAFTA.

"No, no. Some other guy will. A driver for the new company."

Javier wanted to say more, wanted to complain about the unfairness of losing his job to a foreigner, a Mexican. He wanted to hurt the company as it had hurt him—laying him off just two years short of the day he could claim a retirement. He struggled to keep his thoughts to himself and graciously accept the brief thanks and well wishes muttered by his riders as they boarded the bus for his final run.

After collecting the last ticket and climbing back into his seat, Javier was about to close the door when a petite, brown-skinned woman, long black curls falling on her shoulders, appeared at the bottom of the steps.

"Señor, can you help my father with his bags please?"

Javier climbed down from his seat. The trim Latina, wearing a black dress with a scoop neckline and high-heel shoes, stood back. Javier smiled at her, and swung around to lift open the baggage compartment door. But, before he could turn back, a bent, wiry man, wearing a new, cream-colored tejana, appeared at his side and pushed an old tan suitcase into the bay. The cuffs of his stiff new jeans formed a bluish-grey band around the tops of polished-black charro boots. His leather belt, sporting a large silver buckle, held in place a pinstriped western shirt, bunched and tucked in at his waist. Javier shoved the suitcase against the front bulkhead, and when he turned, the old man was at his side again, shoving in a cardboard box neatly bound in heavy twine.

Straightening, Javier found himself staring into the old man's milky eyes. The man smiled. Deep furrows cupped the corners of his wide mouth, and a thin, grey mustache highlighted the dark skin under his broad nostrils. Large ears and fleshy, elongated earlobes framed his worn face.

"¿Para dónde va, Viejo?" Javier asked lightly.

"Ya me voy a mi tierra, señor. Yo no soy un chicano."

I am going home, I am not a chicano. Startled, Javier was uncertain if the remark had been meant as a rebuke. The woman smiled at his discomfort and presented her father's ticket. Javier, noting that it was through to the border, punched it, and turned to lower the baggage compartment door.

I am not a chicano. Not a chicano, Javier puzzled. And then he remembered what his grandfather had told him when he was a child. A chicano is a Mexican who dresses like a norteamericano and tries to act like one, he cautioned. He is a man who has abandoned his roots.

Javier climbed back into his seat and grabbed the handle ready to close the door. The old man patted his daughter's clasped hands, and, stony-faced, grasped the railing to steady himself as he climbed the steps. The woman, clutching a white handkerchief at her slender waist, watched after him, her large brown eyes glossed with tears.

A commuter in the second row gave the old man his seat and moved further back into the crowded bus. Javier pulled the door shut and started the motor coach forward, pulling the steering wheel hard to the left so that the rear tires would not ride up over the curb as he made a right turn onto the exit ramp.

As Javier maneuvered the motor coach into the bus lane, the old man's words weighed on him: *I am going home; I have never abandoned my roots.* Since receiving notice from the company, Javier had tried to temper his resentment of the faceless Mexican who tomorrow would take over his job, but anger welled in him. *That's just great, old man,* he thought. *Come here for a few years, screw things up for everybody else, and then head off for the good life back on the hacienda! I'll bet you get Social Security, too!*

Javier's replacement was not even going to have to leave his home in Tijuana; he would have a visa and simply cross the border every day to drive his route. *Some solution,* he thought bitterly. *Replace the millions of illegal Mexicans working in United States jobs with millions of Mexicans working on visas and pay them all minimum wage. That means minimum wage for everyone here, too. It's like the government built a fence but with a huge gate, a gate they let everybody through so they wouldn't have to jump the line anymore.*

He blamed greedy corporations and bought and paid-for politicians. *It's no different from my father's day,* Javier thought bitterly. *He was always having to change jobs, always moving on, hoping to be able to work at one place long enough to be able to get some money ahead to tide the family over before the farmer gave his job to a wetback. One thing for sure, Viejo,* Javier glanced quickly at the old man reflected in his interior mirror, *you go back to your roots, but I was born here; I've never abandoned my roots, either!*

Javier eased the motor coach to a safe distance behind a white sports utility vehicle. He glanced again into his interior mirror. The old man's tejana and weathered brown face stood out from the sea of passengers uniformly dressed for the business day. He watched the old man pull a scapular from under the collar of his shirt, cross himself three times, kiss the sacred image, and drop it back down inside his shirt. *The old guy never learned a thing here,* Javier thought. *Never changed a bit.*

The old man's leathery face and gnarled, arthritic hands reminded Javier of his grandfather. His grandfather wore a scapular against his breast and professed his faith in God and the church until the day he died. He loved his Mexican roots and kept all the vestiges of the old culture. Javier did not think his grandfather could be called a chicano, concluding that the insult had been meant for him.

Softening, Javier recalled that his grandfather had never learned very much English. When you worked in the fields, there was never time, he reflected. Men like his grandfather, and the old man, too, he admitted, came to California and worked their butts off, making just enough money to feed their families and have a *cerveza* or two. That was their life.

But his grandfather insisted the family's homeland was the United States, not Mexico. He had never wanted to go back. Even though the family had to move from place to place to find work, he insisted that his children and grandchildren attend school and learn English. He raised them to love their family, their church, and their country. Even when World War II arrived and other families, fearing conscription of their sons, returned to Mexico, his grandfather stayed. Javier's father fought in Korea.

When Javier was a young boy, his grandfather, too old to work in the fields, told him countless stories about happy times on the rancho in Coahuila where he grew up, stories of bravado, about fiestas and baptisms and work on the ranch. But when he drank, he told tales about *la revolución*, about machismo and the butchery. Javier found it hard to sort out who were the good guys and who were the bad; it seemed to him that one side was as brutal as the other. His mother explained that his grandfather had come to the United States to escape the violence and raise a family.

My grandfather stayed here because he had something to gain, something besides money, a future for his family, Javier thought. *That's probably the real difference between him and the old man. This old guy has probably found nothing besides work, and at times precious little of that. He probably never had a legal right to stay here, never had a future. That's why the old man's going home. His dreams were never about here. They were always about his family until they too were off somewhere, probably the United States. I guess I would go home, too.*

Still, if he was a wetback, he had no right to be here.

50

 Javier dropped off his commute passengers in downtown Los Angeles, and the sleek motor coach continued down the coast through storied Pacific coast towns: Newport Beach, Laguna Niguel, and San Juan Capistrano. On the run from El Monte to downtown Los Angeles, Javier's passengers had been office workers. The old man's seatmate had been a young business type who worked on a laptop. His passengers now were headed for San Diego or the border, and most chatted in Spanish.

Busy maneuvering on and off I-5, boarding and disembarking passengers, Javier had little time to think about the old man. In his seat two rows behind him, the old man dozed, his tejana dipping forward. From time to time, he would straighten up and stare impassively out the window. Javier had decided that the old Mexican's knock on chicanos was innocent enough, but nevertheless, he continued to regard him as an illegal.

The bus rolled past new housing developments: million-dollar homes, condominiums, and shopping gallerias built for the convenience of the men and women who commuted to jobs in Orange County and downtown Los Angeles. Housing prices were high because little developable land remained available near the coast and the city. "They aren't printing anymore land," the developers boasted, pocketing billions in profits.

Men who never could afford to live in the houses, or even in a much more modest tract home for that matter, had built the developments. Somehow, while the law of supply and demand worked for real-estate developers, it never worked for the men the builders employed, Javier thought. There were always more workers from Mexico, men like the old man, and the contractors hired them whether they had papers or not.

It seemed always to be the case, Javier thought. His father competed for farm jobs against the braceros and the wetbacks. The growers hired the illegals, undermining the decent wages and working conditions César Chavez and farmworkers like his father had won through bitter strikes, boycotts, and fasts. Toward the end of his life, his father found a job as a janitor. But that job, too, vanished; the company contracted the work to a service that employed illegal immigrants.

Corporations did not have to hire illegal immigrants directly anymore; they contracted with middlemen who did. Feckless politicians passed laws that enabled businesses to hire foreign labor. Javier had worked for the bus company for twenty years and was being laid off, his job given to a Mexican citizen on a visa. Men who worked for a living did not stand a chance anymore, Javier thought. Money seemed always to go to the rich. No one appeared to be trying to make it better for the working people.

Janice encouraged him to look for something new, assuring him that she and the children could get along at least temporarily on her salary as a schoolteacher. But Javier knew it would be impossible to get work that matched the pay and benefits he earned as a driver. Replacement jobs for men approaching sixty, clerking at a building supply store or a Wal-Mart, paid little, had few if any benefits, and did not last long.

At San Clemente, Javier pulled the motor coach to the curb in front of a beige, stucco building with a red, Spanish-tile roof. Young men with close-clipped hair, marines from Camp Pendleton, headed to Tijuana for liberty clambered aboard, and stylishly dressed officer's wives on their way to a late lunch and an afternoon of shopping in one of the beach towns along the way or in downtown San Diego stepped on. A short Indian with a round, hairless face, wearing a dark-blue baseball cap and blue work-shirt, was the last to board, taking the vacant seat beside the old man. Neither spoke.

Javier pegged the Indian as one of a recent wave of migrant farm-workers from the south of Mexico or Guatemala who, for the most part, spoke only a native dialect. *I wonder what the old guy thinks about his seatmate,* Javier mused. *I hope he feels as my dad did when the wetbacks showed up and took his job. I'll bet he would if he was still working in the fields.*

Where will the line of desperately poor job seekers end? Javier wondered. *Will the next wave of illegal immigrants be indigenous people from the Andes? Heck, they're already coming,* he thought, picturing the pan-pipe bands that appeared on street corners in tourist places on weekend afternoons.

Bounded on the left by tan bluffs, the dual strands of Interstate 5 traversed Camp Pendleton. On the right, empty savannah extended to the Pacific Ocean, stretching placid and blue to the horizon. The bus swept past the giant canopy covering the checkpoint operated by the US Border Patrol in the northbound lanes. Javier surveyed the long lines of backed-up vehicles on the other side of the mesh fence in the median. The checkpoint had operated for decades, and it never ceased to amaze Javier that hundreds of illegal immigrants and drugs continued to be nabbed there every day.

The border patrol varied their hours of operation, and like a real-life game of roulette, illegal immigrants and smugglers gambled that the checkpoint would be closed when they reached it. When caught, drivers pleaded that they did not know their passengers were illegal or simply abandoned the immigrants and fled. If the vehicle was not itself stolen, the smugglers covered the loss upfront in their fees. *Show me people in need, and I'll show you people making money,* Javier reflected.

The fence in the freeway median extended several miles south of the checkpoint, but fleeing migrants and smugglers often scaled it and darted between speeding southbound cars. Yellow caution signs displaying black silhouettes of a running man, woman, and a small child warned motorists. As always, Javier slowed.

Without warning, a silver SUV in the inside lane braked hard. Instinctively, Javier hit his air brakes. A sickening crash, and a khaki-clad lump, limbs flailing akimbo like a limp scarecrow, hurtled across the pavement in front of the bus. Out of the corner of his eye, Javier saw the crumpled hood and shattered windshield of the SUV, the driver fighting to regain control of his vehicle and bring it to a stop.

The body skidded to a rest in Javier's lane. The steel motor coach shuddered to a halt. Javier set his flashers, and waited for the cars in the lane to his right to stop before opening the door.

The crumpled body on the pavement seemed diminutive, out of scale, like a discarded doll. As Javier stepped down from the bus, he could see immediately that it was an older man, his sparse hair clumped in blood. Blood soaked the man's shirt. The disheveled body lay still, lifeless. He could smell the man's shit. Stooping, Javier found a limp arm and felt for a pulse. There was none.

The old Mexican appeared at Javier's side, peering intently at the dead man's head. The exposed ear, part of an ear, Javier thought, was gnarled. Curious, Javier wondered where he had seen such an ear before. He stood, prepared to take the old Mexican's arm and lead him back to the bus. But before he could act, the old man delivered a swift kick to the corpse's ribs.

"What …!" Javier stammered.

"¡Pendejo!" the old man hissed at the lifeless body, and before Javier could restrain him, the old man lashed out with his boot again.

"Do you know this guy?" Javier blurted, his arms restraining the old man, moving him back to prevent another kick.

"He's a coyote! A worthless pendejo who exploits poor Mexicans!" the old man blurted. "He left my wife to die in the desert."

Javier looked down at the crumpled figure, at the twisted stump of an ear. He caught his breath. *Chuy!* The man who had cost the life of a border patrol officer, sending him to prison for the remainder of his adolescent years, finally had been brought to justice! Muttering, the old Mexican crossed himself and allowed Javier to guide him back to the bus.

The motor coach, its warning lights flashing, remained in the traffic lane protecting the accident scene until Chuy's body and the wrecked

SUV had been removed. After Javier related what he had seen to the California Highway Patrol officers, the bus rolled on down I-5, past a litany of seaside communities: Carlsbad, Leucadia, Encinitas, Cardiff-by-the-Sea, Laguna Beach, Del Mar.

When their jobs permitted them to share a holiday, Javier and Janice had camped with their three children at the state beach at Carlsbad and browsed through the colorful shops and galleries in Laguna Beach. They would still come here, Javier thought, probably less often until he found a new job. He would miss driving this run, miss feeling a part of the daily life of the area.

Javier glanced in his interior mirror. The old man's face was grief-stricken. *Probably reliving the death of his wife,* Javier thought. *I wonder how many other lives Chuy took in pursuit of profit.* The Indian in the seat beside the old man looked perplexed, uncertain. *Funny how we all seem linked together,* Javier thought. *I guess we are. Each of us is powerless, trapped in a system none of us has any control over!*

Many of the Mexican farmworkers now in the United States looking for work were forced off their farms because of NAFTA, the same law that cost him his job, Javier reflected. The treaty required the Mexican government to remove tariff barriers to low-cost American corn, and Mexican farmers could not compete. They became victims, too.

He had nothing to gain by being angry with the Mexicans, Javier realized. Their lives were a tale of good fortune and bad, as was his. *The old man has lost his wife trying to bring her to this country. I can't imagine that. No telling what the Indian has gone through. Was his family still in Oaxaca? He probably lives in a cardboard hovel in a canyon within a stone's throw of a big new housing development on a mesa, not important to anyone here except as cheap labor.*

Our roots are not the same, hombres, Javier thought, glancing again at the old man and the Indian. *But we're being kicked in the ass by the same boot.*

At midafternoon, the coach pulled up to the station at the border at San Ysidro. Javier stood at the foot of the steps while his passengers disembarked.

"*Que le vaya bien, señor,*" he said, grasping the old man's arm until his feet were firmly on the pavement.

"*¡Gracias, señor!*" the old man replied. "*¡Con Dios, señor! With God!*"

THE END

About the Author

Michael G. Harpold began his thirty-five-year career in the US Immigration and Naturalization Service (INS) as a border patrol inspector on the Mexican border at Calexico, California, in 1962, a time when officers were still able to patrol the line alone in a Jeep, armed only with a six-shooter.

In May 1965, he was transferred to a newly opened border patrol station in Bakersfield, California. In nearby Delano, he met César Chavez, and Harpold's involvement with farm workers during the grape strike led to a lifelong interest in their plight. Attending Fresno State University during his off-duty time, he wrote a treatise, "Racial and Ethnic Patterns in Agricultural Employment in the Southern San Joaquin Valley," based on field data he compiled in his border-patrol duties.

Beginning in 1968, Harpold served two years in Viet Nam as an advisor to the National Police with the US Agency for International Development.

After Viet Nam, he returned to the San Francisco District Office of the INS serving first as an investigator and then as an immigration examiner adjudicating petitions for relatives or applications for a green card often filed by farm workers in the northern San Joaquin Valley, Napa Valley, and Monterrey Peninsula. During his years in San Francisco,

Harpold became an officer of the employee union and made frequent appearances before congressional committees testifying on proposed immigration legislation and the INS budget.

In San Francisco and in Washington, DC, he worked closely with the immigrant serving community. In 1975, he was invited by the US Catholic Conference to participate in a meeting of the Catholic bishops of Mexico and the United States in Mexico City. The focus of the conference was to find ways to meet the spiritual and human needs of migrants and migrant families on either side of the border.

In early 1977, newly appointed INS commissioner, Leonel Castillo, asked Harpold to join his staff in Washington, DC. In January 1978, Castillo sent him to Southeast Asia to document the continued flight of Vietnamese from the Socialist Republic of Viet Nam in small boats. In Songkla, Thailand, Harpold, acting on his own, rescued thirty-four Vietnamese men, women, and children on a disabled boat that the Thai Navy was about to tow back out to sea and cut adrift. The State Department had previously called the boat people economic refugees, but the incident in Thailand and the author's report on his interviews of the boat people in refugee camps in Thailand, Malaysia, and Singapore helped lead to their subsequent categorization as political refugees eligible for resettlement in the United States.

In 1979, Harpold was elected president of the National INS Council, American Federation of Government Employees, AFL-CIO. In addition to representing the interests of INS employees, he continued to be an advocate for effective and humane immigration laws.

Returning to the San Francisco district office in 1983, he supervised inspections at the ports of entry and the adjudication of political asylum applications and visa petitions. Late in 1984, he transferred to Ketchikan, Alaska.

In Ketchikan, Harpold was responsible for providing all INS services in Southeast Alaska, including approving visa petitions and applications for immigrant status, political asylum, and naturalization. It was a dream job for an immigration officer, he says. On kitchen tables in people's homes in many of the small island towns he visited, he typed up Certificates of Citizenship for children who were often born in Canadian hospitals. He also arrested illegal immigrants and smugglers and initiated fine proceedings and criminal prosecutions against employers, often in the fishing industry, who hired illegal immigrants.

Prior to joining the US Border Patrol, Harpold served five years in the US Army and was a cadet at West Point, a member of the class of 1961. He completed a Bachelor of Science degree from California State University at Fresno and attended Golden Gate University School of Law in San Francisco. He has also taken writing courses at the University of Alaska.

In retirement, Harpold continues to live in Ketchikan, Alaska, with his wife, Elaine, and has served on the Ketchikan City Council and the Board of Education. He has a basement filled with model trains.

He has five daughters and four grandchildren who live up and down the West Coast, affording him many opportunities to revisit the Mexican border and the California valleys that are the scene of his novel.

In writing *Jumping the Line*, Harpold initially envisioned it as non-fiction but eventually decided on the novel as the appropriate form to convey the many faces of the truth about farm labor and immigration.